# WHEN CARING ISN'T ENOUGH...

Meeting the Need for Long-Term Care
with Long-Term Care Insurance

BY SAMUEL LARRY FELDMAN, CLU
AND THE NATIONAL LTC NETWORK

Laws and compliance regulations vary from state to state and company to company. Please be sure to check with the laws in your state and your company's compliance department before using any new sales material.

ISBN: 1 891042-11-4

Printed in the United States of America.

This publication is designed to provide accurate and authoritative information in regard to the subject matter covered. Although an effort has been made to assure the accuracy of the information in this publication, the Million Dollar Round Table Center for Productivity does not warrant that accuracy, and is not liable for any errors or omissions.

# DEDICATION

To my father, Leo Feldman, who encouraged me to join him in the business of insurance thirty-seven years ago and taught me the value of four "nevers":

Never be late for an appointment.

Never quit on someone or something you believe in.

Never blow out someone else's candle to make yours shine brighter.

Never tell anything but the truth; it's easier to remember the truth than it is to remember a lie.

"If you stick to these nevers, you will never fail," my father said.

I believed he was right then, and I still believe.

# TABLE OF CONTENTS

Rosalyn Carter quotes a colleague in her book *Helping Yourself Help Others*, who said, "There are only four kinds of people in this world: those who have been caregivers, those who currently are caregivers, those who will be caregivers, and those who will need caregivers." Our initial chapter sets out to validate these omniscient statements. Succeeding chapters will document how long-term care insurance can be of benefit to many caught in the web of long-term care needs and long-term care providers.

Although most people who need long-term care are elderly, long-term care is not exclusively an aging issue. These pages take a thought-provoking look behind the statistics. Issues could run the gamut from "When Bad Things Happen to Good People" to "Risk Homeostasis."

The long-term care industry is the fastest growing industry in the United States. The demand for care is far greater than the supply of care. Through modern technology and modern medicine, care can be provided to meet certain needs and/or in special settings. Comprehensive long-term care insurance policies pay for care outside of a nursing facility. The ability to be conversant about alternatives to nursing home care reduces anxiety and creates a positive attitude toward the purchase of long-term care insurance. This chapter examines the multitude of care settings.

In 1935, when Social Security began, the average life expectancy was 63. Today, nearly 80% of all Americans will live beyond age 65. For every ten people who turn age 65, four will enter a long-term care facility sometime in their lifetime.

Based on these statistics and the sheer size of the baby boom generation, long-term care becomes the largest unfunded liability facing Americans today. Many citizens believe the government will provide for their long-term care. In this chapter, the reader discovers why the path to qualify for limited government benefits is difficult and repugnant for most people of ordinary means.

The authors not only explain the government programs available, they also cite several acts of legislation that are clear long-term care insurance buying signals, underscoring the shortcomings of government to continue financing long-term care.

Generally, insurance is bought or sold based on an understanding of one's perceived risk or potential loss. Usually, the purpose of insurance is to maintain status quo or to make whole again. Anyone who has a need for long-term care or the need to provide long-term care has dealt with a roller coaster of financial, physical, and emotional demands. The distance between peaks can be immeasurable. Long-term care insurance acts like a set of disc brakes, preventing total loss of control to those along for the ride. The evolution of long-term care insurance policies since 1990, in design and distribution, is unparalleled in the history of insurance. This chapter examines the various types of long-term care insurance and provides an explanation of each of their benefits.

Is there an agent or financial planner who isn't aware of the value of maintaining contact with his or her existing clients? Most clients reach a point when there is no need to purchase additional life insurance and earned income no longer provides a basis for disability income insurance. Clients fitting these descriptions have normally entered a phase called the "Golden Years." Through long-term care insurance, agents have discovered a new area in which to be of help to their clients. Several proven long-term care insurance techniques for illustrating this need are explained.

Long-term care insurance isn't for everyone. Mostly those who can afford to pay the premiums for many years and who have substantial assets to protect should consider purchasing a policy. Before making a sale, any responsible agent should first assess whether a client needs the coverage and can afford it. If the answer to these questions is yes, the next step is to submit the client's health history to an underwriter. On average, 20% of the applications submitted to long-term care insurance companies are rejected — a precursor to considerable financial, physical, and emotional stress. Several methods for altering the impact to uninsureds are provided.

The assistance policyholders should expect from their insurance companies provides a major advantage to owning a long-term care insurance policy. This becomes evident as clients experience the onset of inability to indulge in the activities of daily living or of general cognitive impairment. Policyholders will have access to Care Coordinators or Care Managers, whose job it is to help them navigate the health care delivery system at a time when the average family is unprepared and hard pressed to deal with the issues of long-term care. Sometimes a care manager's advice, such as an alternative plan of care, allows the insured to stay in their own home longer than anticipated. Understanding the claims process equips the agent to be a better long-term care insurance advocate, ensures a continuum of care for clients' elder years, and expedites professional growth for the agent.

There are several paths that lead to qualifying as a member of the Million Dollar Round Table. The broadest path appears to be as a general practitioner. Some follow the path of pension planning, while others are on the paths of financial planning or estate planning. No matter which path has been chosen, when a client is faced with an uninsured stay in a nursing facility, the likelihood is that the plans developed along these chosen paths are doomed to failure. This chapter guides one how to preserve their planning by shifting the risk for costs of professional long-term care to an insurance company.

Concealed amid the rhetoric of the previous pages is a writer's writer. His mission was to polish and weave the words of more than a dozen National LTC Network members into the fabric of a cohesive professional text. The literary expertise he brings to this task, however, is additionally driven by a personal (and painful) experience, which appropriate long-term care insurance coverage might have made eminently more bearable. The National LTC Network believes it is an experience worth sharing.

This book was written at the request of a 23,000-member international insurance sales organization. Therefore it was incumbent on the author to provide global perspectives of long-term care and long-term care insurance, recognizing that caring is universal.

# ACKNOWLEDGEMENTS

To my family for their love and encouragement. To my office staff for their support and patience. To Paul Elisha, Editor — words cannot express my admiration for Paul's hand in this project. To Louise Beckbissinger for going the extra mile to sequence words and punctuation, over and over again. To Gail Holubinka, former Director of the New York State Partnership for Long-Term Care Insurance, visionary and advocate of the consumer and the LTCI industry, for her continuous support. To Gary Corliss, LTCI Actuary, whose deep sense of commitment and uncharacteristic sense of humor inspired me to keep filling in the blanks. To Terry Haugen for her thorough reporting of LTC and LTCI globally. To the National LTC Network for their professionalism in helping to make this book a reality and for sharing with readers their personal and emotional long-term care experiences. To the Million Dollar Round Table, who had the foresight to engage me in this project, allowing me to reach many more of the "four kinds of people" referred to in Rosalynn Carter's book on caregivers than I ever dreamed possible. To my archangel, without whom the path would have been incomplete.

Paul,

What a beautiful experience when two minds combine in a harmonious sea of creativity to bouy countless Readers from having to shoulder the full burden of caring, "When Caring Isn't Enough!"

Larry

# C H A P T E R   1

## The Need for Long-Term Care

"Just the facts, Ma'am, just the facts." If you are old enough to remember this saying made famous by actor/director Jack Webb in the 1960's television police drama "Dragnet," I encourage you to read this book about long-term care and long-term care insurance. If you are too young to recall this phrase, I applaud your youth, but trust me, you will find the information contained within these pages just as relevant. Information on aging will prepare you to share some of the difficult physical, financial, and emotional experiences your parents and grandparents may encounter during their lifetimes.

Why is information so important to all of us? As former First Lady Rosalyn Carter wrote in her book *Helping Yourself Help Others: A Book For Caregivers,*[1] one of my colleagues in the field of caregiving once said, "There are only four kinds of people in this world:

- Those who have been caregivers
- Those who currently are caregivers
- Those who will be caregivers
- Those who will need caregivers."

In the big picture, long-term care threatens the financial stability of governments and families around the globe, which in part explains why the Health Care Financing Administration and the U.S. Census Bureau continue to focus on the issue of an aging population. The indicators of a pending future crisis are irrefutable. No serious book on the topic of long-term care would be complete without an explanation of the factors rendering this crisis inevitable. The authors of this book are very concerned with the financial consequences of future projections created by the need for long-term care, however, our approach to solving the problem is to train and educate one insurance agent at a time, and one consumer at a time.

There are plenty of facts, figures, and statistics about long-term care and the future of long-term care. Sometimes the figures and statistics are so overwhelming that they cloud the human elements of needing care or providing care. Sociologists, gerontologists, and government economists are currently consumed with future projections regarding the need for long-term care — and with good reason.

My awareness of the problem began at the 1989 Annual Meeting in Toronto, Canada, of the Million Dollar Round Table. The Million Dollar Round Table is an international sales organization made up of more than 23,000 successful life insurance agents, each of whom have met strict ethical and production requirements in order to qualify. MDRT members represent over 458 life insurance companies operating in sixty-one nations and territories. Inspirational morning meetings were held for 6,000 agents from around the world. Many members were observed wearing headphones listening to simultaneous translations of the presentations. Technical breakout sessions held in the afternoon were attended by agents seeking knowledge on specific insurance topics, as well as estate planning, computer applications, business practices, and human development. MDRT believes in the practice of the "whole person concept." Since 1989, the Million Dollar Round Table has continually made long-term care information available to its members at the Annual Meeting, in spite of the fact that credits from the sale of long-term care insurance were not granted towards membership qualification. Beginning with the 1999 Million Dollar Round Table Annual Meeting, sales of long-term care insurance are eligible for qualification.

Among those appearing on the main platform for the 1989 Annual Meeting was Dr. James Bruning, Jr., who after practicing dentistry for two years became paralyzed, the result of a diving accident. He and his wife Mary shared the podium and spoke about the meaning of disability income insurance.

A testament to the miracle of life insurance was delivered by Danny Tzakis, CLU, a twenty-three-year MDRT member. He spoke of the details that led to the sale of a life insurance policy to his friend Dave McClain, head football coach at the University of Wisconsin. I had tremendous empathy for Danny when he said, "I had lost good friends before and since Dave's death, who were also my clients, but never before, and I hope never again, had I lost a good friend in the middle of a life insurance sale." Then he introduced Dave McClain's widow, Judy, to explain how the claim was finally settled and what the life insurance benefits meant to her and her children.

Another main platform presentation that will live in the memories of those attending was delivered by W. Mitchell, who was burned over sixty-five percent of his body in a motorcycle accident. He lost fingers in the accident, and his face was burned beyond recognition, but he recovered enough to become a very successful businessman and pilot, acquiring his own airplane. One beautiful fall morning in Colorado, he invited four people to fly out to San Francisco with him. The plane had barely lifted off the runway when trouble developed and Mitchell had to crash land. His friends escaped injury, but he was left paralyzed and confined to a wheelchair for the rest of his life. Like all of the speakers, W. Mitchell was a success, and when he shared his message, "It's not what happens to you, it's what you do about it with your life," you had to believe.

In between guest speakers, the Million Dollar Round Table Foundation bestowed several grants to deserving groups. The Foundation's mission is to enhance the quality of life by encouraging member volunteerism and by giving funds to charitable enterprises. These funds are raised by the Foundation mainly, but not exclusively, from MDRT members and their companies. The Foundation makes contributions annually to selected nonprofit organizations and institutions that play an important role in strengthening our society. At this meeting, members witnessed the presentation of two $20,000 grants presented to the Amyotrophic Lateral Sclerosis Association (more commonly known as ALS or Lou Gehrig's Disease), and to the National Head Injury Foundation. Long-term care may not have been at the forefront of MDRT's insurance lexicon in 1989 — it would take ten more years for that to happen — but during that meeting, MDRT demonstrated that it does care!

One of the presenters at this meeting would have a major influence on my career. His name is Dr. Kenneth Dychtwald, and he is the author of the 1989 book *The Age Wave* [2]. Dr. Dychtwald explained the factors behind the "Age Wave." The portrait his statistics and observations painted about aging were enlightening as well as unsettling, and his presentation haunted me for months. Not being able to let go of Dr. Dychtwald's message, I sought to identify its significance to me, my clients, and the business of insurance. The first area I discovered relevant to insuring and aging is Medicare Supplement insurance. It seemed that everyone eligible for Medicare (approximately 75% of the U.S. population age 65 and older) owns Medicare Supplement insurance. To my mind, Medicare Supplement insurance qualifies as a commodity and does not require much expertise or background in sales. Digging further into issues, I discovered long-term care insurance and began to research the technicalities and subtleties of this form of insurance. During my research in 1989, I was looking at a product that appeared to carry a great deal of baggage, with detractors on many fronts. Back then, attorneys and accountants were advising clients not to purchase long-term care insurance policies. Bureaucrats cast a jaundiced eye upon the long-term care insurance industry. Articles appeared in newspapers about salesmen preying on the elderly with aggressive sales tactics, and in many instances, overselling. Some senior citizens were reported to own not one, but two, three, or four policies!

I even questioned the value of the policies being sold in the marketplace at the time. To be sure, many dollars in claims were paid on the early generations of long-term care insurance policies. However, if I couldn't convince myself to purchase one of these policies, I certainly couldn't recommend one to a client.

Dr. Dychtwald's message was loud and clear. We are in the throes of an "Age Wave," and there doesn't seem to be anything short of a wave of catastrophic premature deaths that can stem the tide! Assuming the projection that 250,000 "baby boomers" will turn age 50 each month for the next seventeen years is true, the "Age Wave," "Senior Boom," and "Graying of America" will create a demand for long-term care, hence the need for long-term care insurance to improve through competition and legislation.

It hasn't taken long for positive changes in policies to occur. For example, on January 1, 1992 the New York State Insurance Department adopted minimum standards for all long-term care insurance policies sold in that state. In 1993, the National Association of Insurance Commissioners (NAIC) published NAIC Suitability Standards for long-term care insurance. The NAIC is the oldest association of state government officials. Its members consist of the chief insurance regulators from all fifty states, the District of Columbia, and four U.S. territories. The primary responsibility of the state regulators is to protect the interests of insurance consumers. The NAIC lends support to state regulators by providing a forum for the development of uniform public policy when uniformity is appropriate. It does this through a series of model laws, regulations, and guidelines developed for the states' use. States that choose to do so may adopt the models intact or modify them to meet the needs of their marketplace and consumers. In the area of long-term care insurance, the NAIC established a committee that included consumers and consumer activists groups to assist in the policy making. The NAIC began introducing long-term care insurance regulations in 1986, and has done so continually since then.

In 1993, Suitability Standards for the Long-Term Care Insurance Model Act were devised with several goals in mind: to promote public interest in long-term care, to promote availability of long-term care insurance policies, to protect applicants for long-term care insurance from unfair or deceptive sales/enrollment practices, to establish standards for long-term care insurance, to facilitate public understanding and comparison of long-term care insurance policies, and to facilitate flexibility and innovation in its development of long-term care insurance coverage. A few key provisions of the Act were prohibition against post-claims underwriting, replacement notices, marketing standards, and suitability. Most states have adopted a majority of the thirty-two provisions.

One of the biggest issues that members of the NAIC faced in 2000 was to draft model language providing for long-term care insurance premium rate stability. The impetus comes by way of a few companies who have raised LTCI rates high enough to cause more than one policyholder to cancel coverage at the most inopportune time. While there is general agreement among regulators, consumer groups, insurance companies, and agents for some form of rate stability, finding acceptable solutions has been controversial. In the long run, the buying public and the insurance industry will be well served with knowledge that their long-term care insurance policies are adequately priced at time of sale; also, if increases are necessary in the future, they will be manageable. A model regulation was adopted in August 2000.

State insurance departments are responsible for seeing to it that insurance policies meet regulatory requirements, and for reviewing premium rate filings and any subsequent requests to increase rates.

States also establish requirements for agents to be licensed to sell long-term care insurance. Most states today mandate agents to take a series of Continuing Education courses to maintain their license(s) to sell insurance. Consumers who have a complaint with an insurance agent or insurance company should lodge their complaints with their state Department of Insurance. Insurance agents and/or insurance companies proven to be involved in unethical or illegal sales practices can be censured, fined, stripped of their licenses, and even face jail time.

The federal government passed the Health Insurance Portability and Accountability Act (HIPAA) in 1996. This bill, which set minimum federal standards for long-term care insurance, gave a strong endorsement of long-term care insurance by public policy makers. Further, it legitimized the purchase of long-term care insurance policies by increasing public awareness and promoting personal responsibility.

The bill grants long-term care insurance equal tax status with traditional health insurance. (Details relating to HIPAA will be addressed throughout subsequent chapters.) In conjunction with regulatory long-term care insurance advancements or possibly because of these advancements, positive stories about long-term care insurance now appear regularly throughout the media. Objective and knowledgeable attorneys and accountants have been advising clients to contact insurance agents for information on long-term care insurance in order to protect their assets and life savings. In recognition of the value of long-term care insurance, several states have formed Public/Private long-term care insurance partnerships. Approximately twenty states have granted citizens who purchase long-term care insurance policies a state income tax credit or deduction for payment of their long-term care premium.

In less than a decade, long-term care insurance established itself as the insurance with the highest percentage of growth in the insurance industry, assuring policyholders freedom of choice and access to quality long-term care. According to the Health Insurance Association of America (HIAA), in 1996 there were 117 insurers, including Blue Cross and Blue Shield companies, selling individual and group LTC coverage in the United States. Close to six million policies are in effect entering the new millennium. Life Plans published findings through Year End 1997, estimating total new sales for calendar year 1997 at $700,000,000, and total in force sales for all years through Year End 1997 at $2,707,000,000. According to HIAA, the LTC insurance market has grown an average of twenty-one percent between 1987 and 1997.

What factors have combined to influence insurance companies to create new product lines (a costly and time intensive process) and induce insurance agents to learn about a new set of risks, problems, and solutions, with a demanding learning curve?

People are living longer and dying slower. About one in every nine people today is considered a senior, and a "baby boomer" turns age 50 every seven seconds. Factors leading to longevity are healthier lifestyles and personal habits. People are more diet conscious, eating better and healthier foods. Smoking among people age 50 and older in the U.S. seems to be out of fashion. Exercise has taken up a considerable commitment among "boomers" and seniors in the U.S. The results of two long-term studies printed in the December 1999 issue of the *Journal of the American Medical Association*, state that a healthful lifestyle may be worth six to ten extra years of life. The media highlights the virtues of quality standards of living on a daily basis.

If ever there were a poster child for active seniors, it would have to be "Banana George." Banana George — George Blair, is recognizable by his yellow wet suit as he skims along the water, barefoot, holding a tow line between his teeth! He has appeared in ads for the AEtna Insurance Company and Sony Electronics, Inc., among others. Handing people an advertisement with a picture of "Banana George" is a delight, as you watch them take in the activity of the whole ad. The response is always the same. Shocked looks followed by outbursts of loud chuckles, as the observer comes to realize the water skier is no spring chicken. George turned 85 years old in January of 2000! During the winter, George lives in Steamboat Springs, Colorado, and can be seen snowboarding down a hill with his grandchildren wearing yellow boarding attire! A skydiving Banana George gave new meaning to the song "Yellow Bird"! (And how about another George, former President George Bush, who celebrated his 75th birthday by parachuting out of an airplane over College Station, Texas!!)

Modern medicine is allowing people to live longer, more active lives. Consider the gains made through major organ transplant surgery, or cancer defeating treatments such as chemotherapy and radiation therapy. When I entered the life insurance business in 1962, if a person applied for life insurance and had a heart condition, or high blood pressure, or diabetes, I probably couldn't assist them in buying life insurance. With the advent of coronary artery bypass surgery, angioplasty, and a host of modern medications, today a person applying for life insurance, with all three conditions under control, has a good chance of purchasing a life insurance policy.

As a child growing up in Schenectady, New York, it seemed to me there was a neighborhood bar on every street corner. Driving around town today, the bars have been replaced by drugstores. In fact, some corners have two or three competing national drug chains operating across the street from one another. But aging does have its problems. Combined deteriorating mobility and greater use of medications increases the risks of falls and injuries.

Time was when you could go to the human body repair shop just so many times. Today, however, medical scientists are unlocking the mysteries of the human body at an unbelievable pace, going beyond the science of vaccines and antibiotics, and entering the worlds of cell reproduction, genetic engineering, and organ replacement. The future of pharmaceuticals is to develop drugs to prevent or delay disease, rather than just treating the disease.

People are also living longer as a result of improvements in technology. Modern technology has provided us with safer living and working environments, in addition to making our daily tasks easier and more efficient to complete. The time saved provides more time to exercise and manage our lifestyles. Technology to manufacture a robot to assist in human caregiving now exists. This robot could handle tasks such as monitoring human vital signs, helping someone out of a chair, getting a glass of water, and of course cleaning the house. The newest technology will allow care providers to manage homebound patients' needs with chronic illnesses via hook-ups and linking videophones, medical stations, and the Web.

What more proof of an aging society do we need than to tune in to affable television personality and weatherman Willard Scott, who appears each morning on NBC's "Today Show"? It was 1982 when he began wishing people a happy birthday upon their reaching what was then considered the magical age of 100. In less than twenty years, Willard will have uttered those salutations to more than twenty-five thousand of the most cherished senior citizens on the planet.

In the beginning, the wishes were offered sporadically, after awhile increasing to two or three a week. Nowadays, Willard will "do his 100th wish" several times a week, and it could be to wish a happy 100th, or 105th, or 110th! How often have you said to yourself, "Where does Willard find these people?" In fact, according to U.S. Census Bureau estimates, there are nearly 70,000 centenarians living in the United States in 2000, and 250 people a day celebrate their 100th birthday. People over the age of 100 are one of the fastest growing segments of the U.S. population. The Japanese have the longest life spans in the world, with 10,000 citizens 100 years old or older. By the year 2005, there will be more than 100,000 Americans age 100 years or older, and by the year 2020, according to the Census Bureau, it is estimated the number will grow to 214,000. The New York State Teachers Retirement System reports that their oldest retired member is 106 years of age, and fifty-four of those receiving a retirement benefit are over 100 years old. If your view of octogenarians is that of oldsters sitting home in their rocking chairs collecting pension benefits, think again! Take, for example, Ben Levinson, the 103-year-old shot putter in the 1998 World Masters Games. Ben, who also competes in rock climbing and archery, was quoted at the games, saying, "I'm in better shape now than I was at 100!" The oldest living Olympic champion turned age 100 on November 12, 1998, in Maribor, Slovenia. Leon Stukelj won three Olympic gold medals, a bronze medal, and a silver medal in gymnastics during the 1924, 1928, and 1936 games. Stukelj, who developed a strength move on the rings — a move that became known as the Stukelj cross — still uses the rings hanging in the doorway of his home. Even more unbelievable, in the year 2000 a pair of American twins (the Moyer's) celebrated world record birthdays for twins reaching age 105, and another couple, husband and wife, both age 101, celebrated their 82nd wedding anniversary!

According to the U.S. Census Bureau, about 20% to 30% of 100 year olds are able to get around by themselves and are mentally competent. This body of work will deal with the issues involving the 70% to 80% of centenarians who do not possess physical and mental independence. Only a not-so-funny thing happened on the way to the forum. We learned these issues can strike anyone at any age. It is thought women age more slowly than men and the onset of stroke, cancer, and Alzheimer's may be delayed in women by ten years.

For the record, the world's oldest authenticated person, until she died at age 122 in France, was Jeanne Clement. She outlived her husband, daughter, and a grandson. Ms. Clement lived off income from an apartment she sold to a lawyer thirty years before. He agreed to make monthly payments on the apartment in exchange for taking possession when she died, but he never got to do so as he died at age 77, one year before she died. When she turned 122, she said, "I've only ever had one wrinkle and I'm sitting on it!"

Many examples exist of people's awareness to an aging society. Case in point: a survey conducted by Boston's Museum of Science, where visitors choose aging as the number one topic of interest. This led the museum to develop an interactive exhibit titled "Secrets of Aging." In 2000, the show will tour the U.S. from coast to coast. All one needs to do is scan the media to find stories related to aging. Stories abound in print, on radio, and on T.V. about Medicare, Medicaid, Social Security, geriatrics, and gerontology. Movies and T.V. produce dramas and sitcoms dealing with the issues of old age. (Even music videos, intended to play on one's emotions, contain senior care-giving images and messages, whether sung by country, pop, or new age artists.) Bookstores have shelves stocked with books dedicated to Aging/Retirement.

If there still exists a need to emphasize one of the major points in this chapter, it may be satisfied through the following report, sure to send shivers among some of the heartiest and fun-loving seniors on this planet. For more than a decade, Colorado ski resorts granted people age 70 and over the privilege to ski free. Citing advances in fitness and diet allowing people to ski into their 80s, Aspen Mountain officials, worried about the rising number of free skiers, became the first resort to eliminate free daily passes beginning with the 2000-2001 season!

For the purpose of insurance, why should we be aware of an aging population? Because quantity and quality are not synonymous for everyone. A Mankoff cartoon in the *New Yorker* magazine may have stated it best when one patron sitting at a bar said to the other, "See, the problem with doing things to prolong your life is that all the extra years come at the end when you are old!" Mankoff realized the real goal is to stay healthy as long as possible, and that longevity is secondary. With advanced age comes chronic illness, and people near the end of life need more and more care, therefore most people who are living longer lives will do so disabled. It is at this point that we must make the distinction between long-term care and acute care. Long-term care refers to personal care for people who need help and supervision with the ordinary tasks of the activities of living for an extended period of time. Long-term care can be provided for in the home or in a nursing facility. Acute care refers to an illness or injury that develops rapidly, has pronounced symptoms, and is finite in length. Acute care is most often provided in a hospital setting. To the person afflicted, there can be a world of difference between hope for better care, and hope for better health.

Some diseases that result in the need for long-term care remain a mystery to the medical and scientific communities, because there is little known about the cause of the diseases, and there are no truly adequate treatments to prevent or stop them. They include Alzheimer's disease, Multiple Sclerosis, and Parkinson's disease. What does appear apparent, at least with Alzheimer's and

Parkinson's diseases, is that they manifest themselves in old age. This is not good news for an aging society.

Alzheimer's erodes memory, personality, and self awareness. According to the Washington Office of the Alzheimer's Association, one in ten people over age 65, one in five ages 75 to 84, and half of those over age 85 suffer from Alzheimer's. The increasing demographics of aging leads medical scientists to conclude that the current four million Americans with Alzheimer's will swell to 14 million by the middle of this century, and to 45 million people worldwide. It is suspected the sons and daughters with one afflicted parent are three times more likely to develop the disease than those whose parents have no family history. While there are other causes of cognitive dysfunction, Alzheimer's represents more than 50% of the cause of dementia in the elderly.

## Of Presidents...

On November 6, 1994, former President Ronald Reagan, in a handwritten letter to "fellow Americans," disclosed he had Alzheimer's disease and had now begun "the journey that will lead me into the sunset of my life." (Reagan's mother died of the disease at age 77.)

Reagan, 83, wrote he was feeling fine at the time, but he and his wife Nancy had chosen to reveal the diagnosis in hopes of promoting greater awareness of the incurable, mind-crippling disease.

"Unfortunately, as Alzheimer's disease progresses, the family often bears a heavy burden," Reagan wrote. "I only wish there was some way I could spare Nancy from this painful experience. When the time comes, I am confident that with your help she will face it with faith and courage."

The doctors who tested and observed the former President said Reagan's health was otherwise good, but, "it is expected as the years go on it will begin to deteriorate." Alzheimer's is an irreversible, neurological disorder that destroys the brain's memory cells. In addition to memory loss, symptoms include impairment of judgment, disorientation, and personality change, leading to dementia and an almost infantile state requiring twenty-four-hour care. An estimated four million Americans, 400,000 of whom are under age 50, have the neurological disorder known as Alzheimer's. According to an article published in the August 1994 issue of the *American Journal of Public Health*, caring for each American diagnosed with Alzheimer's disease today will cost more than $213,000 on top of other medical expenses.

On the day of Reagan's announcement, while in Oakland, California, President Clinton interrupted a Democratic rally to talk about Reagan, asking everyone in the room "to give Ronald Reagan a hand and wish him well and Godspeed as he deals with this illness." (President Clinton lost an aunt and uncle to Alzheimer's disease.)

An Associated Press release dated January 16, 1995, states that former President Reagan no longer recognizes his biographer Edmund Morris. Morris said, "For all the willingness with which he showed me his framed photographs, his jelly beans jar, and his view of the Hollywood Hills, I did not feel his presence beside me, only his absence."

## And First Ladies...

Rosalynn Carter states in her book: *"My family has had its share of informal caregiving experiences, and more likely than not, so has yours.... You may prove that every day by actively assisting someone who is elderly and developmentally disabled or who suffers from a physical or mental illness. What a rewarding and noble endeavor it is to help another human being!*

*"Yet, I also know from personal experience and from the hundreds of caregivers (especially those caring for mentally ill family members) who have written to me, or whom I have encountered before, during, and since my years at the White House, that caregiving for those who have been thrust into the role can also be an extremely lonely, stressful, and frustrating*

*responsibility. I have seen so many people who have suffered from having always to take care of another. I know that it can tax one financially, emotionally, and physically. It can disturb privacy, sleep, and even health. Caregivers give so much of themselves and sometimes receive so very little in return."*

*"I have written Helping Yourself Help Others to hopefully ease the trauma associated with caregiving and to help you feel not quite so alone."*

Because each of us will fall into one of the four caregiver categories in Mrs. Carter's opening paragraph, this book is worth reading. If you haven't experienced one of the first two situations, you may not share a full appreciation of long-term care insurance benefits. *Helping Yourself Help Others* will enlighten and motivate some to insure for the costs of professional care, thereby preserving and protecting time, energy, health, and emotional reserves. (Former President Jimmy Carter has written a book titled *The Virtues of Aging*, published by Ballantine.)

Parkinson's disease is a mysterious neurological illness that affects almost one and a half million Americans, according to the National Parkinson's Foundation, placing it second only to Alzheimer's disease in frequency as a degenerative disease of the brain and nerves. Parkinson's causes slow deterioration of the nerves' ability to control muscles. Initial signs are tremors in the arms and hands, and muscle rigidity, progressing to a shuffling gait and increasing weakness. Changes in behavior are also associated with Parkinson's disease. Each year, 50,000 new cases are diagnosed, afflicting one in every 100 people over age 65. Many observers have noted Pope John Paul II's hand tremors, and the Reverend Billy Graham's slow leg movements.

The incidence of a stroke occurring is fifteen times greater than being afflicted with Parkinson's disease. At a 2000 meeting of the American Stroke Association, neurologist Robert D. Brown, Jr., of the Mayo Clinic in Rochester, Minn., presented data from two studies that showed Americans suffer more than 750,000 strokes a year. Strokes occur when blood flow to the brain is blocked or when there is bleeding in the brain. When mini-strokes, known as transient ischemic attacks (TIA's), are added to the count, the combined total of people affected by strokes rises to 1.2 million per year. Strokes are the nation's leading causes of long-term disability.

A more common disease associated with old age and requiring long-term care in its advanced stages is arthritis. According to studies by the Arthritis Foundation and the American College of Rheumatology, about 21 million people are affected by the most common form of arthritis, degenerative osteoarthritis.

With improved lifestyles, increased health awareness, and medical science breakthroughs contributing to increased longevity, how much these statistical casualties that increase with age will swell in the near future may be beyond anyone's best guess. Add to the list of debilitating diseases accidents that can cause the sudden and immediate need for the services of long-term care providers, and it's only a matter of time before long-term care insurance becomes the commodity that Medicare Supplement insurance is now.

What is old age? Most people believe old age is ten years older than they are. But no matter where you are on the spectrum of aging, it should be of concern to each and every one of us, because it affects all of us in one way or another.

Social Security and Medicare programs have been geared to provide benefits at age 65, creating a mindset in which many think of this as the benchmark for old age. Yet, for the six thousand Americans who turn 65 years old each day, the average life expectancy is age 82. That's seventeen years at risk for needing the services of a long-term care provider! If you're 65, you have a statistical chance of living seventeen more years. Again I ask "how old is old?" The U.S. Bureau of the Census projects the number of people age 65 and older is close to 35 million or one-seventh of the population. Remarkably, 19% or more of the population in Italy in the year 2003, Japan in 2005, and Germany in 2006 will be over age 65. The odds are that for every ten people 65 years old, four will need long-term care sometime in their lifetime. At age 70, the odds are five out of ten, age 75, the odds are six out of ten, and for every couple age 75, the odds are that one of two will need long-term care sometime in their lifetime.

These statistics bear witness to the biological definition of aging: "A normal phenomenon which results in a decreased overall physiological capacity of a person to withstand the stresses of everyday living." In other words, the older we get, the more we experience chronic illness and reduced physical and mental capacity. From age 60 on, many people will experience difficulty with hearing, vision, mobility, strength, and mental ability.

The quality and quantity of a person's life can be affected by many factors, such as blood pressure, diabetes, cholesterol, smoking, diet, exercise, marital status, and at-death age of parents and siblings. Meanwhile, biomedical research is leading scientists and physicians to the conclusion that 100-year life spans will be common over the next few decades, and a 200-year life span is not inconceivable. The issue for the architects and sales forces of long-term care insurance policies is that old age leads to increased frailty and disability, which leads to the need for care. Care can be expensive, and the longer people need care, or bids for the highest quality of care, the more likely it becomes that they will exhaust their resources to pay for their care.

Standing on the threshold of needing long-term care may be akin to a skier staring down a slippery slope, with one exception. The candidate for long-term care checks his or her financial status: savings, retirement assets, and income. The skier checks his or her equipment: boots, bindings, and poles. The former usually believes someone will be there to bail him or her out; the latter believes getting to the bottom of things is solely his or her own responsibility. Both of these beliefs may be displaced by dire consequences.

Long-term care can be very expensive, whether it is provided at home or in a nursing facility. Personal care at home can range from eight to thirteen dollars per hour, increasing to twenty-five dollars or more per hour for skilled care. It's easy to see how round-the-clock care at home can exceed the costs of a nursing facility. Nationwide nursing home care can cost $32,850 to $150,000 per year, depending on where you live.

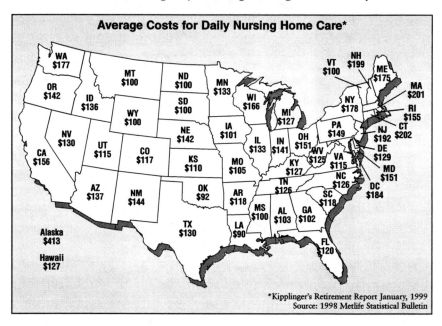

**Average Costs for Daily Nursing Home Care***

|  |  |
|---|---|
| WA | $177 |
| OR | $142 |
| ID | $136 |
| MT | $100 |
| WY | $100 |
| ND | $100 |
| SD | $100 |
| NE | $142 |
| MN | $133 |
| WI | $166 |
| IA | $101 |
| NV | $130 |
| UT | $115 |
| CO | $117 |
| CA | $156 |
| AZ | $137 |
| NM | $144 |
| KS | $110 |
| OK | $92 |
| TX | $130 |
| MO | $105 |
| AR | $118 |
| LA | $90 |
| IL | $133 |
| IN | $141 |
| MI | $127 |
| OH | $151 |
| KY | $127 |
| TN | $126 |
| MS | $100 |
| AL | $103 |
| GA | $102 |
| WV | $125 |
| VA | $115 |
| NC | $126 |
| SC | $118 |
| FL | $120 |
| PA | $149 |
| NY | $178 |
| VT | $100 |
| NH | $199 |
| ME | $175 |
| MA | $201 |
| RI | $155 |
| CT | $202 |
| NJ | $192 |
| DE | $129 |
| MD | $151 |
| DC | $184 |
| Alaska | $413 |
| Hawaii | $127 |

*Kipplinger's Retirement Report January, 1999
Source: 1998 Metlife Statistical Bulletin

According to the New York State Partnership for long-term care, the average stay in a nursing home is two and one-half years. How may people can afford to pay $87,000 or $200,000 for the average stay? Factor in the living expenses of the community spouse — the healthy spouse who remains in their own home — and the seeds for financial disaster have been sown. The uninformed, a major segment of society, believe they don't have to worry about the costs of long-term care. In survey after survey, the prevailing opinions are that traditional health insurance or Medicare will pay for the costs of long-term care.

The following chapters will clear up the falsity of these assumptions. For most of the 1990s, informed consumer activists, who knew better than to rely on group insurance or Medicare, have lobbied the federal government to pay for the costs of care. The federal government, on the other hand, is sending clear and unwavering messages that citizens should become financially responsible for the cost of their own care whenever possible. The first message came with passage of the Health Insurance Portability and Accountability Act, for all intents and purposes endorsing the purchase of long-term care insurance. Another message was delivered by President Clinton in January 2000, encouraging a program to educate Medicare beneficiaries about Medicare's limited long-term care options. The costs of this informational campaign was pegged at $10,000,000.

Wouldn't it be wonderful if the government paid for all of our long-term care expenses and we didn't have to worry about spending our money for long-term care or paying for additional insurance premiums? Sure it would, but the federal government is grappling with how to continue to finance two of the most important social programs ever created, Social Security and Medicare Insurance. The impact of the oncoming "Age Wave" is dealing a devastating blow, because the crafters of these programs never envisioned citizens requiring retirement incomes over the length of current life expectancies, or providing medical care for procedures that weren't even conceived of when these programs were created. The federal government's problem is compounded by the fact that the Social Security system is on a "pay as you go" basis. (Some economists contend the government has spent the money before you get there!) In 1950, when there were sixteen workers to every retiree, the system easily supported itself. In 1996, according to *The New York Times*, the ratio of retirees to workers shrank to three to one. While there is some debate over whether birth rates will continue to fall or if births will be on the rise in the next millennium, the number of aging "boomers" is incontestable. The U.S. Census Bureau, through a study financed by the National Institute on Aging, projects the ratio of elderly people to working-age people (ages 20-64) will nearly double between 1990 and 2050.

With fewer working taxpayers to support their elders in 2020, is it still conceivable that long-term care entitlements will be expanded under the current government assistance programs of Social Security and Medicare? Add to this, most lists of the top ten fastest growing jobs currently include home health aides, personal home care aides, physical therapists, nurses, and/or nurse's aides, all of whom provide care for the elderly.

National LTC Network member J. Eugene Tapper, MS, NHA, who was a licensed nursing home administrator prior to entering the long-term care insurance business, addresses the odds we face for needing long-term care and the purpose of long-term care insurance.

## Long-Term Care: In Your Future?

The subject of long-term care has become an important issue with today's senior population. Will it affect me? Where will I receive the care? Can I stay at home? What is long-term care? What is the cost? Doesn't Medicare pay for these services? What are my choices? What will I need? All these questions are issues on the minds of seniors.

For many, the fear of dying too soon has been replaced by the fear of becoming disabled through a lengthy though frail life. Becoming unable to walk, move from a chair to a bed, perform bathroom functions, bathe, dress, and feed oneself is a matter of immense concern to active adults. Moreover, when we lose these functions, we want to be cared for. This, coupled with the fact that families are geographically separated, makes it more difficult for seniors to receive the traditional support from family members that they have enjoyed in the past. Consequently, seniors are using more services of home health care and long-term care facilities than ever before. It is important to address and plan for these services while good health and a stable mind allow you to implement a course of action to prepare for the future.

Long-term care is also needed for people under the age of 65. Although long-term care tends to focus on persons over the age of 65, more than 40% of persons with disabilities potentially require many of the same services provided to the elderly population.[3] Statistically, a person under age 65 has a 7% chance of having a need to be admitted into a nursing home.[4] At ages 85 to 90, the chances jump to 60%.[5] Nevertheless, when it is your time to need long-term care, it is a 100% chance, not the 7% or 60% chance that statistics give.

The likelihood that an individual will need long-term care is high. Studies show 60% of people over age 65 will require long-term care at some point in their lives.[6] One national study[7] indicates the risk of needing nursing home care is greater for women than men: 13% of the women in this study, compared to 4% of the men, are projected to spend five or more years in a nursing home. The risk of needing nursing home care also increases with age.[8] On average, Medicare pays for only approximately 8% of long-term care costs in a nursing home.[9] Medicaid is a federally funded program, administered by the individual states, which helps pay for the medical care of financially needy people through public assistance, medically needy and medically indigent programs.[10] And, the cost of nursing home care can run from $36,500 to $109,500 per year depending on where you live, with care at home averaging $15,600 to $46,800 per year.[11] At a compound inflation rate of five percent, the annual $36,500 cost in 2000 will grow to $56,575 in ten years, and $92,345 in twenty years. Imagine what your future expenses will be for the higher per-day cost of care!

Medicare coverage only pays up to 100 days of skilled nursing care in a facility, if it is even approved. So, with an average length of facility stay lasting two and a half years[12] to three years, and only some limited home health care, if the care is determined to be medically necessary[13], many older adults will need long-term care insurance coverage to cover the huge gaping hole in the government's reimbursement of cost to the consumer for long-term care services.

The purpose of long-term care insurance is to protect your assets and help you pay for the cost of long-term care. Long-term care insurance may not be for everyone.

You need lifelong asset protection through long-term care insurance if:

- You want to prepare financially now for long-term care needed in your future,
- You want to retain your independence, and avoid depending on family or friends for help, and
- You want to protect your savings and other assets for yourself and your heirs.

The younger you are when you purchase a policy, the less you will have to pay for premiums.

The same policy that costs $480 a year if you buy at age 50 could cost $880 a year if you buy at age 60, or it could cost you $1,750 a year if you buy it at age 70. The same policy benefits could cost you $4,690 a year if you buy the policy at age 80.[14] (As an aside, depending on an insurance company's underwriting guidelines, consumers can purchase policies up to age 100 at the time of application.) Keep in mind that insurers will not sell you a policy if you have a pre-existing condition such as Alzheimer's disease, Parkinson's disease, or deficiencies in activities of daily living such as transferring, ambulating, continence, toileting, bathing, dressing, and eating at time of policy application. Also, keep in mind that long-term care policies pay for services to help you with these deficiencies when you have a policy in place before you become in need of assistance. It's your health that allows you to obtain an individual long-term care insurance policy; it's your money that pays for it.

Consumers considering a plan should think how much they may be able to pay out-of-pocket toward the cost of care before they need a policy to start paying on their behalf. Many questions can be raised when looking at the need for long-term care and long-term care insurance. While no one knows for certain what lies in the future for ourselves, for loved ones, or for clients, the following chapters will help you to consider the possibilities and appropriate alternatives to handle possible future situations.

# CHAPTER 2

## Long-Term Care:
## An Issue of Risk, Not Age

In the minds of most people, the phrase "long-term care" conjures up images of elderly persons confined to a bed, or ambulatory only with the aid of a walker or wheelchair. As you will see in this chapter, nothing could be further from the truth. There are minimum ages to drive, drink, enter the military, and so on, but it is unlikely you will ever see a sign above a nursing facility entrance regarding the minimum age to gain entry. Most likely, a majority of the non-elderly who are in need of care won't be seen in a nursing facility, as families endeavor to provide for their son's and daughter's care at home. So, is long-term care insurance only for the elderly? To answer that question, one need only apply to insurance companies who begin selling long-term care insurance at age eighteen. While few sales are processed for eighteen-year-olds, this does not mean that a young adult should be discouraged from purchasing a policy. Is there an ideal age to purchase a long-term care insurance policy? That question is as easy to answer as the one that noted actress and playwright Ruth Gordon posed: "How old would you be if you didn't know how old you were?" The fact is long-term care affects people of all ages: either as a patient or a caregiver.

Logic would tell us, if there are people residing in nursing facilities or receiving care at home under the age of 65, then everyone is at risk. The business of insurance is to protect against loss or risk, so it is only natural to market a policy to people who could fall prey to a claim and can afford to pay a premium. Hopefully, our sons and daughters will age to normal life expectancies when the odds of needing care are highest. But during the interim, there are more reasons to be insured than not, particularly because major medical insurance plans are *unlikely* to cover custodial care at home or in a facility. It may be difficult to convince most people that debilitating diseases such as strokes occur to children even in infancy, yet research suggests that 1,400 children age 17 and under suffer strokes in the U.S. each year. There is an element of risk for every generation leading to seniority.

The times we live in have brought about risky behavior with consequences to life and limb. Generation X has invented the X (Extreme) Games. Baby boomers are responsible for a new term to describe a conduct called Risk Homeostasis. Risk Homeostasis refers to a situation in which the safer things get, and the more regulators and litigators seek to snuff out any possibility that we can injure ourselves, the more we consciously and unconsciously seek out the exhilaration of risky business.

There are people who go rock climbing, ride the rapids, make ultra-high bungee jumps, go paragliding, swim among the sharks, tee off within sight of African wildlife. It's no wonder those who engage in these activities are required to read through disclaimers and sign releases!

Wealthy people can take risks to even greater heights. For $30,000 to $60,000, one can join an assault on Mt. Everest. Twenty-five thousand dollars can buy you a seat at the controls of a Russian MIG fighter, flying at two and one-half times the speed of sound to experience the affects of zero gravity in the skies above Russia.

If these examples of youthful indiscretion that push the envelope aren't compelling enough, I conclude with the following case in point. The conservative, yet beautifully written and photographed *National Geographic* magazine, which is 110 years old, launched a brand new magazine in April 1999 titled *National Geographic Adventure*, "where the wild and wonderful spirit of adventure is alive and well...and waiting to be shared with daring souls like you. With *Adventure*, you'll get a wealth of ideas for making adventure part of your life, near and far from home, with the promise of "redefining the spirit of exploration for a new generation of adventure." I couldn't wait for my first issue to arrive!

If all this behavior is not risky, an awful lot of stress, anxiety, and worry is wasted by spouses, parents, co-workers, and stockholders. Even less exotic everyday activities engaged in by young people more than oldsters are no less risky and account for thousands upon thousands of injuries per year. In order of most risk, these are ice hockey, football, skiing/snowboarding (acrobatics on ice and snow), soccer, baseball, bicycle riding, rollerskating/inline skating, and ice skating.

A noted example of the type of injury that can occur occupied newspaper headlines across America in 1995. Travis Roy, a freshman hockey player for Boston University, was paralyzed from the neck down, just seconds into his first shift on the ice after crashing head-first into the boards. In spite of being confined to a wheelchair and unable to perform normal activities of daily living without help from home health care aides (costing between $200,000 and $300,000 per year), Roy still earned a college degree from B.U. in the class of 2000.

According to the National Spinal Cord Injury Statistical Center, about 10,000 people a year suffer a nonfatal spinal cord injury, the median age being 26. Leading causes are auto accidents (35%), falls (18%), gunshots (17%), diving (8%), and motorcycle accidents (6%).

Media throughout the United States during 1999 were filled with accounts of school and work site violence at the hands of gunmen. Some of the perpetrators of these shootings were children, and all too often the victims have been children.

School-related shooting deaths naturally garner much attention. One hundred and fifty students have been shot to death since 1992. Several victims, however, have been left paralyzed from these shootings, and little has been said about the struggles they and their care-giving parents are left to cope with. An exception was the report about a mother of one of three students paralyzed during the 1999 Columbine (Colorado) High School shooting who committed suicide five months following her daughter's paralysis. Sometimes, caring just isn't enough.

25

The Consumer Product Safety Commission, which cites nearly 18,000 head injuries per year, advocates the use of helmets for participants of many of the sports previously listed. While Travis Roy's helmet prevented head injury, it's doubtful he would have escaped paralysis from his crash, even if he were wearing a suit of armor! Head trauma injuries are not unusual for people involved in accidents while riding in cars, all-terrain vehicles, snowmobiles, or motorcycles. Proposals to mandate the wearing of helmets spark passionate debates between motorcycle enthusiasts and legislators.

Quoting the C.P.S.C. once again, people have been overdoing physical activities as they age. Over the past ten years, sports injuries have increased 18% for people ages 25 to 64, and 54% for people ages 65 and older. (The November 1999 issue of AARP's magazine, *Modern Maturity*, listed fifty top travel adventures for its members, ranking them by difficulty.) With these activities claiming casualties among people of all ages, there will be those requiring long-term care, some longer than others. No surprise, you say? Then how about the following examples of disabilities that are not of an accidental nature?

Strokes can happen at any age. Twenty-five percent of the time, they occur to people under the age of 40, and about 1,400 children age 17 and under suffer strokes in the United States each year, costing billions of dollars. The average age for those afflicted with Parkinson's disease is estimated to be about 55, with 15% under age 50, and 10% under age 40. Some of the more famous people afflicted at younger ages are actor Michael J. Fox (part of the 5% who are symptomatic at age 30 and under), former heavyweight boxing champion Muhammad Ali, and Attorney General Janet Reno. Alzheimer's disease has been detected among 40- and 50-year-olds. The percentage of those afflicted with Alzheimer's age 64 and younger stands at 8%.

The U.S. General Accounting Office estimates that almost 40% of the 13 million Americans currently receiving long-term care services are between the ages of 18 and 64.[1] If you find that hard to believe, I can furnish proof at a nursing home within a thirty-minute drive of my office. On the third floor, you would discover forty residents whose age ranges from their 20s to their 50s. In other area nursing homes, 10% to 20% of their residents include men and women under the age of 65. There are even plans on the drawing board to build a $4.2 million twenty-bed nursing home just to serve young disabled adults. (I once visited a nursing home and met a mother, father, and son who were all residents of the nursing home.) Such nontraditional residents pose care challenges uncommon to the geriatric population. Younger residents who have lost their independence when their peers are still raising families and moving up the career ladder harbor a great deal of resentment and frustration, with a feeling of "it's just not fair!" The availability of claim dollars from privately owned long-term care insurance provides freedom of choice and access for types of care that could go a long way toward improving the quality of life for young people caught in these circumstances.

To most, the phrase "long-term care" conjures up visions of frail, elderly individuals. For every person receiving care in a nursing facility, there are four to five people receiving care at home. Examples of non-age specific diseases with durations lasting three to five years are cancer, AIDS, respiratory disease, and heart disease. These diseases and many others have caused millions who do not fit the stereotypical "old" mold to seek up to eight, ten, or more hours of care per week at home. And ordinary health insurance and major medical insurance do not provide the means necessary to hire help to provide assistance with symptom management, dressing, mobility, and the myriad other nonmedical needs to get through another day.

The 1998 Million Dollar Round Table Annual Meeting in Chicago, Illinois, featured a very special speaker. Christopher Reeve is known around the world for the roles he has played on the large screen, especially that of Superman. Reeve's handsome good looks and athletic frame made the transition from comic book hero to real live hero incredibly believable.

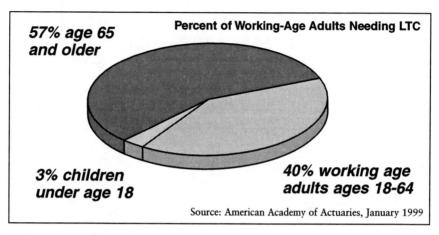

**Percent of Working-Age Adults Needing LTC**

57% age 65 and older

3% children under age 18

40% working age adults ages 18-64

Source: American Academy of Actuaries, January 1999

What made his performances so compelling was the nature of the man himself, who was able to play the mild-mannered newspaper reporter Clark Kent, then in an instant transform himself into Superman, Man of Steel!

However, Reeve's appearance at the 1998 Annual Meeting would prove he is human after all. Daily, people die unexpectedly. Others may cheat death, but in the process be faced with life-long debilitating consequences. This is what happened to Christopher Reeve one May morning. Sports such as tennis, scuba diving, and flying were always an essential part of Christopher Reeve's life.

Anyone participating in these sports will tell you they are accompanied by elements of risk to life and limb. Reeve's new passion was for the world of horses and equestrian riding. It is a sport of grace, power, and beauty that can turn ominous in a moment. So it was at age 42 on Memorial Day Weekend, 1995, during competition Reeve's horse, Buck, instead of going over a jump, stopped without warning. The terrible outcome of this incident was an airborne rider who landed on his head and ended up breaking his first and second vertebrae. A doctor told Reeve that had he landed with his head twisted only a fraction further to the left, he would have been killed instantly. If he had landed with his head slightly more to the right, he probably would have sustained a bruise and been up on his feet within a few weeks, but instead he is a C-2 vent-dependent quadriplegic.

Learning this, Reeve says, "Now I know on a visceral level how fragile our existence is."

Two weeks prior to this tragedy, Christopher Reeve filmed a public service commercial for other riders. His message was, "I would never think of riding without a helmet." Was he wearing a helmet the day of his fall? Of course he was, and his helmet prevented any brain damage, yet his accident is just one more example of how "bad things happen to good people."

The outcome of this event presents one of the most compelling reasons why younger as well as older people should consider being insured for long-term care. In this example, the annual cost of care is reported to be well over $100,000 per year. In Chicago, the star of *Superman* shared with his MDRT audience the fact that he owned life insurance and disability income insurance. He bought the disability insurance, he said "never thinking I would need it, but thinking it was a smart thing to do!" Reeve's body may not be made of steel, but surely his will is. Since that terrible fall, he has directed an award-winning HBO movie, acted in a T.V. remake of "Rear Window," and made numerous public appearances to raise the consciousness and charitable giving of millions of Americans. His incredible desire to survive and achieve earned Reeve a thunderous ovation when he told MDRT members: "My proudest day was when I was able to call my disability insurance company and say, 'Thank you very much, but I can make a living and I won't need your money!' "

Disability income insurance pays when the insured cannot perform the duties of one's occupation. Life insurance pays benefits upon death. Long-term care insurance pays when the insured cannot perform two out of five or six activities of daily living. For Reeve's care, it takes two hours in the morning for a nurse and an aide to help him through the routine of exercising, bathing, and dressing. During the day, others are responsible for his feeding. Required care during the two-hour preparation for bed in the evening includes assistance with toileting, by squeezing the body to empty the bowels.

There are many occasions when Christopher is required to appear in formal attire. At those times, because he pays for his aides out of his own pocket, and can only afford to have them come just twice a day, he spends the day dressed formally for an evening's appearance.

Michael Weintraub, Gene Mahn, Christopher Reeve, and Mitchell R. Stoller, "Million Dollar Round Table," Chicago, Illinois, June 1998

Christopher Reeve believes through modern medicine, modern technology, and determination, he will walk again. His belief is so strong, he was willing to be seen walking in the future, via a computer-generated TV commercial depiction aired during Super Bowl 2000. To that end, the Million Dollar Round Table Foundation presented to Mr. Reeve, Chairman of the Board of the American Paralysis Association, a check for $100,000 so that someday, he and others like him may walk again.

## Still Superman to Me

Heroes come in different sizes, shapes, colors, and abilities. Being "faster than a speeding bullet" has its advantages, but so does the power of the pen.

On a recent trip, I took along Christopher Reeve's book *Still Me*.[2] On the return trip to New York, I had practically finished the book, when I came upon something the author wrote about the pain of sensory deprivation: not being able to hug his son, Will, since Will was two years old. This sentiment struck a nerve in me.

I hadn't hugged my father, Leo, whom I love dearly, for as long as I could remember. From what I have observed in America, this was not unusual for men who raised children during the 40s and 50s. When Dad turned 84 years old in March of 1998, that year, and over the years, I often lamented the fact we had never hugged. Many "what ifs" plagued me on the subject of our not hugging. By nature, I am a touchy-feely person, as my wife and children will attest, compounding my dilemma even more in regard to my relationship with my Dad.

Before my plane had landed, I made a promise to myself to hug my father the next time we met. I was so intimidated by my own promise, I did not share it with anyone. Every Thursday morning, Nancy and I meet my father for breakfast at a local diner. Two days had passed, and I still didn't know how I was going to fulfill my promise. We finished breakfast. Dad picked up the check as usual. When we reached his car, I suddenly heard myself saying out loud, "Dad, on the flight home, something happened up there and I promised myself if I landed safely, I would hug my family, so let me give you a hug!" When I did, I will never forget his look of concern as he said, "What happened up there?" I simply replied, "Let's not talk about it." I am happy to report that was the first but certainly not the last hug between us! Christopher Reeve, a.k.a. Superman, came to my rescue, and I was privileged to have had the opportunity to thank him in person.

## "We All Can Become a Member of a Minority"

Hearing these words, I wondered just what our storyteller was alluding to. There we were, 11,500 feet above sea level, on the Colorado Trail at the timberline just below Jacques' Peak. The horses were tied to the ruins of an old miner's log cabin and we were listening to Bill Miller recount the inspiration that led him to write a song titled "Faith of a Child."

Bill Miller is a walking, talking tribute to the world of contrasts in which we all live. He is of Mohican-German parents, a Native American raised on the Stockbridge-Munsee reservation in Wisconsin.

As Miller tells it, "Faith of a Child" has come to represent "two beautiful children who inspire me daily with their struggles in a world with so many standards of perfection." Therein I found the meaning of the rest of the story, because at any moment, we all can become a member of a minority, *the minority of the disabled!* He sang about the hopes and dreams of a little girl unable to go through life in a way most would consider normal, and oftentimes dependent on the care of others to fulfill her needs.

This day I felt blessed, for as far as the eye could see there was blue sky above and the world below. Breakfast and lunch on the trail were filled with Miller's mesmerizing and inspirational words and songs accompanied by his native flute, guitar, and harmonica. Following lunch, I mounted my horse Stinky to head back down the trail. (Once, Stinky had an abscessed tooth, accounting for a rather foul-smelling mouth, which earned him this unflattering nickname.) Stinky and I came to a small creek loaded with rocks of many sizes and shapes that several horses before us gingerly passed through. Unknown to me, Stinky had his own way of crossing the creek at this point, and in a flash, "we" were leaping from one bankside to the other! That's when Bill Miller's words sprang into my head as quickly as Stinky had sprung into his own agenda: "We all can become a member of a minority, the minority of the disabled!" More than 17% of horse-related injuries are head injuries such as cerebral contusions, concussions, or skull fractures. All can cause permanent damage and, of course, nonfatal spinal cord injuries like Christopher Reeve's.

A year later on the same trail, I had a new mount, and my wife, Nancy, said "Playboy and I should get along just fine."

Well, pardner, I'm here to tell you she was mighty right! Stopping along the trail for breakfast, we were entertained by Colen H. Sweeten, Jr. Colen is a wonderful cowboy poet. Seeing Colen dressed in his cowboy hat, leather vest, leather chaps, and Western boots, sitting atop his mount, one would never guess he would be celebrating his 80th birthday soon!

Colen has given me permission to share a poem called, "Cowboy Without Boots." He wrote this poem after meeting a young cowboy in Elko, Nevada, who had lost the use of his legs.

You should also know Colen had a brother, Lloyd, who was confined to a wheelchair because of an accident he had while picking pears. Lloyd fell out of the tree and became paralyzed from the chest down. Colen's brother spent twenty-eight years in a wheelchair, until he passed away. There is no doubt his brother's plight, combined with his meeting the young cowboy in Elko, Nevada, moved Colen to write the poem.

Colen said he recited this poem to a crowd of thousands, but this particular morning, sitting around a campfire, high atop the Rocky Mountains with twenty-five city slickers, he had to check his emotions to finish the last two verses. I, too, had a lump in my throat, as I began to think of the 200,000 people between the ages of 18 and 64 in nursing homes, and the countless others in this age group who are receiving long-term care at home.

## COWBOY WITHOUT BOOTS

I saw him there at the gathering
With his wheelchair against the wall.
I said, "Howdy cowboy, glad you're here,
Looks like your horse took a fall."

"No, not a horse, but it's all the same.
So I guess that's close enough.
It was an old bull that scoured his plow,
And I tell you that bull was rough!"

"Sorry," I said, "I'll see you next year,
When the wheelchair isn't your seat."
He grinned and said, "Oh, I'll be here,
But I won't be on my feet.

The Doctor tells me I'll never stand,
Nor walk, or sit on a horse.
What's done, is done and I'm O.K.,
And a lot of men have it worse."
He smiled when he said it and offered his hand,
But the grip was much too light.
The hurt in his eyes melted my heart —
Left me lyin' awake at night.
His blue-grey eyes were like a muddied stream,
With no light from the murky skies.
And his voice, when he spoke, was the gentle smoke
Of a campfire when it dies.
I remember the music and laughter,
And the cowboys with Western suits.
But, most I remember the wheelchair,
And the cowboy without boots.

— Colen H. Sweeten, Jr.

My long-term care insurance policy allows me to feel more comfortable on a saddle or on a pair of downhill skis. While Nancy enjoys horseback riding, she does not share my enthusiasm for downhill skiing. I wanted to be sure that if I encountered a severe trauma during skiing (rocks or trees or another skier), she would not have to become a twenty-four hour, seven days a week, three hundred and sixty-five days a year caregiver, with duties such as bathing, changing diapers, food preparation and feeding, management of medications, etc., with no time for her own physical, emotional, or financial well being. Risking the pleasure of life for two people, at the expense of one thrill seeker, hardly seemed fair. Once our long-term care insurance policies were in force, I truly slept better. Providing I haven't had to file a claim sooner than later, the older I am, the more I will value my long-term care insurance to meet the increasing odds of needing care, and I have purchased my policies for a substantially lower premium than if I had waited five, ten, fifteen, or twenty years.

# CHAPTER 3

# Types of Long-Term Care

People in need of long-term care may receive their care in several different settings. New types of care settings will undoubtedly emerge as we learn to meet the needs of the disabled and infirm who live to greater ages with the help of medicine and modern technology. Fortunately for consumers, comprehensive long-term care insurance policies cover care delivered in each of several settings.

Gene Tapper, Product Committee Chairperson for the National LTC Network, who worked in long-term care delivery systems as a nursing home administrator prior to entering the long-term care insurance field, will give a firsthand account of the function of nursing facilities.

Richard Sanford, elder statesman for the National LTC Network, is also intimately familiar with issues that deal with home health care. He will help you to become better informed about home health care, and gain insight into the care conflicts that emerge between desire and denial.

When most people think about long-term care, they think of nursing home care or home health care. Other options for receiving care exist under the banner of community care. A National LTC Network member, Thomas Collica, addresses these options and provides a meaningful example of an alternative to nursing home care and home health care, which he experienced through his clients.

## Nursing Home Care
## by GeneTapper

So many people say to family, friends, health care professionals, and, yes, even long-term care insurance agents, "you will never find me in one of those places."

For many of us, it may not be a matter of choice, but rather a

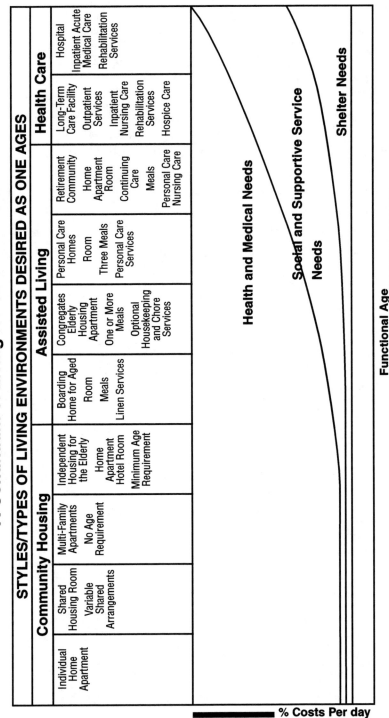

A Continuum of Living for Older Persons

STYLES/TYPES OF LIVING ENVIRONMENTS DESIRED AS ONE AGES

matter of necessity to be in a nursing home. As a licensed nursing home administrator, I was often thrust into a family's dilemma when I became the person who had to deal with a patient's loved one and help a family member understand why a nursing home environment was right for him or her. In most cases, I had to meet with family members in crisis because they were admitting their loved one to a nursing home during a period of extremely high stress. They usually were not informed as to what they could expect from a nursing home, nor were they expecting to be there. In fact, many family members knew only of the negative reports they had heard in the news media about nursing homes. That negative publicity scared many people. My job was to share with them what good nursing homes could provide and to win their confidence as a provider of care.

Here is what happened many times. Can you imagine yourself in this situation? A nursing home residence is the most remote place family members had in mind before admission. Then, because of a sudden change in the condition of the person in need of care, there they were. A case in point: an active, apparently healthy person has a stroke. The person is admitted to a hospital and it is determined the person has paralysis, but there is restorative potential. After a minimum hospital stay of three or possibly five days for stroke, the patient and his or her family find out the patient needs to be in a skilled nursing facility (nursing home). For many, that word is told to them for the first time by a continuity of care coordinator in the hospital. Again, many are told they must leave the hospital because their days reimbursed by Medicare or major medical plan will terminate according to the schedule in their benefit package. Typically, the care coordinator says, "Here is where you need to go — good luck, I'll make the arrangements for you." Wham, bang, you are out of there!

That is the perception that many family members have at the time of discharge from the hospital in these types of situations. Can you imagine the feeling and reaction the responsible party family member must have at that moment? What do I do?

How do I care for my loved one? Where do I go? How do I know the facility being recommended is any good? Do they take care of their patients or do they just let them lie there? How can I check a place out? Do I have time? Are we stuck with this facility just because the hospital referred us to it? Is this the right thing to do? How will we pay for this? Many questions; no where to turn. Panic.

When I saw this occur during a nursing home admission process, I would stop and explain what was happening. I would tell the people what they could expect in the nursing home. I would explain how the different types and levels of care in our health care delivery system fit together so they would know they were in the right place of care. I also found myself having to explain what Medicare and/or their major medical plan was going to pay for and, more importantly, what these insurance plans would not pay for on behalf of the insured in the nursing home.

To the amazement of most, at the time of admission, they were discovering for the first time (and when it was too late to protect themselves financially) their Medicare or major medical insurance plan was not going to pay for needed nursing home care. The reason? Medicare does not pay for custodial care (personal care) if that is the only kind of care you require. Custodial care includes assistance in walking, getting in and out of bed, eating, dressing, bathing, and taking medicine.[1] In addition, most major medical insurance programs follow this same concept when it comes to paying benefits in a nursing home setting. For instance, according to the California Department of Aging, less than 8% of all admissions in nursing homes receive some type of financial support from the government or private major medical insurance plans for what is called "skilled nursing care."[2] Hence, custodial care has a huge financial impact on people in nursing homes. Ninety-two percent of the patients or their families have to pay for the cost of care.

It is important to understand the types and levels of care one can expect from our health care delivery system. We need to plan for long-term care events financially and emotionally while we still have time to act. How do these types and levels of care fit into our health care delivery system and what can we expect from Medicare and major medical insurance plans in payment for these services?

A description of the types and levels of care in our health care delivery system, including acute hospital care, sub-acute care, skilled nursing facility care, and intermediate care, follows:

## Acute Hospital Care

This level of care is short term, and typically for surgery, intensive medical treatment, specialized observation, and other procedures. An acute care hospital is not considered long-term care. It's a place where most of us go hoping for better health, not hoping for better care.

## Sub-Acute Care

This level of care is typically for heavy rehabilitation by licensed persons such as physical, speech, or occupational therapists. Most major medical plans and Medicare in the U.S. pay for this service. Generally speaking, this level of service is not an area of concern with respect to long-term care. Once the therapy is achieved, people are transferred out of this service level, maybe to a home or to a lower level of care in a facility. Sub-acute care has traditionally been provided in a hospital setting, but more recently, nursing facilities have opened their doors to sub-acute patients. Two reasons are responsible for this change: hospitals are releasing patients quicker and sicker, and nursing homes are facing competition from newer types of facilities such as Alzheimer's Centers, Assisted Living Facilities, and so forth.

## Skilled Nursing Facility

This is a long-term care designated nursing facility (or nursing home). Care can be short or prolonged at this level.

Typically, two types of care are provided here. The first is skilled nursing, which is basically described in two parts: skilled nursing care, when, under doctor's orders, a licensed nurse (RN or LVN) must attend to a patient twenty-four hours a day, seven days a week, or a licensed therapist works with the patient, under doctor's orders, every day of the week doing rehabilitation work until the patient has reached his/her restorative potential. When either of these two situations no longer exist, a person is then classified as a custodial care patient, even though physically, they may be housed in a skilled nursing facility. When a person is classified as a custodial care patient, Medicare and most major medical insurance plans do not pay for the services rendered by the facility to the patient. A custodial care patient is generally defined as a person who is not able to perform certain functions that are called activities of daily living (ADL's). Typically, these ADL's include transferring, use of toilet, bathing, dressing, and eating. If a person needs these services for a period of ninety days or more, then they are receiving what the government defines as long-term care. A person might also be classified as a custodial care patient if they need assistance and/or supervision because of an inability to reason correctly or maintain a level of self-safety due to mental deficiencies such as Alzheimer's disease, dementia, or senility. If a person is diagnosed with one of these impairments, they are usually classified as a custodial care patient unless their primary diagnosis is due to some type of care that is restorative in nature. Again, there is no payment or reimbursement of payments for custodial care from Medicare or major medical plans.

## Intermediate Care

This is provided in a nursing home setting, but patients may receive intermediate care services from professional caregivers. Medicare and major medical care insurance plans do not pay the room and board cost for this level of care, as it does not meet the criteria for skilled nursing care.

## Family in Crisis:
## Why I Sell Long-Term Care Insurance Today

It is heavily ingrained in my mind, even today, after actively managing long-term care facilities as a nursing home administrator, that there is a need to have long-term care insurance in one's portfolio.

I vividly recall, on one occasion, when a wife was admitting her husband for Alzheimer's disease care. At one point in the admission process I had to ask the question, "How do you plan to pay for your husband's care in our facility?" Her response was, "Oh, I'm not worried about it. Medicare will be paying the bill." When I heard that answer, I knew I had to explain to her that Medicare would not pay for custodial care, which is the level of care he would be receiving in our facility. To this day, I remember the look on her face when she realized what I was saying — that she would be responsible for the cost of her husband's care.

She sat there for a moment without saying anything. I could see that she was in turmoil. With a look of horror on her face, she told me, "What funds we have are tied up. I will need to mortgage our house to pay this nursing home bill. I'm not sure how I am going to do all this. I've never had to make any financial decisions, nor have I ever had to pay any of our bills."

As I sat there watching her anxiety, I thought to myself, "Why isn't there an insurance policy on the market to pay for the cost of long-term care not covered by Medicare?" Now that there is insurance for this level of care, I have a personal mission to tell people about the need, the cost, and the financing of long-term care and to sell policies to people while they qualify for the coverage. I don't want to experience another wife admitting her husband to a facility without immediate means of being able to pay for the cost of care. The long-term care policy can be a vehicle that prevents any future looks of turmoil and stress on a family, since use of a long-term care policy can prevent unplanned changes in lifestyle and help provide the necessary care.

In 1984, I became aware of nursing home insurance plans that even paid for custodial care. As soon as I learned about the coverage, I sold my first policy to my mother. To my amazement, she had a stroke a year later. She required the services of a nursing home after her stroke and her long-term care insurance policy paid the full cost of care while she lived in the facility. They provided her excellent care, they cared for all her needs, and it was all paid for by the insurance company!

I've been a provider of long-term care as a nursing home administrator, I've been a consumer of long-term care through my mother's experience, and now I sell long-term care insurance so people will not have to experience the turmoil and stress I've witnessed during the admission process into a nursing home. The general public doesn't realize how often families are denied benefits by Medicare and major medical insurance plans for long-term care. In fact, based on information from *Employee Benefit News*, only about eight percent of all costs for a long-term care stay are reimbursed by Medicare.[3] Additionally, Medicare does not pay for custodial care[4] and most major medical insurance plans also do not pay for custodial care services. Custodial care services are what the majority of people require when a prolonged illness places them in long-term care situations. People should consider long-term care insurance to help pay for these services.

If more people understood how often patients do not receive Medicare or major medical insurance benefits for their long-term care stay in a facility or for long-term care at home, they would run to find an agent that offers long-term care insurance while their health permits a policy to be issued. The need is real. A long-term care insurance policy can help a family avoid a stressful financial crisis. A long-term care insurance policy can help a family avoid having to pay out-of-pocket for the cost of long-term care. A long-term care insurance policy can allow a family to select a facility of their choice or receive care at home. A long-term care policy can prevent another spouse from experiencing agony and financial stress during the admission of a husband or wife into a long-term care facility. That's why I sell long-term care insurance.

## Home Health Care
## by Richard Sanford

While most of us think of nursing home expenses when it comes to long-term care, nursing home costs are only 20% of the nursing care scenario, with more than 22.4 million people in the U.S. requiring some kind of care at home. For every person in a nursing home, five others need similar care at home.[5]

Very few of us will escape becoming involved in the long-term care of a spouse, a family member, or loved one. We may be called upon to be a caregiver, financial supporter, or decision maker in the choice of where a person could best be cared for when physical or mental disability requires long-term care.

Caregivers usually pay a price for accepting responsibility: they are three times more likely to seek medical or psychological help for depression and stress-related symptoms than non-caregivers. This occurs even to those who have some paid, formal assistance on a regular basis! For instance, caring for a loved one who has cancer often causes a caregiver to eat poorly, ignore personal exercise regimes, lose sleep, and worst of all, disregard *timely* personal medical advice.

## USA Snapshot

Another example of such care-giver challenges is Barbara Forsberg's story, as told to the House Ways and Means Committee Hearings in January 1995. "Because my husband is in the Sundowning state of Alzheimer's — meaning he wanders throughout the house at night — I do not know how much longer I shall be able to keep him at home. Perhaps for as long as I can subsist on four hours sleep a night. I do, however, want to keep him in his own home for as long as he is able to recognize his surroundings and to recognize his loved ones."

There are three vital issues in all forms of long-term care that affect home health care:

- Who is willing to care?
- Who is able to care?
- Who will pay for care?

The question of willing and able are usually settled, temporarily at least, early in the family discussion. Decisions are often predetermined by external factors such as geography, home size, career demands, etc. Who will pay for care is always the critical question, and the answer will become the linchpin of any care plan.

Why is there even a question of who will pay? Group health insurance, individual major medical coverages, and Medicare pay for nursing care/home health care, right? *Wrong!*

To help you better understand why these familiar funding approaches do not pay for nursing care/home health care, you must become acquainted with two important terms found under definitions of coverable charges — acute care and chronic care.

## Acute Care vs. Chronic Care

*Acute Care* is defined by one insurance company (and is typically defined when used by insurance companies) as "care for illness or injury that has developed rapidly, has pronounced symptoms, and is finite in length."[6]

*Chronic Care* is defined as "care for illness continuing over a long period of time or recurring frequently". Chronic conditions often begin inconspicuously and symptoms are less pronounced than acute conditions. (Long-term care insurance is designed to assist people who have loss of capacity due to chronic illness.)[7]

Thus, acute care is provided in emergency rooms, clinics, and hospitals, and health insurance and Medicare cover some or all of this type of medical service. Chronic care is provided in nursing homes, extended care and assisted living facilities, and at the patient's home or the home of a friend or family member. This type of care is not covered under traditional health insurance and Medicare because it does not meet the definition of acute care. Unfortunately, this comes as a big surprise to many people — and most often not until they are facing the situation of paying for care.

Following an episode of acute care (hospitalization), most people prefer to return home rather than being placed in a nursing facility for a recovery period, physical therapy, or custodial care. Returning to your own home is recognized as a healthy alternative, because being in your own home promotes recovery. Recovery is accelerated by the confidence that comes from knowing where things are located — toilet, refrigerator, telephone, favorite chair — and this confidence promotes a quality of life that aids recovery. It is no wonder that patients with a chronic condition seek home health care when faced with lengthy recovery or periods of incapacity. The critical and determining factor of staying in your own home, or not staying, is frequently whether you have the financial ability to pay for professional support care at home.

## The Two-Edged Sword of Long-Term Care

Why aren't spouses or other family members adequate in providing home health care? An example of the two-edged sword associated with home health care by family members is my own family's experience with home health care for my wife's mother — which is occurring at the very same time this chapter is being written. "Katy," as she is affectionately known to our four children and seven grandchildren, was in great spirits this past October when she traveled from Southwest Arizona to Petoskey, Michigan, for her annual fall visit with family and friends back home. After her visit, my wife and daughter drove her south to Kalamazoo for a brief stopover prior to her return flight to Arizona, and that's when the persistent cough was noticed.

Katy delayed visiting the doctor, but did so in early November, when CAT scans and other tests confirmed a diagnosis of cancer. But the medical community (probably fearful of a mistaken diagnosis) was not definitive about answering specific questions. Is it terminal? How long? What will her capabilities be? Will she be hospitalized? (Rule that out, Katy says.) No hope for a cure? What else can we do to help her? But the information provided was soft and ambiguous. After receiving a delayed "no hope" decree, Katy was given an alternative, last ditch approach. The doctors said, "We can give you chemotherapy and/or radiation, but it won't really help or change your condition. It's too advanced." So, in a desperate attempt to achieve a miracle, Katy chose radiation (because one loses one's hair with chemo!) We sought expert advice from an experienced, professionally licensed caregiver who had experience with the results of radiation therapy administered to the chest area.

I interrupt the story at this point, to say the first edge of the sword has struck. Affairs at home, family relations, business matters, the upcoming holidays raised a constant cacophony of emotions. Give attention to our immediate family and business after an absence of three and a half weeks? Or, continue caring for Katy, who is slowly and painfully dehydrating and starving herself because the radiation has burned her throat and esophagus so badly she can't swallow, and who now requires daily care just to move from the couch to the lavatory to the bed and back again?

What to do? What to do? A quick return to Michigan and family and business, then another call for help from the temporary caregiver (she charges only $100 per part-time day; the full-time, twenty-four-hour caregivers charge $360 per day.) So, a return to Arizona prior to Christmas was appropriate, hoping to provide a family-type last Christmas for Katy, but she was too weak to travel the few miles to join us and asked if we could postpone the celebration and gifts to a day when she felt a little bit better. Holidays are the worst time to find yourself in a caregiver position with someone you love. It's emotionally debilitating I can assure you, but, considering the challenges, stress, and pain Katy was facing every day, hour , minute, we had no right to complain. Damn! The helplessness and despair were beginning to overcome our usually positive attitudes.

Now, the other side of the sword edge becomes apparent...we cannot continue neglecting our Michigan family and business, so we're guided to seek twenty-four-hour care arrangements. Nice, accommodating people, these professional caregiver organizations. So, to Hospice as an interim answer. With their help, a plan is worked out for Katy to get 24-hour home health care from four different sources: Monday through Friday for eight hours during the day; a home health care aide during the night; an RN to perform catheter changes, etc. several times a week; and Hospice support two to three times a week. "How much will this cost?" we asked. A calculator was needed to figure the various sums, and a rough estimate was provided — $10,000 to $12,000 per month! Damn again! Katy can't afford this, not for very long anyway. O.K. It's pony-up time. If needed, we'll pick up the cost differential needed. We're lucky. Many other Katys don't have family in a position to help financially. Another bite of the sword blade is our frustration at having to dissipate principal (particularly after working so hard to accumulate it in spite of the plethora of taxes on income by federal, state, city, social security, and medicare taxes.) The only alternative, though, would hurt Katy, make her condition worse, and intensify the suffering she is already bearing.

So, it's now February, Katy is slipping away fast. My wife is still at her side daily, keeping Katy's personal affairs in order (bills still have to be paid, groceries bought, oxygen supplied, other errands the caregivers don't do). It goes on day after day. The other side of the two-edged financial sword cuts into our love, commitment, and desire to help on one side, and the cost in dollars, emotions, time, and sacrifice on the other. Would Katy have been better off in the hospital? No — they don't accept chronic care patients. A nursing home? She absolutely refused to be "dumped there" — her words. Or at home, where she could find some peace and comfort. Our saga continues at this time, the final chapter to be written some time later.

We are indeed fortunate to have been able to give the time and financial support Katy needed, and we have the support of our Michigan family to aid in caring for her. Many families are unable to do this. And, if those families do not have long-term care insurance, including full coverage for Home Health Care, they face a story similar to the one I've just shared with you.

## A Caution or Two!

NOTE: This would be a good time for insurance professionals to pause and consider recommending 100% coverage for home health care to clients. As more families find themselves in a predicament such as the one as I've discussed — and due to the demographics of the aging baby boomers, there will be many families facing this quandary in the not-too-distant future — there will be more and more claims and lawsuits in an attempt to remedy this situation at someone else's expense.

A further caution for the professional insurance advisor is not to pander to the client's desire for reassurance that home health care will be sufficient in all cases. Cases requiring skilled care and twenty-four-hour care cannot be adequately handled in the home. For example, in New York State and others, when the cost of home health care for someone under Medicaid reaches or exceeds the cost of nursing home care, the patient is required to enter a nursing home. Conditions of chronic care most often include a deteriorating health event eventually ending in skilled care in a nursing facility. Professional advisors who do not fully describe the need for both home health care and nursing facility care and allow the client to insist on purchasing only home health care coverage should consider securing a signed disclaimer. Thus, a nursing care insurance program that does not include *both* home health care and nursing facility care is deficient.

## Medicare and Medicaid

During the search for possible sources of payment for home health care, families quickly learn that neither Medicare nor any major medical insurance will pay the *basic and custodial care* the loved one may need. Medicare and major medical insurance sources *pay only for "skilled care" delivered by a licensed or registered nurse* (and then for only a limited period of time.) Health insurance and Medicare pay for "intermittent" visits by a nurse over a limited time period. Most people assume when they

---

## ACKNOWLEDGEMENT OF RESPONSIBILITY

I understand the risk of needing long-term care as explained to me by
_____. I understand that neither Medicare or Medicaid Supplement policies will satisfy that need.

I choose to decline the insurance protection shown to me at this time and, in so doing, acknowledge that I am assuming responsibility for arranging funding of any long-term care services that I may need in the future.

| | |
|---|---|
| _____ | _____ |
| Name | Date |
| _____ | _____ |
| Signature | Agent's Signature |

---

## WAIVER OF LIABILITY

By my signature below, I acknowledge that I have elected to obtain long-term care insurance that provides less coverage than that recommended by _____, who has offered this coverage as protection for my assets.

The plan recommended would have a daily Nursing Facility benefit of $_____, and a daily Home Care benefit of _____, with an elimination period of _____ days, and a maximum benefit period of _____.

Instead, I have selected a daily Home Care only benefit of $_____, with an elimination period of _____ days, and a maximum benefit period of _____.

| | |
|---|---|
| _____ | _____ |
| Name | Date |
| _____ | _____ |
| Signature | Agent's Signature |

---

are on Medicaid that they can remain at home for care. Medicaid is a state and federal program. There is no guarantee that home health care must be provided for the person on Medicaid. Nationwide, only 10% of Medicaid long-term care services for the elderly are used at home. Some states provide for even less than that. Mississippi, Pennsylvania, and Indiana provide for less than 1% of home health care. The states that provide the most home health care services are Oregon with 39%, New York at 23%, Texas and Missouri at 21%, and Arizona at 17%.[8] This is inadequate to meet the needs of a housebound person.

## What Part Do Activities of Daily Living Play in Triggering Benefits?

Benefits for chronic physical or mental disability are included in long-term care and nursing home insurance policies, and are triggered if the insured requires human assistance to perform two of five or six basic activities of daily living (ADL's).

ADL's are the minimum basic physical skills a person needs to live independently. Activities of daily living are dressing, walking, eating, toileting, transferring, and bathing. Home health care provisions in a long-term care policy will answer the third question in the planning process for long-term care: Who will pay for care? Combining the limited benefits of Medicare and other major medical insurance with long-term care insurance coverage makes it possible to develop a care plan that combines both skilled and custodial care at an affordable cost, particularly when the plan is started prior to retirement.

## In Summary

Many families are now considering transferring the financial risk of home health care from their personal assets and financial plans to an insurance company. The risk of needing home care is becoming more real every day; demographic studies suggest that today 8.1 million people need human assistance in two of their six ADL's.[9]

Also, home care is preferred over post-hospital recovery and is becoming the location of choice for long-term care. The need for supplemental cash to pay for supportive custodial care is a realistic concern for all future financial planning. Current trends in long-term care show that home care is the first step in a continuum of care that allows an individual to move from a low level of care in the home setting into the more intensive levels of care provided in skilled nursing facilities.

Home care insurance is part of the protective cover every financial plan needs.

**NOTE:** When hiring an independent contractor to provide in-home care or respite care for 40 hours or more a week, it is advisable to call a general lines insurance agent to inquire about the necessity of purchasing Worker's Compensation insurance. (At least a half dozen states may also require statutory Disability Benefits Law insurance as well.)

## Community Care Settings
## by Thomas Collica

After living in the same home for fifty-two years, Steven S., age 87, wants to move. Yard care for him is overwhelming. The extra space in his two thousand square-foot home is more than he needs or can maintain. He has already taken a fall in his garage and spent six months recuperating from a broken hip. If he stays, he risks more physical injury and certainly more mental anxiety trying to cope with a life he can no longer handle. This is a very common scenario facing seniors.

Ruth G. had an unfortunate tragedy of the type we all hope to avoid. Fifteen years ago, her husband Sy was struck by a paralyzing stroke. Because of this misfortune, Sy was confined to a wheelchair and unable to speak, requiring a considerable amount of home health care. Ruth, being a committed, loving wife, acted as her husband's primary caregiver. It totally exhausted her, and the toll on her health since his passing has manifested itself. At age 87, Ruth could no longer function independently because of her declining intellectual capacity. Consequently, she was no longer able to stay at home. Since her children lived three hours from her, it was difficult for them to manage her bills and see that her personal needs were attended to.

As Ruth's agent, I researched her long-term care policy and began the claim process. Evaluations were done to determine her cognitive abilities. Because it was concluded she was impaired (in need of supervision, and reminders to take her medications), her claim was approved. We had a care coordinator make arrangements for her to move into an assisted living facility, which was a tremendous relief to her family. She calls it her home away from home, and her life is very comfortable now.

## Find the Proper Setting

There are several types of community care settings and an equal number of different terms for similar care. One that you will hear frequently is the term *residential care communities*. This term is the same as *community care*. However, depending on what part of the country you are in, some types will be licensed and required to follow set regulations and will vary from state to state. The cost of care is expensive as well, and will range in price from $2,400 to $5,000 per month, depending on the needs of the individual. Facing such cost has caused an alarming number of older Americans to remain in their homes, regardless of the consequences.

Most of the long-term care services provided in community care settings are covered by today's comprehensive LTCI policies. What is important to remember as you understand the different types of community care is that not all settings within any category will be appropriate for all people. Some individuals may require more assistance, or a secured environment, and if there is a mental or physical progression of deterioration, then there is need to consider what the facility has to offer for the future of the resident. For this reason, people should consider how long the facility will accommodate their loved one's needs and when another move may be required. The following is a synopsis of the types of facilities available in the community:

# Retirement Housing, Senior Apartments, Senior Living

These settings provide a place for individuals to live and are designed for those who are totally independent, or nearly so, and who choose to live in a community with other seniors. These facilities generally offer a common area to gather and organized social programs. The services offered may include prepared meals, transportation, recreational activities, and access to health and shopping facilities. Nursing services are not usually offered. This type of housing is not licensed and usually will not have staff on-site twenty-four hours a day. In addition, staff will usually have little or no knowledge about any specific illness. Some individual apartments or rooms may have call cords, usually in the bathroom, that may be monitored by a nearby hospital or nursing facility. There is usually no assistance with medication management for a resident, however, the person may be able to get in-home services for this type of requirement. There is an ancillary charge for this extra service, and the amount of service available is usually limited. Generally there is no financial assistance to pay for the rent, but some places may determine the monthly rent based on income.

## Residential Care Facilities

These are also known as personal care facilities and are residential-type homes licensed to care for a relatively small number of residents who are able to care for themselves in a protected environment. Most of these facilities provide residents with basic needs such as room and board, laundry, cleaning, and assistance with the taking of medications, bathing, and dressing. Most will accept at least some residents who are non-ambulatory. This type of care facility may be required to be licensed by the state in which it is located. The rates can range from $1,200 to $3,000 per month and usually no public financial assistance is available.

# Alzheimer's Living Choices

Alzheimer's disease can be challenging both for people with the disease and for their loved ones. As one of the nation's most common diseases among seniors, the need for assisted living with this group has increased dramatically, and more and more assisted living facilities are being built on a daily basis. There are four residential options available to people with Alzheimer's disease: supervised living, assisted living, skilled nursing, and special care units. The appropriate setting is dependent on the specific need of the individual, and can be determined based on the answers to questions including: how much help does the patient need with activities of daily living, such as dressing, bathing, or eating? Can he or she be considered somewhat independent? Does the patient need skilled nursing care? Let's look at the options more closely.

*Supervised living* allows a house or apartment-like environment to provide safety and security with supervision. Caretakers check in on residents, provide assistance arranging for household maintenance tasks, make arrangements for transportation, and help with other tasks as they arise. Some retirement communities offer residents the option to move from their homes into such supervised living areas.

*Assisted living facilities* provide increased supervision for frail elderly who want to remain in a homelike environment and don't require full-time nursing care, but who require help with daily tasks. This type of environment, is usually appropriate at the beginning to middle stages of the disease. Many such facilities provide group social activities, communal eating areas, organized activities and excursions, housekeeping assistance, and help with personal tasks such as dressing, bathing, or hair styling. These facilities offer all meals and are usually in a secured environment, so there is no danger of the resident leaving the facility and wandering off into the nearby neighborhood, which can be a common occurrence if elderly patients are left alone or in an unsecured area.

*Skilled nursing facilities* provide a third option, offering round-the-clock supervision and care from licensed registered nurses and other staff. Nursing homes are appropriate for people whose condition has begun to affect their physical well-being or who have developed other medical problems in addition to Alzheimer's. This type of facility is usually reserved for the advanced or later stages of the disease.

## Assisted Living Facilities (ALF's)

For many, assisted living facilities are meeting the needs of the growing elderly population, and for this reason seem to be the most popular elderly care option. They are often referred to as board and care, group home, community based residential facility, or foster home. These facilities are on the cutting edge, and are a rapidly expanding service, with the concept of assisted living beginning its development in the United States in the mid-1980s. ALF's provide residential care for seniors who require some assistance and supervision with activities of daily living (such as reminders to take medication or assistance with bathing) but do not require the intensive services of a nursing home. The goals of a good assisted living facility are to promote each resident's independence, preserve his or her dignity, and provide appropriate individualized assistance as needed. Some ALF's may have nursing services on staff with emergency call systems installed in each resident's room and may include amenities such as housekeeping, linen service, and all daily meals. There is usually twenty-four-hour staff, but not necessarily twenty-four-hour active staff. The amount of care provided by staff will vary greatly from setting to setting. Most places will provide some type of structured activity program. The rates for this type of facility range from $1,200 to $4,000 per month. There is generally little or no public financial assistance available to pay for rent, but Medicaid waivers may be available in some states. The relative newness of assisted living facilities combined with rapid growth has led to an industry lacking standardization or uniformity. On the other hand, LTCI policies are usually specific as to what qualifies as an ALF. Quite often healthy people, as well as people needing assistance, choose to live in an ALF. In either situation, LTCI policyholders looking for an ALF should check with their insurance company to determine if a particular facility meets their insurance policy definition as an ALF, and what charges would be covered.

The three following levels of care are typically covered in comprehensive long-term care insurance policies:

## Respite Care

Respite care is temporary care designed to care for an individual the way a day care does, only the stay is usually a minimum twenty-four hours up to a maximum of thirty days. This care can be offered on an Assisted Living basis or with an Assisted Living Dementia Specific area basis. The focus is on the type of care and the individual needing the care. The marketing is targeted to the caregiver, who needs more than the standard eight or twelve hours of time away from the senior or the person needing respite care. The rates range from $100 to $200 per twenty-four-hour period, but usually not more than the one-month rate at an assisted living facility.

## Adult Day Care

These facilities are usually for seniors who need support during the day. Services generally include meals, snacks, medication supervision, stimulating activities and interaction with peers. The adult day care is an alternative to having someone come into your home and assist in the supervision of the senior. This allows the caregiver time away for work or personal business, with the knowledge that his or her loved one is cared for in a safe environment filled with social interaction and quality care. The programs are usually very flexible to fit the needs of a variety of seniors and their lifestyles. The average cost for these facilities is between $35 and $50 per day and prices vary greatly across the country.

# Hospice Care

Hospice care revolves around a terminally ill person. One of its major goals is to help the individual remain at home so long as they wish during the final stage of his or her life. Hospice is a combined effort of family, friends, and professionals, including volunteer caregivers, working together to offer the patient with a life-limiting illness an effective alternative to routine home care and repeat hospitalization. Hospice programs can provide patients with state-of-the-art pain and symptom management from teams of compassionate health care professionals including physicians, registered nurses, home health aides, social workers, chaplains, and bereavement coordinators. With the help of the family and this team of professionals, the patient is able to live each day to the fullest, while sharing the time that remains in the supportive circle of the family and friends. Many Hospice care programs are run by nonprofit organizations, affiliates of hospitals, or charity organizations.

## Continuing Care Retirement Communities

Continuing Care Retirement Communities are life care communities which are defined to include full coverage for nursing facility services as part of the entrance fee and monthly fee. Entrance fees range in the six-figure plus category, and typically entrants are required to be in reasonably good health.

The resident pays the same monthly fee regardless of his or her location in the community. This extensive long-term care coverage adds a level of risk to the operation of a retirement community which many otherwise qualified sponsors are unwilling to take. CCRC's can be established as campus-like settings, offering stimulating social and physical activities. From the entrant's perspective, long-term care insurance is not a high priority, because all events are covered from the entrance and monthly fees. Some owners of CCRC's, however, may require long-term care insurance upon entrance, to shift the risks for the higher costs of skilled care to an insurance company.

# LTC: Today/Tomorrow

The wish to move into community housing places Steven S. on the threshold of a continuum of care for older persons. Ruth G. has begun to utilize the early stages of care provider services through her long-term care insurance policy. By knowing what a client's or family member's needs are, or knowing his or her degree of frailty, we can enlist him or her in an appropriate continuum of care, from the full range of services available.

We do know that today's comprehensive long-term care insurance enables policyholders to obtain appropriate care, in the right place, at the right time. As recently as ten years ago, assisted living facilities were practically nonexistent. Today, they're an accessible reality. Who can say what resources will be available ten years from now? Long-term care insurance policies that offer *alternative care benefits* should be flexible enough, in most instances, to address new developments in the field of care management, to meet the needs of future policyholders.

# CHAPTER 4

## Government Related Long-Term Care Programs

Whenever the general public is surveyed about the financing of long-term care expenses, the results are overwhelmingly identical. A great majority of those surveyed falsely believe Medicare will pay for their long-term care. Susan Palla, Chairperson of the National LTC Network's Education Committee and a speaker at the 1997 Annual MDRT Meeting held in Atlanta, describes what Medicare does cover.

Speakers on the topic of long-term care often will use the term Medicare when they mean Medicaid, and vice-versa. When this happens, you can observe knowledgeable people cringing at the error. Medicaid is for people who are indigent and cannot afford to pay the cost of their own care. Because of the demographics of aging, Medicaid threatens to break the budget of almost every state in the union. Many people working in the field of private long-term care insurance believe that if they are successful promoting long-term care insurance, the insurance industry can preserve the integrity of the Medicaid system for the truly needy. In addition to describing Medicare benefits, Susan also covers Medicaid and Veterans Benefits.

Recognizing the threat posed to the financial stability of federal and state governments by the impending explosion of the need to care for the baby-boom generation turned elder boom, Congress has passed tax legislation to promote the purchase of private long-term care insurance. Jonathan Spilde, the National LTC Network Legislation Committee Chairperson, explains the advantages of the new LTC tax incentives to individuals and businesses to purchase a long-term care insurance policy for themselves and their employees.

Individual states have also passed legislation to promote the purchase of long-term care insurance either through income tax credits, income tax deductions, or in several instances

Public/Private LTCI Partnership Programs. This chapter will conclude with an explanation of the measures states have taken to become proactive to promote the purchase of long-term care insurance among its citizens.

# Medicare/Medicaid (Palla):

**Important Points**

- Administered by the federal government, Medicare is a health insurance program for all persons 65 and older, persons of any age with permanent kidney failure, and certain disabled persons.
- Medicare consists of Hospital Insurance protection (Part A) and Medical Insurance protection (Part B).
- For the purpose of qualifying for Medicare, the definitions of home health care, skilled facility care, and skilled nursing care are very stringent.

# Medicare: An Overview

Medicare is a federal health insurance program for all persons 65 and older, persons of any age with permanent kidney failure, and certain disabled persons of any age. The program is administered by the Health Care Financing Administration within the Department of Health and Human Services.

People who are entitled to or who are receiving Social Security or Railroad Retirement benefits when they turn 65 will automatically be enrolled in Medicare upon turning 65. If not enrolled, individuals will need to contact the Social Security Administration to apply. Upon becoming eligible, enrollment rules limit when a person may apply for coverage.

Medicare consists of two types of coverage: Hospital Insurance protection (Part A) and Medical Insurance protection (Part B). Hospital Insurance Part A is financed for the most part by Social Security payroll tax deductions, which are deposited in the Federal Hospital Security Trust Fund. Part B is funded in part by the monthly premiums paid by those who purchase the coverage.

As with other types of insurance, some people will need to pay a premium for Medicare coverage. Those who are entitled to Social Security or Railroad Retirement benefits or worked in local, state, or Federal government for a long enough period of time will receive Part A coverage at no charge. Part B coverage is optional and requires a monthly premium. This premium changes every year.

The Balanced Budget Act of 1997 has recently been noted for having a chilling effect on reduced skilled nursing care benefits and restrictive caps for physical and speech therapies.

# Medicare Part A: Hospital Insurance Protection

### A Definition

Medicare Part A helps to pay for medically necessary inpatient care in a general hospital, skilled nursing facility, or psychiatric or hospice care.

### Benefit Periods

Medicare Part A benefits are paid on the basis of benefit periods. A benefit period begins the first day that a patient receives Medicare-covered service in a hospital or skilled nursing facility. It ends when the patient has been out of a hospital or skilled nursing facility but does not receive any skilled care there for 60 consecutive days. If the patient enters a hospital again after 60 days, a new *benefit period* begins. All Part A benefits are renewed with each new benefit period, except for any lifetime reserve days or psychiatric hospital benefits that are used.

# Inpatient Hospital Care

When an insured is hospitalized, he/she is responsible for meeting the Medicare *deductible* (an initial dollar amount, which the individual must pay before Medicare starts paying.) Medicare will then pay for all covered hospital services for the first sixty days. In addition to the deductible, the insured will be responsible for a share of any hospital costs that occur during days sixty-one through ninety of hospitalization.

# Skilled Nursing Facility Care

A *skilled nursing facility* may be a skilled nursing home or a distinct part of an institution, such as a ward or a wing of a hospital. Not all nursing homes will qualify, and those which offer only custodial care are excluded. The facility must be primarily engaged in providing skilled nursing care or rehabilitation services for injured, disabled, or sick persons. The facility must be certified by the state.

It also must have a written agreement with a hospital that is participating in the Medicare program for the transfer of patients. NOT all skilled nursing facilities are approved by Medicare.

*Skilled nursing care* is care that can only be performed by or under the supervision of licensed nursing personnel. Skilled nursing care and skilled rehabilitation services must be required and received on a daily basis at least five days a week, or the patient will NOT be eligible for Medicare coverage.

As the patient gradually recovers, he or she may move from one level of long-term care to another. Once out of the skilled care level, Medicare no longer pays.

Medicare will pay the entire amount of eligible skilled care charges incurred during the first twenty days only if the patient has been in a hospital for three days and received skilled care in an approved facility. However, the individual is required to pay a coinsurance amount during days twenty-one through one hundred. If an individual is confined for more than 100 days during a single benefit period, Medicare provides no further coverage.

# Home Health Care

Home health care is exactly what the name implies: "care at home." Nursing homes are not the only possible sources of care for the elderly and impaired. In some cases, a nursing home is not the appropriate setting to provide for a person's needs or medical care. Home health care services include skilled nursing care, speech and occupational therapy, as well as domestic services like housekeeping.

Most would rather stay in their own environment, "Home Sweet Home," but let's examine the realities. What does Medicare pay for?

The following services are covered under Medicare Part A (Home Health Care):

- Intermittent part-time skilled nursing care
- Physical therapy
- Speech therapy

If a person needs intermittent **part-time** skilled nursing care, physical therapy, or speech therapy, Medicare also pays for:

- Part-time services of a home health aide
- Medical supplies
- 80% of the approved cost for durable medical equipment (e.g., wheelchairs, etc.)
- Occupational therapy

Medicare provides extremely limited coverage, and only if the need is certified by a doctor. The care includes part-time skilled nursing care, physical therapy, or speech therapy if the patient is confined to his or her home and the agency providing the care participates in Medicare. Otherwise, the patient and/or his/her family may be responsible for paying the entire amount.

Medicare does not pay for custodial care, home health aides, or housekeeping services.

## How to Receive the Medicare Home Health Care Benefits?

Medicare recipients must be qualified as "homebound," which will entitle them to thirty-five hours a week to receive skilled nursing home health aide services and skilled therapy services, provided they are documented by a physician as *reasonable and medically necessary.*

Care must be required for fewer than five days per week, which can be once in every sixty or ninety days, and must be for less than eight hours per day, part-time only. Skilled nursing services include administration of medications, tube feeding, catheter changes, training the caregiver, and management and evaluation of patient's care plan.

Medicare home health care is one of the least understood and most abused benefit, subject to fraud and overutilization.

## Additional Coverage Provided Under Part A

In addition to providing coverage for inpatient hospital care, skilled nursing facility and home health care, Medicare Part A will also pay for psychiatric hospital care and hospice care.

---

### Home Health Care —
### Largest Growing Medicare Costs in 1996

- Home Health Care cost was 16.7 billion
- Nursing Home cost was $11.1 billion
- Rising costs for nursing home and home care costs, including HMO's used to cut costs, are straining the Medicare budget. Double-digit growth is expected through 2002.

Source: Congressional Budget Office, January 1997

---

## Medicare Part B: Medical Insurance Protection

**A Definition**

According to the *Guide to Health Insurance for People with Medicare,* Part B coverage is defined as follows:

"Medicare pays for a wide range of medical services and supplies, but the most significant coverage is for doctor's bills. Medically necessary physician services are covered no matter where (they are) received — at home, in the doctor's office, in a clinic, in a nursing home or in a hospital. Part B also covers:

- Outpatient hospital services
- X-rays and certain laboratory tests

- Certain ambulance services
- Durable medical equipment, such as wheelchairs and hospital beds used at home
- Services of certain specially qualified practitioners who are not physicians
- Occupational therapy — $1,500 limit (moratorium 2000 + 2001)
- Speech/language pathology services and physical therapies — $1,500 limit (moratorium 2000 + 2001)
- Partial hospitalization for medical health care
- Mammograms and Pap smears
- Home health care for those without Part A coverage."[1]

## Part B Enrollment

As noted above, Part B coverage is optional. However, since the Federal government subsidized 75% of the coverage, it is an excellent buy for most individuals. An individual is automatically enrolled in Part B when he/she becomes entitled to Part A unless he/she declines the coverage.

An individual may delay his/her enrollment in Part B. If an individual continues to work after age 65 and chooses to be covered by an employer's insurance plan or is covered under a spouse's employment-related insurance plan instead of Medicare Part B, he/she will have a special seven-month enrollment period for Part B, beginning with the month he/she stops working or the month during which he/she is no longer covered under the employer plan, whichever comes first.[2]

## Deductibles and Co-Payments

Individuals using Part B coverage still will be responsible for an annual calendar deductible of $100. After satisfying the deductible, Medicare Part B usually will pay for 80% of the remaining approved and covered services. The insured will be responsible for the remaining 20%, plus any charges over the

Medicare-approved amount. There is no deductible for home health care services. However if the doctor or supplier does not accept the "assignment" or charges more than the Medicare-approved amount, the individual will be responsible for the difference. In addition, the insured is responsible for 20% of the Medicare-approved amount for durable equipment.

---

### 2000 Medicare Deductibles and Copayments

**Part A Hospital**
Deductible                                           $776
Copayment      Days 61 - 90  You pay $194 per day
Life Reserve Days                    Copayment $388

**Skilled Nursing Home Care**
When hospitalized for at least three days and enter a Medicare approved skilled nursing facility within 30 days after hospital discharges and is receiving skilled nursing care.

Copayment      Days 21-100    You pay $97 per day

**Part B Doctors**
                                              $100 deductible

**2000 Part B Premium**
The Part B premium payment automatically deducted from Medicare recipient's monthly Social Security check during 2000 will be $45.50.

---

### Help for Low-Income Medicare Beneficiaries

For some people who have low incomes and few resources, the state they reside in may pay Medicare premiums and, in some cases, other "out-of-pocket" Medicare expenses such as deductibles and coinsurance.

Only the state in which an individual resides can decide if the individual qualifies for help under this program. To find out if an individual qualifies, contact the state or local medical assistance (Medicaid) agency, social services, or welfare office.

For more information, contact Social Security to request a copy of the leaflet *Medicare Savings for Qualified Beneficiaries* (HCFA Publication No. 02184.)

# Medicare: What It Pays & What It Does Not Pay

**Medicare will not pay for long-term care unless:**
1. You have a three-day prior stay in a hospital and you are admitted to the nursing home within thirty days for the same medical condition.
2. You require daily skilled nursing or rehabilitative services.
3. The skilled nursing facility is Medicare approved.

Your physician must certify that you need and that you receive skilled nursing or skilled rehabilitation services on a daily basis. The care also must be for the condition for which you were treated in the hospital.

## SKILLED NURSING FACILITY SERVICES

**Allowed**
- Semi-private room
- Meals
- Regular nursing services
- Drugs provided by family
- Blood transfusions
- Medical supplies
- Wheelchairs, walkers, etc.
- Rehabilitation services (physical, occupational therapy) $1,500 limit

**Not allowed**
- Personal items (TVs)
- Private nurses
- Special diets

- Custodial/intermediate nursing care provided to individuals with chronic illnesses or disabilities (i.e., walking, getting in and out of bed, bathing, dressing, and feeding)

## HOME HEALTH CARE SERVICES
### Allowed
- Part-time care
- Physical or speech therapy — $1,500 limit

### Not Allowed
- Homemaker services
- Meal services
- Custodial services
- Full-time nursing care in the home

## HOSPICE SERVICES
### Allowed
- Nursing services
- Physician services
- Drug therapy

### Not Allowed
- Physical/speech therapy
- Custodial care
- Homemaker services
- Counseling
- Medical supplies

# Medicare/Medicaid

## MEDICAID: ELIGIBILITY & SPEND DOWN RULES
### Important Points
- The Medicaid patient may not select the nursing care facility of his/her own choice.
- A patient in a nursing home facility will need to deplete most of his/her assets before Medicaid will begin to pay for his/her care.

- In the case of a married couple, if one spouse enters a nursing home, assets of the at-home spouse will be used to pay for the cost of care if the couple's assets exceed the maximum "protected" amount.
- The OBRA '93 rules have increased the need for LTC insurance.

**"The Payer of Last Resort"**

According to the *Guide to Health Insurance for People with Medicare*, "Medicaid is a joint federal and state program that provides medical assistance for certain individuals with low incomes and limited assets."[3] Medicaid is a needs-based program. In actuality, Medicaid is the "payer of last resort."

In order to receive Medicaid, recipients must be destitute. Their life savings are no longer available, their lifestyle has probably changed. They have no choice about where they will receive the care that they need and they must rely on the state for assistance.

In order for Medicaid to pay for nursing home care:

1. the facility must be a certified Medicaid provider in the state,
2. the patient must be in need of the level of medical care provided in the skilled care facility, and
3. the patient must be financially destitute.

Although discrimination is illegal, in many Medicaid nursing facilities it has been known to happen. Medicaid recipients are by definition the lowest-paying persons in the facility and are usually the last in line to be accepted into nursing facilities. There is a good chance that the Medicaid bed is not going to be available (when needed.)[4]

**Health Eligibility**

An individual will be determined to be presumptively eligible for Medicaid if the following conditions exist:

1. The applicant is receiving care in an acute care hospital at the time of application.

2. A physician certifies that the applicant no longer requires acute hospital care but requires the type of medical care provided by a certified home health agency (CHHA), long-term home health care program (LTHHCP), nursing home, or hospice.

3. The application or his or her representative states that there is insufficient insurance coverage for this type of care and that the applicant would not otherwise be able to pay for the type of care required.

4. It reasonably appears that 65% of the cost of care provided by certified home health care, nursing home, or hospice will be less than the cost of continued hospital care computed at the Medicaid rates.

5. The applicant reasonably appears to meet all the criteria, financial and nonfinancial, for Medicaid.

When the applicant is on Medicaid, services will be covered, except the following:

1. Hospital-based clinic services,

2. Acute hospital emergency room services, or

3. Acute hospital inpatient services (except when provided as part of hospice care).
   The Medicaid bed will not be held for individuals leaving a nursing home for any reason. Medicaid does not cover custodial-level home care, or provide coverage for any community based facilities.

### Financial Eligibility

In order to be eligible to receive Medicaid, a person would need to have not only a limited income, but limited assets as well. For the purpose of Medicaid eligibility, assets include cash, securities, income, money in the bank (including savings and checking accounts), stocks, bonds, mutual funds, certificates of deposits, and other liquid assets. Additionally, any real personal property, including automobiles, homes, and any other personal belongings (with a few exceptions), is considered to be an asset.

Income rules do not apply to the at-home spouse. He or she is free to continue working and keep all salary and other monthly income, such as Social Security.

Although financial criteria for eligibility is different for each state Medicaid program, there are certain exemptions that are standard.

For exemptions, please see the *$pend Down Quick Reference Guide* on pages 78–80.

## Eligibility for Married Individuals

### Limited Income

The eligibility rules for married persons are almost the same as those for individuals. The spouse entering the nursing home has to qualify based on his or her income.

There is no "his assets" and "her assets," "his pension," "her house." The pension is not exempt. Neither are IRA's, TSA's or 401(k)s. Prenuptial agreements don't work when it comes to Medicaid. Divorce is one way, but neither practical nor probable. Everything both spouses own either singly or together, directly or indirectly, will be counted. The rest will be split in half with one half provided to the Medicaid applicant.

The majority of states will determine eligibility by the "name-on-the-check" rule. Often, couples will have their income in both names; this would be considered "joint income." For example, if Betty's husband received a pension or Social Security check in his name, this income would be considered his alone, even if Betty and her husband jointly use the income.

California and Washington have slightly different guidelines. These states have "community property rules," which means that spouses are considered to own one-half of any income, regardless of whose name is on the check. Since some states are changing these rules, it's worth taking a few minutes to confirm which rules your state now uses to determine income for Medicaid eligibility.

Joint income, such as income earned on joint investments, is shared equally for the purpose of Medicaid eligibility.

## Resource Assessment or Medicaid Snap Shot

If married individuals are not yet impoverished when one spouse enters the nursing home, Congress has made sure that the at-home spouse will soon become broke. Federal law has established minimum and maximum asset amounts for the at-home spouse.

$84,120 is considered the "ceiling" for the community spousal resource amount (CSRA). There is a floor. However, the states have the option to raise the floor. For example, New York and Massachusetts have raised the floor to $84,120. Therefore the community spouse gets to keep the first $84,120 in combined assets. Please check your state for exact figures.

Meeting the asset limit is the most difficult criterion when applying for Medicaid. The following is a general rule of thumb to use:

1. "Resource Assessment" is basically a balance sheet or "snap shot" of the combined assets on the day the spouse goes into the nursing home or a hospital for thirty days or more.

2. Medicaid requires that the couple list all their countable assets regardless of in whose name they are listed, including all transfers within the past thirty-six months (sixty months for certain trusts).

3. The value of those assets is divided in half.

4. The at-home spouse is then allowed to keep one-half of the total amount of the assets, but not less than the floor nor more than $84,120. These figures will increase annually and are different from state to state.

Assets in excess of $84,120 are referred to as "spending down" and will be used to pay for the nursing home or institutional spouse. All nonexempt resources held by either one spouse or both must be totaled and then divided equally between the spouses. Should the at-home spouse's total half exceed the state's limit, the excess will go toward paying the bills for the spouse receiving care in the nursing home. If both spouses are in the nursing home, there is no spousal protection.

When one spouse enters a nursing home, the spouse remaining at home may not have sufficient income of his/her own to maintain the standard of living to which he/she has become accustomed. The following example shows how little the couple will have before Medicaid becomes a factor.

The home is exempt when it is the principal residence for the applicant, the applicant's spouse or children if these children are under the age of 21 or are disabled or blind. The home remains exempt until it is verified that none of the above persons intend to live there or that none are physically able to live there.

**Example:** Bill and Betty are married and are residing in New Jersey. Bill enters a nursing home August 1st, and applies to Medicaid. Their assets are as follows: CD's, bank accounts, and investments totaling $150,000. Medicaid will take a snapshot of the couple's combined assets on August 1st, the day they applied for Medicaid. Betty will be allowed to keep one-half of $150,000. Since $150,000 is over the maximum limit of $84,120, Betty must pay the nursing home until she has spent down her assets to the $84,120 maximum.

Fortunately, individuals like Bill and Betty are allowed to keep their home, household goods, personal belongings, and an automobile. As long as they are married, the house is their most valuable asset. The home is exempt when it is the principal residence for the applicant or the applicant's spouse or children (if these children are under the age of 21 or are disabled or blind.) The home remains exempt until it is verified that none of the above persons intend to live there or none are physically able to live there. There exists no limit on the price of the home. However, under the OBRA '93 Act, a lien can be placed on the home once the Medicaid patient dies.

**Eligibility for a Single Individual**

Many people assume that they don't need to worry about LTC insurance, because the combination of Medicaid and Medicare will take care of long-term care expenses. Well, they are wrong. Under the Assets Limitations Standard, a single individual must "spend down" most of his/her assets before being eligible to receive Medicaid assistance.

- The individual may keep a personal allowance (usually between $30 and $60 per month to cover incidentals such as clothing, toiletries, and medical expenses not paid by Medicare or Medicaid.

- A deduction for amounts withheld to pay for federal or state income tax in Tennessee, Georgia, Kentucky, Mississippi, and South Carolina.

- The insurance premium needed to maintain the care recipient's Medicare Part B coverage and Medicare supplement policy.

**Transferring of Assets[5]**

Transferring of assets is one way to divest the money instead of paying Medicaid. The state in which you live will evaluate an applicant's financial picture before granting you eligibility. They will be looking at any transfer of countable assets within a certain period of time called a "look-back" period.

The look-back period in 2000 is thirty-six months for outright transfers (to family) and sixty months for transfers to a trust. The period begins only when an individual *applies* for Medicaid application for benefits, not when the transfer takes place.

The transfer of assets for less than fair market value within the application look-back period creates a period of ineligibility from Medicaid benefits.

The following formula is used by all states: assets made inaccessible, divided by what the local Medicaid office considers the average monthly cost of nursing home care in that community. For every state, ineligibility begins on the *date of transfer.*

Do not confuse the look-back period with the ineligibility period. The look-back is simply a span of time that begins on the day Medicaid was applied for and looks back either thirty-six or sixty months.

Ineligibility for transferring of assets during the look-back period is determined by the above formula.

Medicaid is very confusing and should not be taken lightly. Under OBRA '93, if someone transfers a large amount of assets and applies *within* the applicable look-back period (either thirty-six or sixty months), the applicant will be ineligible for benefits, since the time will extend past the look-back period and the applicant will not qualify for benefits until he or she spends the money that was transferred on his or her care.

## 1996 Law Strengthens Penalties for Medicaid Fraud

Individuals with money have been known to "hide" assets in order to qualify for Medicaid benefits to pay the costs of long-term care. The idea is to divest or transfer assets in order to shield them for heirs, instead of using them to pay for nursing home costs. Congress in 1993 extended the waiting or "look-back" period between the date of asset transfer and eligibility for Medicaid benefits to thirty-six months or three years. The 1996 Health Insurance and Portability/Accountability Act strengthens that statute by adding criminal penalties under USC Section 1320(a), to be explained later in this chapter.

## With the Recovery Against Your Estate Section of OBRA '93, LTC Becomes Even More Important

The OBRA '93 rules have increased the need for LTC insurance in order to protect assets in this day and age.

A major fact overlooked by many is the Recovery Against Your Estate Section of OBRA '93. The new law requires states to seek recovery of medical assistance paid to individuals who were 55 years of age or older when the assistance was paid (42. U.S.C. 1396p(b)(1)). The following is an oversimplified version of this new rule:

- Requires states to recover nursing home and long-term care Medicaid expenses from the estates of deceased recipients. (Yes, they even come after the dead.)

- States can go against any real personal property or other assets in which the individual had some property interest, including the home held in the individual's own name.

- In some cases, the state may even recover assets the individual gave away or otherwise disposed of prior to death or from property held jointly with someone else. Some states are utilizing the Debit/Credit law to obtain the property.

- No recovery is made from long-term care insurance payments!

Each state designs its own recovery programs, and no two are alike.

Homes represent the lion's share of assets recovered by states from the estates of Medicaid recipients. The reason is simple: A home is the single largest asset you can keep and still qualify for assistance. Bank accounts of less than $2,000 and cash accounts at nursing homes (also exempt under Medicaid eligibility rules) are also targets of recovery.

States use a variety of methods to track deaths of nursing home residents whose bills are being paid by Medicaid. These include collecting notices from probate courts. Most states place liens on the homes to protect their interest. Federal law prohibits the forced sale of a home if there is a surviving spouse, an adult disabled child, or a child under age 21.

"Compared with the total of nursing home bills paid by Medicaid — $32.5 billion in 1997 — the amount recovered by state programs is a tiny drop in the bucket. But it's growing: from $62 million in the 1992 fiscal year to $176 million in 1997. Arizona recovers the highest percentage of Medicaid nursing home expenses (7.9%), followed by Oregon (5%), Idaho (2.8%), New Hampshire (2.6%), and Maine (2.4%)."[6]

States are finding that the programs are extremely cost effective, collecting $10 to $12 in assets for every dollar "invested." With numbers like these, no wonder the states are using private collection agencies and letting them keep a portion of what they recover.[7]

**Annuities May Affect Medicaid Eligibility[8]**

The Department of Social Services, which administers the Medicaid program, states that annuities created so that an individual's assets are reduced to an amount where they would become eligible for Medicaid will be subject to a five-year-look-back period. Therefore, an annuity created within five years of someone applying for Medicaid will be deemed an ineligible transfer of assets. The individual will be denied Medicaid coverage for a period of time determined by the amount transferred into the annuity.

In simplified terms, the penalty period is the amount of the transfer divided by the average cost for nursing home care in the state.

If an individual chooses to use an annuity for the purpose of sheltering assets, it may be in the person's best interests to add long-term care insurance to the plan. The treatment of annuities when determining Medicaid eligibility has been a strong reason why long-term care insurance is a viable solution and a safe and sound addition to retirement plans.

IRA's (owned by either spouse) are usually considered nonexempt. The dollar value of an IRA is the total IRA amount minus any penalties for early withdrawal of the entire IRA account. Other types of retirement funds (pensions, annuities, disability plans, and some profit sharing plans) would be considered nonexempt if the person has the option of withdrawing a lump sum for any reason, even if he/she is not yet eligible for periodic payments. However, a retirement fund is exempt if employment must be terminated in order to obtain payment. (These exemptions could change in the future, based on changes in federal or state laws.)

Check with a tax advisor or Elder Law attorney for details in your state.

# $PEND DOWN QUICK REFERENCE GUIDE

Under the Assets Limitations Standard, almost all of the assets you own must be "Spent Down" before you are eligible for Medicaid assistance. The following are important exemptions:

**Single individuals qualifying for Medicaid**

| | |
|---|---|
| $ Home: | regardless of income (some states protect the home for a period of up to 6 months only if you are single). |
| $ Automobile: | one automobile. |
| $ Personal Belongings: | household goods and other personal items up to $2,000. |
| $ Wedding Ring: | one wedding ring and one engagement ring, unlimited value. |
| $ Property: | up to $6,000 equity in personal and real property, if essential for support. |
| $ Life Insurance: | cash surrender value of $1,600. |
| $ Assets: | about $2,000. |
| $ Burial Costs: | funeral and burial plots up to $2,500. |

$ Personal Needs:    allowance is $35 to $70 per month; moneys spent for personal expenses are not covered by Medicaid.

$ Home Maintenance:    allowance of about $2,000 per month.

## COUNTABLE

Vacation Home
Second Car
Certificates of Deposit
Investment Properties
Savings Bonds
Cash Value Life
    Insurance

Bonds/Stocks
Keogh Plans
IRA's
Single Premium-
    Deferred Annuities
Whole Life Insurance
    (above a certain level)

## NONCOUNTABLE

House (When Spouse
    is living)
Automobile
Household Goods
Jewelry

Personal Effects
Prepaid Burial
Prepaid Funeral
$2,000 in cash
Term Life Insurance

## INACCESSIBLE

Gifts

Jointly Held Irrevocable
    Trust

# $PEND DOWN QUICK REFERENCE GUIDE

Under the Assets Limitations Standard, almost all of the assets you own must be "Spent Down" before you are eligible for Medicaid assistance. The following are important exemptions:

**Married couples, qualifying for Medicaid when one spouse enters a nursing home***

| | |
|---|---|
| $ Assets: | half the couple's combined assets up to approximately $84,120, regardless of value. |
| $ Home: | regardless of value. |
| $ Household: | household goods regardless of value. |
| $ Personal Belongings: | regardless of value. |
| $ Automobile: | one automobile only, regardless of value. |
| $ Property: | up to $6,000 in personal and real property, if essential for support. |
| $ Life Insurance: | cash surrender value of $1,600. |
| $ Burial Costs: | funeral and burial plots up to $2,500. |
| $ Basic Living: | allowance for the at-home spouse is up to $2,103 per month. |
| $ Personal Needs: | allowance for the nursing home spouse is $35 to $60 per month to be used for medical expenses not covered by Medicaid. |

* Since the figures are periodically adjusted for inflation, the current figures for your state should be verified.

Half the couples' assets are countable at the time of admission to the nursing home (up to $84,120 in 2000), but not less than the floor. Additional assets can be protected for the community spouse if needed to produce income to meet the minimum protected income levels.

**Veterans' Long-Term Care Benefits**

Most of the twenty-five million veterans who served in the military think they have special privileges for nursing home or home care. "According to the U.S. General Accounting Office, the VA operates 173 hospitals and 136 nursing homes. The VA also has developed innovative health care programs that mirror efforts in the private sector. The agency provides or facilitates the delivery of home health services to more than 40,000 veterans, allowing them to live independently, rather than caring for them in institutional settings. Many are older adults with chronic medical conditions, such as heart disease, that only require periodic attention to remain at home. Others have been discharged from VA medical centers following treatment and need continuing care, such as the changing of dressings or administration of medications."

The occupancy rate at VA facilities is more than 90%, making access difficult. This situation has created a desire on behalf of the administration to contract with multi and regional providers for nursing facility care for veterans. Unfortunately, certain provisions of the contract create a disincentive for prospective bidders.

Veterans' health care benefits include medically necessary hospital and nursing home care and some outpatient care. Those known as "Category A," or mandatory care veterans, have a higher priority for receiving care and are eligible for a wider range of services.

**Category A:**
- have service-connected disabilities,
- were discharged from the military for disabilities incurred or aggravated in the line of duty,

- are former prisoners of war,
- were exposed to certain toxic substances or ionizing radiation,
- served during the Mexican Border Period or World War I,
- received disability compensation, or
- received non-service-connected disability pensions benefits; or have incomes below the means test threshold ($22,888 for a single veteran or $27,469 for a veteran with one dependent, as of January 2000; these rates change yearly).

**Categories B and C**

Veterans who were not disabled in service or with higher incomes might receive care on a space available basis. The co-payment or deductible is based on their level of income.

To learn more about your eligibility benefits as a veteran, contact your local Department of Veterans Affairs Regional Office, or write to:

Veteran's Benefits Department
Paralyzed Veterans of America
801 18th Street N.W
Washington, D.C 20006
or call: 1-800-424-8200

For veterans with higher incomes who do not qualify under these conditions, the VA may provide hospital care if space and resources are available. These "discretionary care" veterans must pay part of the cost of their care.

The Department of Veteran's Affairs can provide information on how to reach the closest VA medical center or nursing home in your area and how to apply for the programs.

# A Personal Story
## by S. Larry Feldman

The services of a VA medical center, though both conscientious and comprehensive, still can have long-term care patients lacking in areas of need. This personal story is one similar to the experiences of thousands of veterans and their families, caught in the web of caregiving for loved ones needing it, long-term.

My father's brother Jack, a World War II veteran, was also a one-time boxer. Not nearly as successful as Abe, their younger brother, who once had been ranked World's Number One Light Heavyweight. Jack's problem was the proverbial "glass jaw." Ring knockouts cause temporary memory loss to some; eventual long-term injury to others. No one can tell its origin, but for sure Uncle Jack's ultimate onset of Alzheimer's disease stripped him, bit by bit, of memory and then the capacity for independent living.

In some, independence dies hard. Jack's wife refused my father's offer to help finance his nursing home care, instead, opting for placement in a VA hospital's long-term care wing, causing a family rift. Despite a regimen of conscientious care, it was frustrating and painful for Jack's family to see him housed in a ward with five other unfortunates — all in varying stages of functioning loss — in a severely restricted area of the hospital. This is in no way meant to impugn the programs or efforts available to veterans in such circumstances. It is merely an unvarnished view of the extent to which financial shortcomings restrict one's options for long-term care. Under government programs such as Medicare, Medicaid, and Veterans Benefits, freedom of choice is directly affected by the fiscal resources available to meet such needs. Given the extent of deterioration possible, over time, long-term care can be both extensive and expensive.

## Cost-of-Living Adjustment (COLA)

Based on the increase in the Consumer Price Index (CPI-W) from the third quarter of 1998 through the third quarter of 1999, Social Security beneficiaries and Supplemental Security Income (SSI) recipients received a 2.4 percent COLA for 2000.

Other important 2000 Social Security information is as follows:

| Tax Rate: | 2000 |
|---|---|
| Employee | 7.65% |
| Self-Employed | 15.30% |

Note: The 7.65% tax rate is the combined rate for Social Security and Medicare. The Social Security portion (OASDI) is 6.20% on earnings up to the applicable maximum taxable amount (see below.) The Medicare portion (HI) is 1.45% on all earnings.

**Maximum Earnings Taxable**

| Social Security (OASDI only) | $76,200 |
|---|---|
| Medicare (HI only) | No Limit |
| Quarter of Coverage: | $780 |

Up until December 31, 1999, senior citizens who kept working between the ages of 65 to 69 faced a Social Security earnings penalty of $1 in benefits for every $3 in earned wages over $17,000. The House of Representatives and the Senate by unanimous vote repealed this provision in the law during the first quarter of 2000, retroactive to January 1. (For early retirees beginning at age 62 and under age 64, their Social Security benefits are subject to $1 withheld for every $2 in earnings above $10,080 in 2000.)

**Maximum Social Security Benefit**
**Worker Retiring at age 65 in January of 2000:**
$1,433/mo.

**SSI Resources Limits**

| Individual | $2,000 |
|---|---|
| Couple | $3,000 |

**Estimated Average Monthly Social Security Benefits After the December 1999 COLA:**

| | 2.4% COLA |
|---|---|
| All Retired Workers | $804.00 |
| Aged Couple, Both Receiving Benefits | $1,348.00 |

| | |
|---|---|
| Widowed Mother and Two Children | $1,611.00 |
| Aged Widow(er) Alone | $775.00 |
| Disabled Worker, Spouse and one or more children | $1,255.00 |
| All Disabled Workers | $754.00 |

*Fact Sheet, Social Security, Kenneth S. Apfel, Commissioner, Social Security Administration, 2000.

## State and Federal Tax Initiatives for Long-Term Care Insurance
### by Jonathan Spilde

Dr. Fernando Torres-Gil, former Assistant Secretary on Aging and current Director of the Center for Policy Research on Aging at UCLA, puts the issue of long-term care financing into proper perspective. Speaking at the National Summit on Retirement Savings held June 1998 in Washington, DC, he likened LTC to "the elephant at the dining table. We can choose to ignore it, but it *is there*, and it will not go away, and we cannot push it aside." Such is the nature of the situation local, state and federal governments find themselves in as they search for solutions to ballooning Medicaid budgets, where far and away the largest share goes to LTC expenses. The best solution for many of us continues to be insurance. With that in mind, the move is on by governments to create attractive tax incentives for consumers to buy LTC coverage. A portion of this chapter will look at what has been done thus far on both the state and federal levels, as legislators attempt to give a nod of acknowledgement to the LTC elephant, and examine the opportunities and responsibilities these initiatives present to agents and consumers alike.

### State incentives

Because state budgets fund roughly 33 cents of each Medicaid dollar, there are a growing number that have passed incentive legislation allowing for either an income tax credit or tax deduction for their residents. Where tax credits have been granted, they are generally based on a percentage of premium not to exceed a certain limit. For example, my home state of North Dakota allows a credit of 25% of premium not to exceed $100 to residents filing long form state returns. Such a credit may not sound like much of an incentive to purchase LTC coverage, but as a consumer it means the net cost of owning coverage gets easier to handle.

The same holds true for a tax deduction. Some states have chosen to create an incentive in this manner. Usually, this method involves simply allowing filers to subtract all or a portion of their long-term care premium expense as a line item from their gross income prior to figuring net tax due. Depending upon the average income of residents, and what the average tax rate of the particular state is, a line item deduction may actually work out to be less costly and, therefore, more attractive to budget-conscious legislators than the credit approach. Yet, to the average taxpayer, the sound of the words "tax deductible" can have a powerful effect.

At this point, it is impossible to assess which method is/has been the most effective incentive for taxpayers. Evaluation of the data to determine the ages of those claiming a credit or deduction has not been done up to this point. One thing, however, seems clear. If we as a country are to successfully point to LTC insurance coverage as a meaningful part of the solution to the national crisis in LTC funding, tax incentives are sure to play a very important role in getting the message out.

## The Federal Role

Several states express their tax levels as a percentage of federal tax, and thus have been reluctant to address the issue of incentives until the federal government gets into the act. This entrée by Congress has now materialized in a very big way with the passage of a bill known as Kennedy-Kassebaum (or, depending on one's politics, Kassebaum-Kennedy.) As we can infer from its sponsorship, this landmark piece of legislation was approved with bipartisan support and became the Health

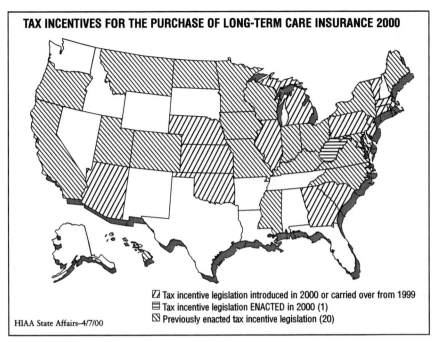

**TAX INCENTIVES FOR THE PURCHASE OF LONG-TERM CARE INSURANCE 2000**

⊿ Tax incentive legislation introduced in 2000 or carried over from 1999
⊟ Tax incentive legislation ENACTED in 2000 (1)
◺ Previously enacted tax incentive legislation (20)

HIAA State Affairs–4/7/00

Insurance Portability and Accountability Act of 1996 (HIPAA). Here at last, contained within a massive tax bill, is the federal government's first major acknowledgement that they have no intention of picking up the LTC tab for millions of financially able individuals. Instead, HIPAA addressed this very thorny subject by providing tax breaks for people purchasing LTC insurance as either individuals or as part of voluntary or employer group plans in the workplace.

Following is a brief description of HIPAA highlights regarding long-term care and LTC insurance. If for no other reason than space limitations, it is not intended to be the last word on tax treatment of long-term care. Indeed, HIPAA itself creates as many questions as it provides answers, and Congress and the Treasury Department will be occupied for some time to come as they attempt to further define and clarify LTC tax issues.

### Asset Transfers

The subject of transferring assets with the intent of qualifying for Medicaid benefits has attracted a great deal of attention in our nation and in our Congress as we attempt to come to terms with

LTC financing issues. HIPAA originally addressed this activity by including language prohibiting such transfers, complete with monetary fines and prison terms for everyone involved.

The pertinent section of the law (USC Section 1320(2)) began with the words "Whoever: (6) knowingly and willfully disposes of assets," etc. This section quickly became known as the *Granny Goes to Jail* provision, and became a rallying point for many Elder Law attorneys and others actively involved in the advice of *artificial impoverishment*. Much effort was made to paint grim scenes of removing elderly and disabled from the care of nursing homes and casting them into federal prisons — there to reside with the most hardened of criminals.

Congress, hearing (and visualizing) these impassioned cries, repealed the offending section — replacing it instead with language many dubbed *Granny's Attorney/Financial Advisor Goes to Jail*, leaving little doubt as to the legislative mindset in this regard. Finding this turn of events equally distasteful, a lawsuit was filed by the New York State Bar Association against U.S. Attorney General Janet Reno seeking to prevent her from enforcing the law on grounds that it was an unconstitutional restriction of the right to freedom of speech. The State court agreed and granted an injunction prohibiting the federal government from enforcing asset transfer restrictions in New York.

It is noteworthy, though, that even prior to the Court's decision Attorney General Reno had indicated her agreement with the Bar in a letter to the Speaker of the House. She then went on to offer the Justice Department's assistance in drafting new asset transfer legislation that could pass Constitutional muster. Thus it would appear that — one way or another — the days of Medicaid asset transfers are numbered, putting even further importance on the message of individual responsibility fostered by the favorable tax treatment granted LTC insurance by HIPAA.

## Tax Treatment of LTC Insurance Premiums

HIPAA created a new type of long-term care insurance called *tax-qualified* (TQ). The law essentially treats tax-qualified LTC insurance like accident and health insurance. To the extent that unreimbursed medical expenses exceed 7.5% of an individual's adjusted gross income, those expenses are considered deductible. The premiums paid for tax-qualified LTCI policies are now considered to be eligible medical expenses. The deduction is subject to the limitations found in Chapter 6.

At the same time, *benefits received* from tax-qualified LTCI policies are guaranteed not to be taxable. An exception to this would be per diem benefits received from what are commonly known as indemnity policies. Here, benefits may be taxable if they are in excess of $190 per day in 2000 and are more than actual incurred expenses. To minimize the possibility of confusion, industry product trends are moving away from the indemnity model policy in favor of a "pooled benefit" approach payable on an expense-incurred basis.

Following is a capsulated breakdown of the tax treatment of tax-qualified LTC insurance (TQ LTCI) purchased in common scenarios other than on the individual basis discussed above. Acknowledgement and thanks are given in advance to TransAmerica Occidental Life for their Worksite LTCI Tax Guide — from which much of this was sourced.

*Self-Employed.* Here, eligible TQ LTCI premiums are treated as medical insurance premiums up to the same limits as listed for individuals. The percentage of premium eligible will be found in Chapter 6.

Any premium amounts over the allowed percentages may be deducted as unreimbursed medical expenses (as outlined previously for individual taxpayers). Benefits received are excluded from gross income subject to the same limitations as other individual taxpayers.

*Sole Proprietors.* Benefits received by employees of a sole proprietor under an employer-paid TQ policy are treated as any other employer-paid health insurance benefit and are not includable in the employee's gross income. Premiums paid for the policy by the sole proprietor are fully deductible if they retain no interest in the policy.

Tax treatment of a policy for the sole proprietor and their family members is subject to the same rules as self-employed individuals.

*Partnerships.* A partnership purchasing a TQ LTCI policy for a non-partner employee and/or a spouse may deduct the entire premium as a business expense, provided the partnership does not retain any interest in the policy.

If a partnership buys TQ LTCI for a partner (or spouse), the entire premium amount would be included in the partner's gross income. The partner is treated as self-employed, with the same tax rules applying as for self-employed individuals. Any balance of eligible premiums above the amount deductible as self-employed health insurance may be added to other unreimbursed medical expenses and deducted subject to the 7.5% of adjusted gross income threshold rule.

Benefits received either by partnership employees or partners are excluded from income in the same manner as any other employer-paid health insurance benefit.

The same rules apply for limited partnerships and family limited partnerships.

*C-Corporations.* Where the Corporation buys a TQ LTCI policy for an employee (may also include the employee's spouse and dependents) the Corporation may deduct the entire premium as a business expense, so long as they retain no interest in the policy. Premiums paid by the Corporation are excluded from employees' income.

Benefits paid from the policy for expenses incurred are also excluded from income — just as with any employer-paid health insurance benefit.

*S-Corporations.* The Corporation may deduct any premiums paid for TQ LTCI as a reasonable and necessary business expense. The amount excludable from income to the employee differs depending on whether they own more or less than 2% of the stock in the corporation. Shareholders of more than 2% are required to include the entire amount of premium paid by the corporation in their gross income, while shareholders of less than 2% may exclude the premiums.

As with C-Corporations, benefits paid for expenses incurred are excludable from income.

*Limited Liability Corporations (LLC).* For non-owner employees, spouses, and dependents, the entire amount of premium can be deducted by the LLC as a business expense. Owners and part-owners (2%+) of the LLC will be considered as self-employed individuals.

Here again, benefits reimbursing expenses incurred are excluded from income.

## More Positives

While HIPAA expressly excludes LTC insurance premiums from being offered under cafeteria plans (Sec. 125(f)), support is growing on Capitol Hill for the opportunity to do so. Nevertheless, Congress has created worksite opportunities, and most LTCI companies believe that HIPAA allows employers to selectively choose participants in providing TQ LTCI as an employee benefit without jeopardizing the exclusion from income. This opens the way for what many call the executive "carve-out" sale, enabling a company to offer richly designed TQ LTCI coverage for key employees.

To accommodate and reward consumers with the foresight and personal responsibility to purchase LTC insurance even without the encouragement of tax incentives, Congress chose to "grandfather" all such policies with an effective date on or before December 31, 1996. That means all those plans will automatically qualify for favorable tax treatment! Care must be taken, therefore, to honor the integrity of grandfathered coverage, as any increases or additions will generally be considered by Treasury to be a *material change* and, as such, destroy the contracts' grandfathered tax advantages. Any additional coverage enhancements or additions to existing coverage should be done via a separate "supplemental stand-alone" policy, with the grandfathered contract considered as an underlying foundation.

On December 9, 1998, the Treasury Department published Final Income Tax Regulations regarding TQ LTCI contracts. In response to consumer and insurance industry concerns the term *material change* was further defined.

All this is *very good news!* Prior to HIPAA, the tax treatment of LTCI benefits was virtually unknown. Pending Congressional clarification and/or guidance from the Treasury, this remains the case for all plans sold after January 1, 1997, but which are not tax qualified as defined by HIPAA standards. Because such plans may still be purchased, it is important to understand the distinction between them. For lack of any better term, these plans have been dubbed *non*-tax-qualified, and are best described as the way LTC insurance was before HIPAA came into existence.

The virtues of tax-qualified vs. non-tax-qualified have been and will continue to be the topic of many a spirited debate among agents and other industry professionals. At great risk of oversimplification (and certain criticism from both viewpoints) the essence of the issue is as follows: Conditions under which benefits would first become payable are generally conceded to be more liberal under a non-tax-qualified (NTQ) than its tax-qualified (TQ) counterpart. On the other hand, the tax status of these same benefits is only guaranteed in the TQ version of events.

There have been many articles written attempting to explain what Congress did or didn't intend to accomplish with more rigid benefit qualifiers for TQ LTCI. The fact is, no one can speak for them, and until such time as official clarification is offered, consumers should examine all options open to them and choose the product that will best serve their individual situation.

In the final analysis, it is important to recognize and remember that it is much better to have coverage for most of our LTC expenses than not. Accordingly, agents and consumers should be focused and prioritized on the *overall need* for LTC financing. In order to take advantage of the individual and worksite tax breaks created by HIPAA, the agent must sell (and the client must purchase) tax-qualified LTC insurance coverage. Where tax advantages are not meaningful, non-tax-qualified coverage remains available. The politics of the particulars is best left to the policymakers in Washington.

When an insurance company pays benefits on behalf of an insured, the insurance company must report payments to the Internal Revenue Service.

**IRS LTC 1099 Reporting Form**

## State Partnerships

Whoever coined the phrase, "Success is in the eye of the beholder," could have had their eye on the public/private long-term care insurance partnership programs. People within the insurance industry consider each new insured a success, while the lobbyists who believe the government should pay for all long-term care, will have difficulty acknowledging the gains achieved under the partnership programs. Many sales interviews have been initiated because of the public's confidence in a state's sponsorship of a public/private LTC insurance program, resulting in the purchase of non-partnership policies.

Wealthy prospects can afford to protect assets *and income!* Policyholders who retire to a non-partnership state may not wish to return to a nursing facility in a partnership state for the Medicaid asset protection following maximum payout of insurance company policy benefits.

And some citizens may find applying to Medicaid, even under the best of circumstances, repugnant.

Fifty to sixty percent of all New York State applications processed in our office are for New York State partnership policies, so we know partnership policies offer a great deal for a majority of New York consumers. If partnership policies offer such an excellent value for the premium paid, why are only four states participating? The answer or blame if you wish, can be placed in Washington, D.C., at the hands of Congress.

The Omnibus Reconciliation Act of 1993 (OBRA '93) grandfathered the four operating state partnership programs, and created language that put the brakes on new state partnerships by mandating states to recover assets from the estates of all persons receiving services under Medicaid. In other words, Congress tore the heart out of one of the most innovative legislative initiatives of the decade of the '90s!

Mark R. Meiners, Ph.D., Associate Director, University of Maryland Center on Aging and Director of the Robert Wood Johnson Foundation Partnership for Long-Term Care, highlighted the case for shared responsibility when he wrote, "Long-Term Care is important but expensive, and neither the public nor the private sector alone is capable of providing adequate funding for that component of the health care delivery system."[9]

Some issues inhibit realization of the extensive possibilities of the long-term care insurance market. The most immediate are probably the best known — denial and lack of knowledge. Together, these factors can create an almost impenetrable barrier to consumer demand. The facts regarding the risk and expense of long-term care are just beginning to reach audiences outside government and academia. Though it may seem media attention to the problem has grown commonplace, for many people, education is gained through personal experience. It is not until it happens to them or a loved one that the enormity of coping with the emotional, physical, and financial implications becomes clear. Even then, for a large number, the lesson may miss the mark, as the event is perceived as isolated. Millions of families around the globe are struggling with the effects of long-term care. Yet it appears they must imagine their situation unique. Given the numbers sharing the experience, it is difficult to understand how this could be. But the lack of public outcry seems to imply a lack of a sense of the universality and probability of the need. Even firsthand knowledge may be misunderstood because knowing and believing can be very different.

This leads to the second barrier to the growth in long-term care insurance sales — denial. In the future, there will probably be a study about why, when it comes to long-term care, even informed people — including those who sell insurance — often fail to apply the facts to themselves. The reasons could range from paradigms of social expectations (families take care of their own) to the personal (fear of aging, loss of control, power, or independence.) In any case, whatever the reason, the worth and therefore salability of any product is based on its perceived value.

The framework demonstrating that public/private long-term care partnerships can and do work is in place.

Although the cost of long-term care insurance is as reasonable as any other coverage when compared to actual risk, without acceptance of the risk, it may appear unaffordable. However, affordability is not absolute. Often it is a flexible concept that depends on priorities, which in turn are based on perceptions of need. Simply put, the more the perceived need, the more affordable the purchase becomes.

While formidable, the problem of increasing public awareness about the risk of long-term care is being addressed. The insurance industry is not alone in its efforts to educate the public. Government, through Medicaid, a program originally designed to provide health care for the poor, is now responsible for over one-half of all long-term care expenditures. The general consensus is that a national social insurance system to cover these costs is not anticipated, so the only alternative is to increase private coverage. And, in spite of discussions regarding medical savings accounts and small tax credits to informal caregivers, most experts agree the most cost-effective solution is to encourage the purchase of insurance. To that end, clarification of the tax status of policies and benefits was a significant step forward. Recently, a seemingly simple but actually more important proposal was made by Washington — a campaign to inform the public that Medicare does not cover long-term care costs to any real extent. In the over thirty-five years of Medicare's existence, this fact has never been acknowledged. In extending this proposal, the seriousness with which the government is viewing the problem of financing long-term care is notable. Since at least one of the hoped-for outcomes of the proposed educational campaign is to increase the purchase of insurance, a singular opportunity is taking shape on a national level. It is the chance for government and the insurance industry to work together to reach a mutual goal.

It is not unusual for the private and public sectors to seek each other's support. It is unusual for the confluence of need to be as complete as it is in the case of long-term care. To avoid possible fiscal crisis, the government must expand the private financing offered through insurance. To realize market potential in expanding private financing, the insurance industry would benefit from the credibility and reach of the government. Unlike most needs that draw the public and private sectors together, the objectives of each sector are not centered on a product as much as an idea — shaping the future in regard to a social problem. The end goals of each sector differ and the parties could work separately. However, maximum success in terms of cost avoidance by government and sales growth for the industry might be more likely and timely if they worked together. This sets the stage for considering a unique, symbiotic relationship not based on the customary roles of oversight and governance — a partnership. This is the opportunity of a public/private approach to the problem of long-term care.

Government intervention through increasing public awareness could eliminate a major obstacle to the common acceptance of private insurance as protection against the cost of long-term care. However, it can not resolve the largest barrier — cost. While affordability can be subjective, there are limits to what individuals can spend without sacrifice. The parameters of affordability depend on the age and/or location of the potential purchaser. The older the buyer or the more expensive the care where they live, the higher the premium. This means that there is no single income amount that can define affordability. Nor is relative financial security a useful index. A 75-year-old living in rural mid-America with an income of $40,000 might be considered quite comfortable and easily afford coverage for care in an area where $100 a day was sufficient. The same person in urban New York could be less comfortable financially, and the cost of a premium to purchase coverage for care averages nearly $300 a day — prohibitive. The question of who can or who cannot afford long-term care coverage can be illustrated by imagining a continuum with poverty (cannot under any circumstance) at one end and wealth (can under any circumstance) at the other. As outlined above, most of the population will fall between the two ends in accordance with age and/or location. The objective of a public/private partnership might be to increase the number of persons toward the "can afford" end of the continuum.

The advantage of partnering instead of independent action to reach the objective of broadening the long-term care insurance market can be seen by examining the possible outcomes of more traditional approaches. The private sector usually addresses cost barriers by lowering price. However, due to actuarial expectations and the need for solvency, insurance costs are less elastic than those of other commodities. Therefore, the usual approach is to reduce benefits or coverage. Although this will have the effect of lowering premiums and perhaps increasing insurance sales, the result may not be consistent with public sector goals. Inadequate coverage might be considered better than no coverage, but the inadequacy could be a problem for government. Private coverage that pays too little might reduce reliance on Medicaid, but not to the extent necessary. Impoverishment due to out-of-pocket expenses to compensate for daily benefits bearing no relationship to anticipated costs or coverage of lengths of stay below expected averages may be delayed, but not necessarily avoided.

Government usually encourages private behavior through tax incentives. However, tax incentives are effective only if (a) the item that can be purchased (is affordable), and (b) the purchaser's tax situation gives value to the incentive. The current deductibility of long-term care insurance premiums is an example of how these two conditions may have limited the efficacy of the tax incentive approach. The vast majority of taxpayers do not meet the 7.5% medical deduction standard. As a result, while sales increased after the legislation was enacted, growth was not sustained. Tax credits could be a more attractive incentive, but they could also increase public expense without a guarantee of commensurate reduction. So there is a risk that those who would have purchased anyway would receive a reward, while the market and Medicaid expenses would remain constant.

If tax incentives are flawed vehicles for promoting long-term care insurance market growth, and if the availability of limited coverage is truly unlikely to alter public dependency to a significant degree, is there a possible solution for both? The answer is yes, and prototypes already exist — the partnerships for long-term care financing currently operating in California, Connecticut, Indiana, and New York.

Saving the details on the specifics of these programs for the moment, each program combines private insurance with Medicaid without the requirement of impoverishment. The general design includes the promise that if specific, approved insurance is purchased, and the coverage is not sufficient, the buyer will be permitted to enroll in Medicaid. However, persons enrolled in Medicaid who participate in the partnership program will not be held to state limitations on assets. Depending on the state, these enrollees are permitted to keep assets equal to benefits paid under their insurance up to unlimited amounts. Although program designs, limits, and results vary, their one commonality is the acceptance of a set of powerful yet rational assumptions regarding market behavior, human nature, and the expectations of government. It is these assumptions that could form the basis of an effort to realize the goals of both the insurance industry and government — lowering the final barrier to the growth of long-term care insurance sales and reducing future dependency on public funds.

1. The concept of insurance should be neutral — neither inherently positive nor negative. Shared risk as used in insurance is an effective way to manage the unmanageable expense of the individual. Private insurance that is based on sound financial principles, ethical sales practices, and legitimate operating procedures can be a valuable tool in handling the risk that government cannot or does not want to undertake.

- *Translation: A well-run insurance company should be no more suspect than any other organization. And, as insurance is needed to make the partnership work, political rhetoric and wishful thinking about alternatives should be left at the door.*

2. Private insurance is a business. To remain effective, rules and requirements that protect profitability and the likelihood of profitability must be considered.

- *Translation: Business is not the public sector. Profit is important. Profit can be limited to a degree, but not eliminated.*

3. Government has more of an obligation to its constituents than does the insurer to its customers. To retain credibility, government sensitivity to this obligation must be considered.

- *Translation: Government must govern. Caveat emptor does not apply.*

4. Government currently pays the majority of long-term care costs. It is not probable that all responsibility can be eliminated. Reduction is a feasible and desirable goal.

- *Translation: The poor will always require support, some people will not be helped, and it is possible that some people will gain unnecessarily. These are issues for another day. Waiting to do anything until everything can be done means nothing will be done.*

5. Partners are equal, and their respective limits, needs, and considerations have equal validity.

- *Translation: Neither sector should forget that the other does not really need to be there. But once there, actions are not only jointly decided but jointly enacted.*

6. Negotiated agreements promote better results than mandated settlements.

- *Translation: Pulling rank or weight settles disputes but does not guarantee cooperation once everyone leaves the table. Regulation does not touch the heart of the marketplace, as personal gain does. Not every action involving government requires legislation. Consider alternatives.*

7. Everyone, including businesses and governments, are more likely to behave appropriately as a result of inducements, than from fear of punishment.

- *Translation: Even donkeys work harder on the promise of a carrot than the threat of a stick.*

8. There is a common value system. It is not reasonable to ask of others what the asker would not do if the situations were reversed. Concurrently, if something appeals to those who ask, it will probably appeal to others.

- *Translation: Fairness and the perception of fairness count. A truly good deal will appeal to everyone.*

9. It is the nature of the American public to be independent. Given the choice between relying on themselves or government, they will choose self-reliance. However, it is the duty of government to identify those instances where self-reliance requires support.

- *Translation: For the most part, the public will do what it can to solve its own problems. Always assume the best approach is supportive rather than proscriptive.*

What is possible, then, if public and private sectors can meet under the aegis of the above assumptions? Operating under these assumptions, in one state sales of long-term care insurance jumped almost seventy percent in one year. A survey of purchasers indicated that one in four would have relied on Medicaid in the absence of the partnership program — a figure that could be projected to equal more than $90 million in Medicaid savings. If one state alone can do that much, the potential of many states joined is extraordinary and worth consideration.

It takes only an open mind to verify the magnitude of the impact that the financing of long-term care is having and will have on society, unless meaningful changes are made. But also in crisis is opportunity — an opportunity with many facets — to shape the fiscal future for ourselves and our nation, to bring an exciting market to maturity, and to make all this possible through a new idea of public/private cooperation. The methods have been tested, the lessons learned and experience gained. What is needed now is a willingness to try that is equal to the urgency of the demand to try.

The sooner concerned citizens, representatives of the health care delivery system, and members of the insurance community involve themselves to restore the original public/private LTCI concept, the closer we will come to preserving an individual public benefit program.

### State Public/Private LTCI Partnership Profiles

Two models have been created: the Dollar for Dollar model and the Total Assets model. The Dollar for Dollar model must cover at least one year of benefits at issue for a minimum per day indemnity amount (variable by state). Every dollar of benefits paid out by the insurance company will be deducted from the resources counted toward Medicaid eligibility. The Total Assets model, also known as the Time Element model, must cover three years of nursing home care or six years of home care or a combination thereof. Every two days of home care count as one day of facility care. Once the total benefits of the insurance policy have been paid out, Medicaid eligibility is granted without regard to assets. Neither model protects income; only assets are protected.

**California Partnership for Long-Term Care**

| | |
|---|---|
| Model: | Dollar for Dollar, 2000 Minimum Daily Nursing Home Benefit — $90 |
| Agent Training: | At least eight hours mandated, depending on year of licensure |
| Comments: | State conducts consumer advertising programs. Eight LTCI companies approved to market Partnership policies. |

**Connecticut Partnership for Long-Term Care**

| | |
|---|---|
| Model: | Dollar for Dollar, 2000 Minimum Daily Nursing Home Benefit — $118 |
| Agent Training: | Seven and a half-hours mandated |
| Comments: | In addition to general public availability, the State offers voluntary payroll deduction partnership policies to state employees through a private carrier. Nine LTCI companies approved to market Partnership plans. |

**Indiana Long-Term Care Program**

| | |
|---|---|
| Model: | Originally only Dollar for Dollar. Today: both Dollar for Dollar and Total Assets Models available. Dollar for Dollar — 2000 Minimum Daily Nursing Home Benefit — $85 Total Assets Protection 2000 Minimum Policy Benefit — $154,350 |
| Agent Training: | Seven hours of ILTCP continuing education mandated |

Comments: State is very proactive in assisting agents to market Partnership plans. State publishes qualified Partnership Agents List, issues Agent I.D. cards, and conducts annual seminars for agents. Ten LTCI companies approved to market Partnership plans.

**New York State Partnership for Long-Term Care**

Model: Total Asset Protection, 2000 Minimum Daily Nursing Home benefit — $141

Agent Training: No state requirement; left to the insurance companies to provide agent training

Comments: Though not the first state approved, New York leads all states in total number of policies in force. Ten LTCI companies approved to market Partnership plans.

**Variations of Partnership Program States**

Illinois and Massachusetts

# Never Underestimate the Power of an Idea

Early in 1992, it became apparent to perceptive observers that the New York State Partnership for Long-Term Care Insurance would soon make this critical need available to consumers throughout the state. Living and working in the shadow of the state capital provided me with access to various state agencies and a broad base of insurance and financial planners. With this in mind, I approached the Partnership to ask if they would participate in a seminar to describe the Partnership and its purpose to an audience of related professionals: insurance agents, lawyers, and accountants.

I proposed the seminar be conducted by a panel that would be made up of representatives of the Partnership, the nursing home industry, and the insurance industry. Since most bureaucrats tend to view private industry with a jaundiced eye, I was prepared for a negative response. To my surprise they were eager for such a forum to take place and replied they'd be happy to participate. With several hundred professionals expected to attend, we knew it would be impractical to accommodate the general public. Still, we wanted much of the vital information generated to be made available to a wider audience. So I approached the local public broadcasting television station to see if they might be interested in taping the session for airing to their viewers. Their response was an enthusiastic "yes." As their executive director put it: "Medicare, Medicaid, long-term care, and aging are hot topics." He even offered to help arrange distribution to the eleven PBS stations throughout the state! With help from insurance carriers and the Partnership, this was arranged. The Governor's Office also cooperated, with a press conference at which the Governor announced the event. In sum, New York's Public/Private Partnership had become a living, breathing example of what it was truly meant to be.

## Some Closing Thoughts

It's now apparent that Medicare cuts in the Balanced Budget Act of 1997 had the effect of balancing that budget on the backs of elderly and disabled patients, nursing homes, and other types of fee for service long-term care providers. Headlines announcing the forced closure of 2,500 home care agencies attribute a major share of blame to the Medicare cutbacks. Nursing homes have also been affected, with four of the largest chains and nearly ten percent of facilities nationwide in bankruptcy. According to the American Health Care Association, states in which facilities have been hurt include New Mexico and Nevada, where close to 47 percent of the 128 facilities have declared bankruptcy. No region of the country has escaped unscathed.

Inadequate reimbursement, coupled with stringent limits on levels of care mandates, has created staffing dilemmas. These are especially severe in areas of extremely low unemployment.

Without relief, countless numbers of patients will be facing long-term care crises.

When discussing veterans' benefits, I am curious as to how many veterans will qualify for benefits under tough criteria for service-related disabilities, and whether they will be able to readily obtain occupancy in a facility without being placed on a waiting list.

Case studies by psychiatrist Devidre Johnston of Wake Forest University in Winston-Salem, N.C., suggest a high correlation between violent episodes of post-traumatic stress disorders and the number of veterans now suffering from dementia who experienced combat in World War II or Korea. The findings published in the January 2000 *Journal of the American Geriatrics Society* theorize the outbreaks stem from the possibility that cognitive functions are not intact enough to prevent memories of War from being unlocked and sometimes played out. In addition to concern for the health and welfare of these combat veterans, there must also be concern for the safety and well-being of their spouses and caregivers. No long-term care insurance underwriter with whom I've spoken has suggested adding "history of combat duty" to its list of uninsurable events.

Mention also should be made of the long-term care insurance opportunity afforded seniors through Congressional passage of a bill repealing the Social Security earnings penalty in 2000. Nearly 1,000,000 workers between the ages of 65 and 69 will receive up to an additional $6,700 in Social Security benefits. Other seniors not yet 70, who might have worked in the past but were discouraged by the earnings penalty, will surely welcome this reversal. In either event, "new" dollars to purchase the benefits of long-term care insurance that did not exist before, plus additional dollars in reserve accounts to fund future LTCI premium payments, may now be available.

And finally, there are signs on the horizon the federal government, the insurance industry, and the senior coalition can work together to help solve the nation's mounting long-term care crisis. During March of 2000, a consensus proposal by the

Senate Special Committee on Aging sponsored legislation called the Long-Term Care and Retirement Security Act of 2000. The announcement was released with a joint letter of support from the Health Insurance Association of America and the American Association of Retired Persons. This landmark event has the potential of elevating LTCI to the status of a commodity and at the same time, preserve the system of Medicaid for which it was originally intended.

# CHAPTER 5

## Long-Term Care Insurance: The Policy

Discounting certain ineffective look-alikes, long-term care is the newest form of insurance. Like other distinct types of coverage, such as property and casualty, life and health, it has been created in response to a specific need of a large portion of the general population. For reasons already stated, it can be argued that the need driving the individual purchase of long-term care insurance is often more compelling than that of other insurances. For most people, health insurance coverage is secured as a rite of employment, or upon eligibility for Medicare. Life insurance needs accelerate in early adulthood and begin to wane following middle age, except for owners of large estates, or executives in key positions. Disability insurance protects against the loss of employment income. Fire, auto, and liability insurance are dependent on ownership. But long-term care insurance, with a 50 percent probability of occurring to older people who live long enough, and costs of care that often exceed a quarter of a million dollars or more, is a universal risk too significant to escape the attention of the insurance industry. Given these facts, long-term care insurance has the potential of posting the highest percentage of new policies sold among all insurance in the new millennium.

Competition, creativity, and consumer demand are compelling long-term care insurance companies to offer a plethora of benefits and options. Comparing the policies of three different insurance companies is like comparing apples, oranges, and peaches. This point is demonstrated with a side-by-side analysis.

Members of the National LTC Network are long-term care insurance specialists, hence they are often asked which company has the "best" policy? If there were an absolute best policy, members could make a lot of material and storage space accessible, as well as freeing up space on their hard drives. But the answer is not that simple. The best policy for one client may be inadequate for another. Guiding us through this maze, Everett Thorne's "how-to" approach will assist readers to focus wisely on a meaningful way to select benefits and options for personal use.

Thorne shares his insight into "why people are persuaded to buy long-term care insurance and how this is similar to placing the horse before the cart."

In addition to the question "which is the best company?" Network members are often asked, "which company has the lowest premiums?" The answer to this question depends on several factors, including the applicant's age, health, marital status, and, primarily, benefits applied for, as well as available discounts. Premium comparisons will be graphically charted to demonstrate how, by altering the factors from one situation to the next, each company illustrated in the policy comparison can claim to offer the least expensive policy.

Several of the insurance companies who have built their book of business through the sale of life and disability income insurance are now seeking ways to protect their customary lines of business by combining them with elements of long-term care insurance. Hal Stone and Gregory Hill describe a few of the schemes created to maintain the sales momentum of a company's traditional product line in conjunction with long-term care insurance.

## Why People *REALLY* Buy
## Long-Term Care Insurance
## by Everett Thorne

When I started selling long-term care insurance ten years ago, I soon found that the easy part was talking about policy benefits and provisions. I could wax eloquent about the wonderful benefits my lucky prospects would enjoy if they just gave me a little information about themselves and wrote out a check. When product information alone didn't motivate purchasers, I discovered more success by adding statistics and sad testimonials. But my approach still lacked something.

Then one day I discovered the missing ingredient — a good reason to buy. My enlightenment began when a rather blunt prospect disregarded emotional appeals and exclaimed, "Everett, if I must, I'm prepared to spend it all and then go on Medicaid; so tell me why I should spend good money for your insurance." "To save your assets, of course," I answered. "What for?" he asked. "For your children," I retorted. "I'm only concerned about my wife and myself. The kids can fend for themselves." I was stunned. It hadn't occurred to me that not passing on assets to young people might be a reason not to buy long-term care insurance. I have since found that many prospects feel the same way. For some, giving more money to the kids may be a reason against paying additional premiums for many years. I had to seek other reasons.

The solution came in bits and pieces. I learned firsthand that confidence levels tend to drop with the onset of old age. People become less assured about climbing ladders, going down stairs, driving cars, and trusting their memory. However, I am convinced that they fear the loss of their independence more than they seek support. Let me give you an example.

I remember trying to take the arm of my aging father to help him out of the car. He vigorously shook his elbow from my grasp and gave me a glare, as if to say "I'll do it myself, thank you." My father was very proud of his ability to manage his affairs at the age of 85. He had been an athlete in his youth, and he was particularly proud of winning a gold medal in the state senior track and field championships for the age 80 and over group. He was unwilling to admit that he was now becoming frail, and unsteady on his feet. He wanted to remain in command.

A streak of independence runs deep in Americans, perhaps second only to a desire for freedom. It is no accident that you will frequently find those two words in the founding documents of this nation. These attitudes constantly face you across a kitchen table strewn with brochures. Those who have acquired enough assets to capture attention as prospects are used to calling the shots. They are accustomed to being the boss. Their greatest unspoken fear is the loss of control.

It is enough to suffer the indignity of losing control of bodily functions, and to be dependent on others, but to lose control of finances is the final disgrace. The question is not about having sufficient assets to weather a long-term care stay; the real question is having sufficient liquidity. Liquidating assets, any financier will tell you, is a matter of timing. Buy low and sell high, right? But what if the nursing home wants their money now? You have no choice but to sell now to get the dollars they want. It makes no difference to them if there are early withdrawal penalties, if the stock market is down, or if real estate is depressed. You take your losses when you need the money — now. Having money, insurance money, activated at the time of need solves this problem and keeps finances under your control.

I have a saying, "Plan for what you want, or else settle for what you get." Medicaid is settling for what you get. In a majority of states, you get crowded conditions, discounted care, and the humiliation of demonstrating need. Don't get me wrong — Medicaid recipients should be appreciative of the services they receive, but Medicaid is intended to provide a floor of protection for those who have no other resources. People of means rarely got that way without planning and some sacrifice. The premium for long-term care insurance is a small sacrifice indeed to get you what you want — your own private room where you choose, and appointed with furnishings of your choosing, rather than being stuck four to a room in a nursing home you couldn't select, where you have no privacy, no dignity, no visitors, and no control.

I found that while most people fiercely resist becoming a burden to others, they also fear the possibility of becoming powerless and abandoned. Putting a long-term care insurance policy in force while one is as young and healthy as possible represents the most affordable and complete solution to these concerns. Would you wait until the house is on fire before you make your plan of escape? Then why wait until the family is thumbing through the yellow pages to find the cheapest care available? Why wait until your kids are fighting over what asset to sell next? Instead, formalize a plan now and remain in control, now and later.

### Forecasting Long-Term Care Protection

Forecasting long-term care insurance benefits can be a challenge. Such objectives as how much, how long, how soon, how broad, and how current policy benefits should be, must be decided twenty, thirty, or even forty years before the fact. Mistakes can be costly.

How much, or the daily benefit allowance, is the heart of every policy. How long is established by determining whether an unlimited benefit length or some lesser amount is acceptable. How soon depends upon the length of the elimination period before benefits begin. How broad depends upon what benefits and options are included in the nursing facility and/or home health care policy, and how current would depend upon what kind of inflation protection is selected.

A careful look at personal resources should help define how much insurance is needed. A good rule of thumb is this: the more income you have, the lower the daily benefit allowance (DBA) you need. The more assets you have, the shorter the benefit length required. The greater the short-term savings, the longer the elimination period you can get by with. The interrelationship between resources and insurance begins with a close look at income, both current and anticipated.

### Three Types of Daily Benefits: Reimbursement, Indemnity, and Per Diem

Most LTCI policies are reimbursement-type contracts where benefits are paid for billed professional care services up to a target benefit, not to exceed the actual charge. Indemnity contracts pay the target benefit or scheduled daily benefit allowance as long as some charge (generally at least an hour through a home health care agency) is incurred. The per diem or disability approach pays the scheduled amount whether charges are incurred or not. Some agents are concerned that the indemnity and per diem contracts present a high potential for future premium increases. Claimant thrift is not rewarded, since cash is received up front.

If per diem benefit payments are not dependent on proof that care has been provided, the insurance carrier has little way of determining if actual care was rendered. This lack of ability to be proactive in the management of the policyholder's care is equivalent to issuing a blank check and encouraging what could end up into an abusive situation.

Take as an example: a per diem policyholder with a $6,000 per month nursing facility benefit and a $3,000 per month home care benefit. Dad needs care and son agrees to become dad's caregiver and have dad move in with him. Six months later, dad needs more care than son is capable or willing to provide. Dad is malnourished, he is not bathed daily, and his diapers are not changed as often as they need to be. Maybe a professional caregiver needs to be brought in or, more likely, the best care for dad is in a nursing facility. However, as soon as the son makes the decision to place dad in a nursing facility, the $3,000 a month check stops coming to the son's mailbox — not much incentive for the son to do the right thing.

The attraction of having family members eligible to be paid a flat amount under a per diem policy sounds warmly appealing at time of issue. It is easy to promise one's parent, "Sure, I'll be happy to care for you." This commitment is made when mom or dad is healthy, active, gardening, doing their own shopping, etc. But wait until circumstances change — when they are confused, cantankerous, and need help bathing, toileting, and other activities of daily living. There is no room for a casual commitment here. It is time for a trained, dedicated caregiver.

What quality of care can be demanded from family caregivers when the disincentive not to give up the per diem payment is greater than doing what is best for the parent? Mom or dad can get exploited. (See material in Chapter 9 on Elder Abuse.)

Some insureds favor the per diem contract because extra money beyond care may be used for other essential items to make the insured comfortable. Studies show, however, that the per diem and indemnity contracts promote greater utilization, which is not surprising, and rate increases soon follow. The per diem approach can ultimately be very expensive for the nominal advantage of getting money above and beyond costs.

Reimbursement-type policies will typically leave unused daily benefits in the pool of money, which could extend benefits beyond the initial number of benefit days stated in the contract. The reimbursement approach has better cost containment advantages for policyholders as a whole, because unclaimed benefit reserves act as a hedge against future rate increases.

## How Much? Setting the Daily Benefit Allowance

### Calculating Daily Benefits for a Single Person

Begin by pricing desirable local long-term care facilities, and compare this with how much personal income would be available to cover these costs. The difference should be insured. Assume the daily cost of a private nursing home room in your area is $140 (see box about the importance of a private room) and your net retirement income is $1,825 per month ($60 per day.) On the surface, it may seem logical to select a DBA of $80 ($140-60=$80 DBA.) In a static world, this combination of income and insurance should cover the daily cost of private care. However, as years go by and inflation takes its toll, this plan may become less sufficient. As an example, if you are 62 years of age when you buy a policy, and age 82 before you need it, benefits may have eroded significantly over the intervening years.

To calculate how five percent inflation would affect the cost of care at the end of twenty years, consult the "Compound Interest/Inflation Table"(see Appendix A later in this chapter), which reveals that a five percent annual inflation increase would expand the base amount by a factor of 2.65. This means that the daily cost of a private room at the end of twenty years would be $371 ($140 x 2.65). If a five percent compound inflation rider were added to the $80 DBA at the end of twenty years, benefits would be $212 ($80 x 2.65). The $60 difference when the policy was first taken out has now increased to $159

($371-$212). Where will the extra money come from? Unless the current $1,825 monthly income expands to $4,770 ($159 x 30) over this time period, assets may have to be accessed — assets that insurance was purchased to protect.

Personal income must expand significantly over time to keep up with the growing gap between costs and policy benefits. How predictable are such increases in income? It is a stark reality that Social Security increases are rarely more than two percent per year, and pensions, installment sale contracts, and other income sources rarely have inflation increases built in. This leaves investment income to take up the slack. Income from conservative investments might be more secure, but it may not be aggressive enough to keep up with inflation. Yet more aggressive investments aren't as predictable. What to do? The answer is to rely more upon insurance than personal funds. Insurance is more predictable. Also, keep in mind it is cheaper to buy a higher DBA when one is younger and healthier than to attempt to increase benefits at an older age. Not only will subsequent policy increases require new underwriting to qualify, but new policy premiums will be increased to reflect the attained age rather than original age.

### Best Time to Purchase LTCI

Some people considering the purchase of long-term care insurance have a tendency to procrastinate. Since most long-term care occurs late in life, the assumption is that the longer you can push off the decision to buy, the more premiums can be saved. So why not wait and buy this coverage as late as possible? One fallacy in this thinking is that the cost of care does not remain static — it continues to go up with inflation. Another fallacy is that the cost of insurance increases about 7% over the previous year as the potential applicant ages. Even worse, while uninsured, health can decline and eliminate insurance as an option altogether.

The following table shows how a $120 per day long-term care insurance plan escalates in price from age 50 to age 75. Even using conservative mortality tables, it becomes obvious that due to the increasing costs of insurance, particularly with a five percent annual inflation assumption, premiums may be paid for a shorter period of time, but the cumulative cost is higher.

There appears to be no rational basis for delaying the purchase of a LTCI policy.

## Cost of Delay

| DBA | Age | Years Life Expectancy | Annual Cost | Accumulative Cost |
|---|---|---|---|---|
| $120 | 50 | 25.5 | $1,260 | $32,130 |
| $153 | 55 | 22.3 | $1,695 | $37,798 |
| $195 | 60 | 18.2 | $2,527 | $45,991 |
| $250 | 65 | 15.0 | $4,625 | $69,375 |
| $318 | 70 | 12.1 | $8,681 | $105,045 |
| $406 | 75 | 9.6 | $17,620 | $169,152 |

$120 Daily NF Benefit/5-yr. Benefit Period/100% Home Health Care Option/30-Day Elimination Period/5% Compound Inflation Benefit/ Preferred Health Risk

### Calculating Daily Benefits for Couples

Couples have an added problem when factoring the daily benefit allowance. They must decide how much income will be available to pay long-term care costs for each spouse. If income is split equally between husband and wife, this presumes that while one spouse is away in a nursing home, the other can survive on half the customary household income. If this were true, on a combined income of $1,800 per month each spouse would have $30 per day accessible for care costs ($1,800 divided by two = $900, divided by thirty days). The problem with this assumption is that maintaining a house and standard of living for one spouse on $900 may not be possible.

Household expenses don't necessarily drop when one spouse is away in a nursing facility. The utilities, property taxes, home maintenance and food costs probably won't be any less. Eating out more, and the healthy spouse's travel to and from the nursing home will actually expand domestic expenses. In addition, previously shared household chores must now be done by one person or hired out. With one mate ailing, prescription drugs and other nonreimbursed medical expenses are also likely to grow. Don't count on a budget surplus to contribute to the cost of care when one spouse is still living at home. The reverse is more likely to be true.

Since husbands are typically older than their wives, and women live longer, one possible solution is to purchase a full daily benefit allowance for him. He will likely need care expenses before his wife dies, and she will have to maintain the household on the income that is left. In our example, he should consider taking a full DBA of $140 to eliminate the possibility of depleting her income during his nursing home stay. In this way, she will be left with sufficient income to live on without liquidating assets.

In summary, the daily benefit allowance must be determined based on realistic income projections. To hedge against a shortfall in income, buying a bigger daily benefit is advised.

## The Importance of a Private Room

The place you call home gives definition to your privacy. Each room has a function and a level of formality or informality that you assign to it. You are master of your domain.

First, no one gets into your home legitimately unless you give him or her the privilege. When the doorbell rings you are careful whom you let in. You ask yourself: is it a friend or is it a stranger? Do they look harmless or menacing? Is this a convenient time or am I too busy? You control the entry into your private world.

If this is someone you want to impress, you invite them into the living room. Generally, this is not only the neatest place in the house, it also probably has the finest furnishings. Your taste in décor is represented, the style you feel comfortable with is apparent, and something of your interests and personality is conveyed. This is the room where you put your best foot forward.

The dining room has a similar air of formality. Here the finest china is used, the choice silverware is resurrected from its velvet hiding place, and you bring out your best tablecloth and centerpiece. The formal you is now on display as you direct a culinary experience, have an unhurried cup of coffee in a porcelain cup, or snack on designer cookies with a friend.

The kitchen is more informal. You may have a breakfast nook here where you use the stainless steel flatware and eat out of everyday dishes. Milk and ketchup are served out of the containers they come in, and you may serve your friends a brew straight from the bottle. During parties, this is the space your guests gravitate toward. The mood is more casual and furnishing more serviceable.

Your bedroom is a personal and private space, but even more private is the bathroom. All rooms in your house are not created to be equal. You designate the formality, informality, or intimacy of the occasion by directing your guests to the appropriate room. Whether you live in an apartment or a mansion, you expect this kind of control over your dwelling space.

But when you are in a nursing home, nearly everything occurs in one room. You entertain visitors there. You are fed there. This is done in the presence of roommates and the door is generally wide open. You are deprived of privacy and dignity. You are powerless in this setting. Depression and physical decline are accelerated. The culture shock is overwhelming. The loss of control is demoralizing.

This need not be so. A private room, where the door can be kept closed to keep strangers from wandering in, is a start in the right direction. Aesthetic improvements such as drapes, plants, wallpaper, and paint brighten the ambiance. Pictures and familiar furnishings from home link you to your past. Your privacy and dignity can be maintained. Visitors return. You are less likely to be abandoned and alone. Great improvements can occur with the choice of a private room.

## How Long? Establishing the Benefit Length

If we consider the length of benefit needed for a long-term care policy to be reduced by assets available, we must also look at the composition of these assets. Some, like checking or savings accounts, are totally liquid, yet others, such as an office building, may take years to sell. Some assets appreciate, like a residence in a desirable neighborhood. Others, like a motor home, constantly depreciate. Considering the overall mix of holdings, the growth of an estate may be slow or fast, predictable or unpredictable. The real issue is which assets will be expendable for long-term care costs.

Converting a fixed asset into cash can be both costly and time consuming. Finding the right buyer for a piece of property, art, fine antique, or Winnebego can be a laborious process. Waiting to sell stocks or bonds when the market is most favorable requires careful timing. Even withdrawing certificates of deposit prematurely can invoke penalties. Patience and skill are essential to get the best price for an asset. Added to this, taxes are a further expense that must be assessed on most gains.

For peace of mind, this issue comes down to how much can be placed in assets, as opposed to insurance. Rather than endure uncertainties of the future and the probable shrinkage that could result from a quick sale of an asset, it is better to have long-term care insurance that activates at the time of need. Even if assets are sufficient to cover the entire cost of care, it makes sense to have at least a two- or three-year benefit. This provides time to optimize liquidation of fixed assets. Even people who have a net worth over $5 million will be well advised to purchase long-term care insurance, not necessarily to shift the risk, but to reduce shrinkage of an estate for which more profitable uses could be made.

Predicting the length of time a person may need long-term care suggests a look at national trends. The most commonly quoted study identifying the frequency and length of care comes from a 1991 article in the *New England Journal of Medicine*. In that study, it was revealed that forty-three percent of those reaching age 65 will spend some of their remaining life in a nursing home. Half of the elderly in nursing homes will stay six months or less, but the other half will average two and one-half years (912.5 days) of nursing home confinement. A later study increased that figure to three years (1,095 days.) At $140 per day, a two and a half year stay would cost $127,750 (912.5 x $140) and a three year stay would cost $153,300 (1095 x $140.) An even more alarming possibility would be a stay as a result of Alzheimer's disease, which average eight years (2,920 days) for a total expense of $408,800 ($140 x 2920.)

Also revealed in this study were figures showing that men were found to stay in a nursing home more than five years only four percent of the time, while women were found to do so thirteen percent of the time. This gender difference suggests that a man could have a five-year plan with a ninety-six percent assurance that these benefits would not be exceeded. A woman has only about an eighty-seven percent assurance that the same plan would be sufficient.

With stays for Alzheimer's about eight years, and with women at significantly higher risk for this condition, an unlimited plan holds greater promise for a female. A man can more realistically get by with a five-year plan. Ideally, if the premium can be budgeted, both husband and wife should have unlimited plans. One of the first ways of cutting costs, however, could be to reduce the man's plan to five years, while keeping the woman on an unlimited benefit. New shared benefit products should also be considered. One method of calculating a shared benefit is to create an eight-year plan for two, rather than four-year plan for each. Unfortunately, with this approach, one person could use most of the benefits and leave little or nothing for the survivor. A better option is the shared benefit approach that gives the couple exclusive rights to their own four-year individual benefit but an additional four years to be shared between them. Either spouse can withdraw from this pool of funds.

Originally, policies had a time value approach. For instance, a four-year plan simply meant that once eligible care started, benefits would continue until four years had elapsed, regardless of whether days, weeks, or months had been skipped in the process. The pooled money approach converts the benefit length from a time period to a formula that is a multiple of the daily benefit. In this way, there is a total benefit dollar amount to be drawn upon, like a bank account.

An example of this would be conversion of a five-year benefit into 1,825 days (5 x 365), then multiplying this by the DBA to arrive at an aggregate figure. If the DBA were $120, the total pool would be $209,000 (120 x 1,825.) If $100 per day was used, benefits would last 2,090 days ($209,000 divided by $100), thus extending the benefit period by almost a year. The result of a large DBA is to allow the benefit length to be extended. This flexibility makes the pool of money approach the preferred method of calculating benefit length.

In summary, the greater the assets, the shorter the benefit length needed, but for convenience even those with high asset levels will find at least some long-term care insurance a valuable benefit. A shared benefit and pooled money approach adds important flexibility at a time of claim.

### How Soon? Selecting an Elimination Period

It is common practice to carry elimination periods or deductibles on most forms of insurance. In this way, the policyholder agrees to pay a defined affordable amount on the front end of a claim in exchange for a reduced premium.

The cost saving technique may not work with long-term care insurance, because the elimination period is set in days, not dollars. If the deductible were a flat amount, say $1,000, it would be a simple matter to keep that amount of money continually on hand to cover initial expenses. However, long-term care insurance has an elimination period defined in days such as zero, twenty, thirty, sixty, ninety, one hundred, one hundred eighty, three hundred sixty-five and so one. Shorter elimination periods increase the premium rate. For example, a thirty-day elimination period would cost roughly twelve percent more than a ninety-day elimination period. An elimination period of zero days would increase premium rates at least twenty-five percent. With each passing year, the deductible gets bigger as prices grow higher. Stated in dollars, a ninety-day elimination period, when daily costs are $120, would be $10,800. Assuming five percent annual inflation, twenty years later the same daily care costs would inflate to $320 ($120 x 2.65), for a ninety-day deductible of $28,800. If the policyholder saved only $5,000 in reduced premium over a zero elimination period, the savings do not appear to justify the risk. It is rare that a carrier's coverage adequately compensates for a high deductible. Be sure to calculate the premium savings over time, before being too eager to go for the long elimination period. Usually, a twenty- to thirty-day elimination period provides a sufficient premium saving to substantiate the additional risk assumed.

Another reason a shorter elimination period may be desirable is that insurance companies require out-of-pocket expenses to be documented. One must establish not only that the necessary level of impairment existed, but also receipts and care charts must be retained for each day, to satisfy the elimination period. A shorter elimination period requires less record keeping. Daily nursing home confinement over a sustained period is easy to document, but home health care is often irregular and intermittent. Tracking these expenditures can be an ordeal. One helpful benefit design may be to have a waived or shorter elimination period for home health care. This reduces the need to track a long elimination period when care is less predictable, and to provide some premium relief in the process.

In short, be sure policyholders realize that sufficient short-term savings must be available to cover the initial stages of a claim, and this amount must grow as costs increase. Second, be careful that the premium saving justifies the out-of-pocket risk taken. Third, alert claimants that they must keep records to substantiate each day of an elimination period. In case of intermittent home care, this can be a challenging process. In general, shorter elimination periods are best.

## How Broad? Including Home Health Care and Other Options

Comparing a comprehensive long-term care policy to a nursing home only policy, the nursing home only policy will be less expensive — approximately seventy percent the cost of the comprehensive long-term care policy. It is equally true that a comprehensive long-term care policy will be more expensive than a home care only policy. However, a comprehensive long-term care policy will be less expensive than a nursing home policy with optional home care rider, or a home care policy with optional facility rider.

A nursing home policy without home care coverage (or vice versa) would leave out needed protection. It is impossible to know in advance what configuration of benefits will be needed. Guess right and all is well; guess wrong and regrets abound. Only in retrospect can a limited benefit plan such as a nursing home only or home care only plan be defended. After the fact, it is easy to say that certain benefits were a waste of money, but when the future is uncertain, all bases need to be covered for peace of mind to exist.

Here's a pointed example: If there are motivated and capable children who live locally and are available to care for an invalid parent, perhaps the home health care portion of the contract can be omitted. The policy then would be utilized only where confinement is needed. However, a key inducement to buy a long-term care insurance policy in the first place is to keep from being a burden to one's family. Why obligate them to be part of the solution? A stand-alone home health care only policy makes even less sense. The objective of a long-term care insurance policy is to provide funds for protracted debilitating conditions. Though convenient and cozy, a home eventually ceases to be an appropriate site for such care — often sooner rather than later. To have continued peace of mind, a full continuum of benefits is required. Anything less can spur nagging doubts about the future. Insurance is supposed to give you the assurance of security. It's hard to feel warm and secure when there are holes in the blanket. People who do purchase a nursing facility only policy or a home care only policy should expect the representative who sold them their limited benefit policy, to ask the policyholder to sign a disclaimer letter (sample provided in Chapter 3). This disclaimer letter is for the agent's (or financial advisor's) protection from future questions either from the policyholder or from family members when they have doubts about the original benefits selected. The disclaimer should state that the policyholder was advised to purchase a comprehensive policy, the reasons why, and that the policyholder elected to do otherwise.

Even if a comprehensive plan is decided upon, it still must be determined whether home health care is to be paid at the same level as nursing home confinement. Most companies allow a choice of home health care benefits to be paid at fifty percent, seventy-five percent, or 100 percent of the daily benefit allowance. On average, a seventy-five percent home care benefit results in a ten to twelve percent increase in premium rates. The 100 percent home care benefit increases premium rates twenty to twenty-five percent over the fifty percent home care benefit premium rates.

If a fifty percent home health care benefit is chosen, this doesn't mean that care costs are paid at a coinsurance level of fifty percent. Home care benefits may be paid at eighty percent or 100 percent, but only up to fifty percent of the DBA. Continuing our example of a $140 DBA, a fifty percent home health care benefit would be $70. This would be very close to covering three hours of care.

When a person needs more than three hours of care at home, one might wonder whether they are beginning to lose their ability to live alone. At that point, they may be better off moving into an assisted living facility or congregate care setting, rather than increasing the hours of a home health care nurse. Be sure to investigate the hourly home care rates in your area. For instance, if charges are $25 per hour, with a three-hour minimum house call, this means $75 would be the basic daily charge for an RN, LPN, or CNA to come bathe, count out medications, run the vacuum cleaner, put the soup on, and leave. If claimants can turn the stove off, answer the phone, and put themselves to bed, chances are that they can remain at home unmonitored for the rest of the day. However, as their conditions fail, it's questionable whether they should continue to stay home alone. When the patient needs more than three hours of care, will four hours be enough? Why not five, six, or seven hours? There comes a point when even a 100 percent home health option is insufficient. At $25 per hour, having a trained licensed caregiver around the clock could cost $600 per day ($25 x 24). Where does one-on-one home care cease to be economically feasible to insure? Let the client decide. Often, when confronted with the financial realities of what it takes to stay home at a severely impaired level, an assisted living facility looks like an attractive option. Although 100 percent home health care benefit is probably the best choice for strong benefit design, to economize on a premium, reducing this benefit 50 percent is probably the first step to take. However, this should be done only with the understanding that an assisted living facility or congregate care facility will be an acceptable option, when care beyond the minimum three-hour basic level is needed.

The critical question arises: Does limiting the home health care to fifty percent of the DBA also limit such options as assisted living, adult foster care, and alternate care? If so, this reduction in benefits may be too great a price to pay for the modest premium savings that result from accepting a fifty percent rather than fifty percent home-health care reimbursement.

Other options which can broaden the benefits of a policy include a survivorship benefit, restoration clause, dual waiver of premium, shared benefits, and a nonforfeiture provision. Since these enhancements can increase the cost of coverage, the clients must decide whether to increase the core benefits or add ancillary benefits. The decision to add these provisions may be at the expense of strengthening policy characteristics, increasing daily benefit limits, or increasing the benefit length. This should be done with caution.

**Survivorship benefit** provides a paid-up policy for the survivor of a couple after the policy has been in force for a certain period of time. This length of time can be as short as four years or as long as ten years. In some cases, this benefit will be paid only if there have been no claims by either party prior to a death. Survivorship benefit options usually require both individuals to purchase identical coverage.

The survivorship option is appealing because when the first spouse dies, if it's a husband, he will often leave his wife with less to live on. The cessation of a long-term care insurance premium surely would be a welcome relief from the widow's diminished income. The problem is whether the insurance company has charged enough for this provision. The premium calculation depends on the age of the older spouse and can increase pricing to ten percent. Since wives typically outlive their husbands and present greater risk for a long-term care stay, the great risk survives. Because the insurance company no longer gets a premium to cover this risk, the company must look to active insureds for rate increases. If rate increases become severe, this could drive healthy risks back into the market, as they drop their now expensive policies and shop for new coverage. The survivorship benefit could be a time bomb. Properly rated, it can be a great idea for the first people who take advantage of it, but costly for policyholders who remain.

**Benefit restoration** may come with a policy automatically. Depending on the overall plan design, an appropriately priced restoration feature could add anywhere from two to twelve percent to the overall premium rates. Very rarely will an individual be able to use this benefit to restore the overall maximum benefit, which requires at least 180 treatment-free days following a period of care. This benefit may be more smoke than fire.

The **dual waiver of premium** eliminates the premium on the healthy spouse when the other spouse is on claim. Again, this can be a gender issue. Since men are generally older than their wives and spend less time on claim, it is typically the wife who stands to benefit by this waiver, and then only while the husband is on claim. The charge for this benefit should be nominal, because he is less likely to go on claim, and then for shorter times than she. After his death, her premiums would resume. In short, it is difficult to imagine when this benefit would provide a predictable return of any substance.

It has always been risky to buy short benefits to save premiums, but with the advent of the **shared benefit** concept, added flexibility has been introduced. A shared benefit allows husband and wife to combine, say, two three-year plans into a six-year plan to be used by either or both spouses. The problem here is the first person to use the benefits could use up all the benefits. Another drawback could be in getting stuck with a partial benefit and paying for a full one. Assume that the husband uses four years of a six-year benefit during his lifetime. After his death, his wife has only a two-year benefit, but must continue the original premium as though the full three-year benefit were in force. It is better to purchase a benefit that adds to the length of the original individual benefit.

An example of this would be if the husband has a three-year plan, the wife has a three-year plan, and there is an additional three-year plan that can be shared between them. Each person will always have the original three years of benefits, which cannot be reduced with a claim by the other spouse. In this case a total of nine years of benefits would be available. Assuming a reasonable premium is charged, a shared benefit approach (in which there is a third pool of money equal to the other two) is superior to a combined pool from which benefits are shared.

Under tax qualified guidelines, a **nonforfeiture provision** must be offered and officially rejected or accepted by a long-term care insurance applicant. Should the policy be cancelled, this provision allows for the receipt of benefits equal to the greater of all premiums paid or thirty days during the lifetime of the policyholder. Cash will not be refunded to the policyholder at termination, nor will the unused premiums be paid to heirs at death. Depending on the definition of the nonforfeiture lapse benefit and the issue age of the insured, this benefit option costs an additional twenty to fifty percent of the basic annual premium rate.

This provision is seldom selected, because at the time a policy is being purchased, there is no intent to cancel it. The substantial additional premium that nonforfeiture adds could be applied to strengthening the benefits to protect assets, a plan more in keeping with the central objective for purchasing this insurance in the first place.

As an example, if the annual premium for a policy is $2,000 and was paid for ten years and then cancelled, the policy benefits would be frozen at that level to be paid up to a maximum of $20,000 ($2,000 x ten years) during the remaining life of the policyholder. If the DBA had grown to $200, this means that there would be a total of 100 days ($20,000 divided by $200) of benefits payable under the guidelines of the policy. Considering that this amount is not likely to preserve an estate from being devastated by long-term care costs, its value as insurance is limited. The question is whether this rarely purchased benefit is worth the expense, and apparently few people think so.

## How Current? The Role of Inflation Protection

The prime focus of plan design is to posture a solution that will stand the test of time. Over time, the cost of care can inflate to double or triple what might be needed today. There are essentially three options for increasing benefits that can be employed to keep the daily benefit allowance current: simple automatic, compound automatic, and periodic adjusted. Each has distinct advantages and disadvantages.

**Simple automatic** inflation protection was the earliest attempt to deal with this problem and is still incorporated in some plans being written today. This method adds a percentage, usually 5 percent of the daily benefit allowance, to the DBA each year. A $140 per day plan would add $7 ($140 x 5 percent) each year. By the end of twenty years, the DBA would have doubled to $280. If actual inflation were to continue at five percent for the life of the plan, the $140 cost today would be $371 ($140 x 2.65) at the end of twenty years. Obviously, our simple inflation plan would not keep up. The problem with this method of augmenting benefits is that the increase is a static amount that actual inflation compounds upon itself. Budget limitations often prompt a choice for a simple inflation rider, but chances are it will be insufficient. This choice is more tenable for those of an older age, because life expectancy is less and there is less time to lag drastically behind the inflation curve.

**Compound automatic inflation** protection is often resisted because of the higher cost. The cost of a five percent inflation protection feature could be as high as sixty-five percent of the annual premium for an insured person who is 45 years of age, and fifty percent of the annual premium for an insured person who is 65 years of age. An elemental payback test will demonstrate the value of adding the compound inflation benefit. If the premium for identical long-term care insurance plans is $2,700 with compound inflation protection, and $2,250 with simple inflation protection, opting for the latter would result in annual savings of $450. At the end of twenty years, the compound method would have a $350 daily benefit while the simple approach would pay $280, a $70 daily advantage for compounding. The total premium paid for those twenty years would be $54,000 ($2,700 x 20) and $45,000 ($2,250 x 20) respectively. Yet, should a claim occur, the total premium cost for the compound plan would be paid back in 154 days ($54,000 divided by $350) while the simple plan would take 160 days ($45,000 divided by $280.) The $9,000 ($54,000-$45,000) in savings would be used up in 120 days ($9,000 divided by $70.) Beyond that, for every month of care, the compound approach would pay $2,100 more ($70 x 30.) This advantage would grow every year. At the end of fifteen years, the advantage would be $4,000 per month.

The **periodic increase** method can take several different forms, but essentially this option allows a policyholder to add additional amounts to the daily benefit allowance at specified intervals. Typically, the method of calculating these available increments is based upon the Cost of Living (COL) Index. For instance, if a policy was purchased with a $100 DBA and had a three-year COL option, and the cost of living had increased by seventeen percent during a three-year period, a policyholder could purchase an additional $17 DBA. This would be executed without evidence of insurability, but this increment must be purchased at attained age. On the surface, the ability to buy only as needed seems like an ideal method of keeping up with inflation.

However, two major problems exist. First, the COL index is based on pricing specific commodities or products that are unrelated to the cost of long-term care. Keeping up with the "cost of living" may not be keeping up with the inflating cost of care. The process has little chance of being accurate. Second, the cost of the additional insurance grows with advancing age. A typical cost curve, which adds five percent to the daily allowance each year, would increase the premium sevenfold in twenty years. For a plan that costs $700 at age 65, the premium typically would be about $5,000 in twenty years. A comparable benefit under a compounded approach would remain at the $1,500 level.

The periodic increase method eventually becomes too expensive to justify, and should be avoided. The compound automatic inflation benefit generally is the best bet. Its higher costs will be returned in the form of higher benefits. Even at an advanced age, a time when simple automatic inflation protection is often recommended, the rates should be checked carefully. The premium for this benefit is generally discounted to reflect diminished life expectancy.

## Conclusion

In his book *Seven Habits of Highly Effective People*, Steven Covey lists one effective habit as "beginning with the end in mind." When it comes to designing a long-term care policy, this means beginning with the policy you want to end up with. Put benefits together that will grow with inflation and operate in tandem with income, assets, and short-term savings. The function of insurance is to be the predictable element in an unpredictable world. If you pick a solid company, you can rely more heavily on it than on personal resources.

At the end of twenty years, when the cost of care has inflated from $140 per day to $371 per day, a three-year nursing home stay will have increased from $153,300 to $406,245. For a married couple, these costs could double. Even if this risk could be covered by personal funds, is this the most effective use of what has taken a lifetime to accumulate? This disaster need not occur, particularly if it can be prevented by an affordable premium.

In the attempt to reduce long-term care insurance premiums, don't rely too heavily on income that may not grow with inflation, and assets that lack liquidity and may shrink when sold. The premium dollars saved now may not compensate for financial losses later.

## COMPOUND INTEREST/INFLATION TABLE

| COMPOUND INTEREST RATE TABLE AMOUNT OF ONE DOLLAR | | | | | |
|---|---|---|---|---|---|
| Year | 5 | 10 | 15 | 20 | 25 | 30 |
| 1% | 1.05100 | 1.10460 | 1.16096 | 1.23239 | 1.28243 | 1.40122 |
| 2% | 1.10408 | 1.21899 | 1.34587 | 1.48595 | 1.64061 | 1.81136 |
| 3% | 1.15927 | 1.34392 | 1.55797 | 1.80611 | 2.09318 | 2.42726 |
| 4% | 1.21665 | 1.48024 | 1.80094 | 2.19112 | 2.66584 | 3.24340 |
| 5% | 1.27628 | 1.62890 | 2.07893 | 2.65330 | 3.038636 | 4.32195 |
| 6% | 1.33283 | 1.79085 | 2.39656 | 3.20714 | 4.29188 | 5.74350 |
| 7% | 1.40255 | 1.96715 | 2.75903 | 3.86969 | 5.42744 | 7.61226 |
| 8% | 1.46933 | 2.15893 | 3.17217 | 4.66096 | 6.84848 | 10.06267 |
| 9% | 1.53862 | 2.36736 | 3.64249 | 5.60442 | 8.62309 | 13.26769 |
| 10% | 1.61051 | 2.59374 | 4.17725 | 6.72751 | 10.83471 | 17.44942 |

## Policy Comparison

The following policy comparison contains most of the categories established by StratiCision, Inc., of Needham, Massachusetts. The long-term care insurance companies, identified as Companies A, B, and C, were selected by the author on the basis of having a Best's Rating of A+ and a Standard and Poor's rating of at least AA.

Best's Rating definitions reflect the ability of a life and health insurance company to meet policyholder and other contractual obligations, as well as the company's overall performance. The ratings range from A+++ to F. Standard and Poor's rates insurers' claims paying ability. Duff & Phelps Credit Rating Company also rates insurance companies on claims paying ability. Moody's Investors Service offers financial strength ratings of life insurance companies. All ratings are independent opinions and not warranties.

A word of caution to agents and consumers before embarking on a comparison of policies: paralysis by analysis can be critically debilitating and never serves a client's best interest!

## Policy Comparison

| COMPANY | A | B | C |
|---|---|---|---|
| Tax Qualified | Yes | Yes | Yes |
| Issue ages | 40-84 | 18-90 | 40-79 |
| Premium Classes Standard | Preferred, Standard Class 1, 2 | Preferred, Standard, Substandard | |
| Spousal discount | 20% | 10% | 20% |
| Disc. for unmarried live together | No | See Comments | No |
| Upgrade to newer policy | Yes | No | No |
| Nursing home daily benefit range | $30-$250 | $50-$300 | $50-$300 |

| Benefit period (years) | 2, 3, 4, 6, L | 1, 2, 3, 4, 5, L | 2, 3,5, L |
|---|---|---|---|
| Benefits for Age 80+ | Benefit period 2, 3, 4, 6 | All options available Only 2 year benefit period; 60 or 100 day elim. period | Will insure when spouse 79 or younger |
| Elimination periods, NH | 50, 100 days | 0, 30, 60, 90 | 20, 60, 100 days |
| Accumulation period | 2 years | 4 x elim. period | Lifetime |
| Elimination one-time | Yes | Yes | Yes |
| NH Premium waiver wait, days | 0 | See Comments | 0 |
| Waiver wait begins with | Benefits | Benefits | Benefits |
| Bed reservation | 21 days | 21 days | 20 days |
| Surviving spouse paid up | Yes | Rider | No |
| Years held up for paid up | 10 | 10 | N/A |
| Benefit transfer option | No | No | No |
| Alternate Plan of Care | Yes | Yes | Yes |
| Must be on claim for APC | No | No | No |
| % for Assisted Living Facility | 100% | 100% | 100% |
| ALF Elimination Period | Same as Nursing Home | Same as Nursing Home | Same as Nursing Home |
| ALF Waiver Wait Time | 0 | See Comments | 0 |
| ALF Waiver Wait Begins | Benefits | Benefits | Benefits |

| Home Health Care Covered | Policy | Policy | Policy |
|---|---|---|---|
| Homemaker covered | Yes | Yes | Yes |
| Adult day care % | 100% | 100% | 100% |
| Respite care days per year | 21 @ 100% | 21 @ 100% | 20 @ 100% |
| Hospice Care % | 100% | 100% | 100% NHDB |
| Equipment Amount | 50 x DB | 50 x MDB under AH Plan of Care | May be covered |
| Caregiver training lifetime max | 5 x DB annually | 2 x DB lifetime max | 5 x NHDB lifetime max |
| Paid from care benefit pool | Yes | Yes | Yes |
| Other home care benefits | In-home safety devices; home delivered meals | Medical Alert system up to policy limit of 50 x MDB @ $50/month | Emergency medical response system. Home modification for wheelchair access |
| HHC daily benefit % of NH | 100% | 50, 100% | 50, 75, 100% |
| Copayment Provision | 20% some HHC w/o Care Co. | None | None |
| HHC daily benefit $ range | % of NH | % of NH | % of NH |
| HHC Daily, Weekly, Monthly | Wkly if Care Coord. | Monthly | No info from Insurer |
| Combined ben. for HHC + NH | Yes | Yes | Yes |
| HHC benefit period, years | Same as NH | Same as NH | Same as NH |
| HHC elimination periods | Same as NH* days | Same as NH days | Same as NH days |
| HHC days/wk for elim. | 7 | 7 | 1 |

| | | | |
|---|---|---|---|
| HHC Premium waiver wait, days | No Waiver | See Comments | 0 |
| HHC Waiver wait begins with | No Waiver | Benefits | Benefits |
| ADL's needed for NH benefits | 2/6 | 2/6 | 2/6 |
| ADL's needed for HC Benefits | 2/6 | 2/6 | 2/6 |
| Is bathing an ADL? | Yes | Yes | Yes |
| ADL includes supervision | Yes | See Comments | Yes |
| Mental illness covered | Not excluded | Not excluded | Not excluded |
| Wait for exist. condition (mos) | 0 | 0 | 0 |
| Look-back exist. condition (mos) | 0 | 0 | 0 |
| Simple inflation % per year | 5% | 5% | 5% |
| Compound inflation % per year | 5% | 5% | 5% |
| Inflate original or remaining | Original | Original | Remaining |
| Increase coverage later | No | No | Annual increases to DB based on increase in CPI. Option not available after 4 refusals or claim payout. |

| CareManagement | Optional. Privileged Care Coordinator assesses need, develops plan of care, helps choose and monitor care. Benefits Enhanced if Priveledged Care Coordinator used: no copayment for homemaker or home health aide, elim. period waived for HHC, elim. period for NH or ALF stay reduced by # of days HHC received, HHC weekly max at 7 x HHC DB — No daily max., Premiums waived while receiving HHC. Reduce max. benefits. | Required. Care Coordinator chosen by Company, does initial assessment, develops Service Plan, may refer to providers, and reassess at least every 6 months. All benefits must be in Service Plan to be paid except confinement in a NH, for which you may be certified as chronically ill by a physician. Does not reduce max. benefits. | Optional. Independent Care Coordinator assesses need, writes and implements Plan of Care, reviews periodically. Annual max benefit is 20X NHDB. Reduces max. benefit. |
|---|---|---|---|
| Restoration of benefits | Rider | No | No |
| Return of premium | No | Option | No |
| Return prem. at death | N/A | Yes | N/A |
| Return prem. at cancel | N/A | No | N/A |
| Percent of prem. returned | N/A | 100 | N/A |
| Other nonforfeiture | Shortened benefit period | Shortened benefit period | Shortened benefit period |
| Care outside U.S. covered | Territory/ possession | Canada, territories | Territories |
| Paid-up options | None | Single payment | None |
| Standard and Poor's Rating | AA | AAA | AA |
| Moody's Rating | Aa2 | Aa3 | Aa3 |
| A.M. Best's Rating | A+ | A+ | A+ |
| Duff & Phelps Rating | AA | AA+ | AA |

| State differences | Simple inflation protection N/A IN, DE, IA, ID, OH,WI. 2-yr. plan N/A in AZ, FL, WI. No Survivorship Benefit in FL, MD, SC. Rates N/A in IN, KS, NM, ND, OR. 3 ADL trigger in CA. Elim. period is 30, 90 days in CA. Elim. period waived for HHC in CT. No caregiver training benefit in WI. Max. DB $350 in certain NY counties. | Not available in NJ, NY. No 1-yr. benefit period in AZ, FL, GA, SD. No 2-yr. benefit simple infl. protection N/A in AZ, IA, ID, IN, OH, WI. Return of premium N/A in AR, SC, NH. No 365 day elim. period in FL, GA, KS, MA, SD, VT. No 365 day elim. period FL, GA, KS, MA, SD, VT. No 180 day elim. period in GA, KS, MA, SD,VT. Single premium pay option N/A in FL, IN, MD, PA. In MA, accum. DB is 365 days. No Survivorship rider in MD, SC. No Contingent Insured rider in MD, TX, WI. In CT, GA, waiver of premium included. Standby assistance included in GA, MD, PA, WI. In WI, home modification is 200 x MDB. Non-forfeiture required in NM. Rates N/A in CT, GA, PA, TX, WI. | $100 in metro NY. Not available as of 1/1/99 in WA. Not sold in WI. In MN, bed reservation is 30 days. 2-yr. benefit period N/A in AZ, FL. CPI annual increase offered must be at least 5%. Simple inflation N/A in DE, IA, ID, IN, OH. Min. eligible age is 18 in PA. Non NM reduced and standard HHC option N/A in RI. |
|---|---|---|---|

| Comments | Premiums A have 100% HHC since no 50% HHC option. Elim. Period waived for HHC, waiver of premium for HHC, HHC paid on weekly basis if Privileged Care Coordinator used. | Relatives living together, such as brother, sister, or parents and children, eligible for 5% family discount. Contingent Insured Rider is available — pays benefits when both primary Insured and contingent Insured are simultaneously eligible for benefits. Waiver of Premium for NH or HHC is a rider. Premium is waived on the first monthly due date after you receive benefits. Standby Assistance Rider expands the definition of Substantial Human Assistance to include supervision or standby assistance. | If both spouses apply together and qualify for coverage, each will get 20% discount. If only one spouse applies or qualifies, will get 10% discount. Custom Community-Based care benefit allows flexibility to receive benefits for multiple HHC services in one day. If in Plan of Care, Policy will pay up to 7 x HHC DB for services incurred in one week. Supplemental Benefits, up to policy max. of 50 x NHDB, covers home modifications and Emergency Medical Response Systems. |
|---|---|---|---|

*Information as of 1/1/1999. Premiums are for least expensive premium class, but do not reflect couples or group discounts. WARNING: Premiums of different policies may not be comparable, because benefit levels may differ. All options not available in all states, or over age 79. California requires seven ADL limitation in non-TQ policies. In Pennsylvania and Minnesota, ADL's must include bathing. Policy information is believed accurate as of the above date. Policy issuers are asked to review their data in all cases. However, no warranties of accuracy or completeness are made by StrateCision, and the policy issuer should be consulted for final determination of features and premiums.

# Premium Comparison

Rightly or wrongly, depending on a person's point of view, most often a buying decision is made on the bottom line. There are certain common denominators that are necessary to generate a premium quotation, such as date of birth, number of nursing home benefit days, maximum daily dollar benefit for nursing home care and home health care, and the number of days during the elimination period. Finally, if inflation benefit increases are included, are they based on five percent simple interest or five percent compounding interest?

These premium comparisons are provided by R. Wright Solutions, of Parsippany, New Jersey. Common data input for all three illustrations was a maximum daily benefit for nursing home care and home health care of $150, and five percent automatic compound inflation benefit.

Illustrations for Companies B and C were based on sixty day elimination period. The closest elimination period offered by Company A is fifty days, which gives them a $1,500 benefit advantage. (Ten additional benefit days at $150 per day equals $1,500.) On the negative side of the comparison for Company A, it will not waive premium when on claim for home health care benefits, unlike Companies B and C, which will waive premiums during a claim for home health care. All quotes are for husband and wife, with maximum spousal discounts included, assuming both spouses apply and pass underwriting on at least a standard risk basis.

The envelope, please!

Exhibit I for husband or wife age 50 shows Company B with the least expensive annual premium. The couple in Exhibit II are both age 65, and for each of them the lowest premium is offered by Company C.

The couple in Exhibit III come from families with a history of longevity and are concerned with the possibility of running out of benefits, so they asked for a lifetime benefit illustration. Because of their gene pool and excellent current health, they qualify for preferred risk discounts. The lowest premium

Exhibit I
Husband or Wife
Spouse Discount: Y
Age: 50
Rate Class: Standard

# Long-Term Care Comparison

## Coverage

| | | |
|---|---|---|
| **Company A**<br>$1068<br>3 Years LTC, 50 Day Elimination<br>Compound Automatic Increase<br><br>$150 LTC/100% HHC | **Company B**<br>$1992  3 Years LTC,<br>60 Day Elimination<br>Compound Automatic Increase<br>60 Day HHC Elimination<br>$150 LTC/100% HHC | **Company C**<br>$1020<br>3 Years LTC, 60 Day Elimination<br>Compound Automatic Increase<br>$1275 W/Nonforfeiture<br>$150 LTC/100% HHC |

## Lifetime Maximums

| | | |
|---|---|---|
| Limited =<br>Daily Maximum x # of days<br>-or-<br>Unlimited | Limit =<br>Daily Benefit x Policy Period<br>-or-<br>Unlimited | Limit =<br>Daily amount x benefit period<br>NH & HHC benefits<br>are integrated<br>(50%, 75% or 100% HHC Avail.)<br>One time elimination period |

## Benefit Trigger

| | | |
|---|---|---|
| Need Substantial Assistance<br>with 2 of 6 ADL's<br>-or-<br>Substantial Assistance due to<br>Cognitive Impairment | Substantial Assistance with 2 of<br>6 ADL's<br>-or-<br>Cognitive Impairment | Substantial Assistance<br>performing 2 or 6 ADL's<br>-or-<br>Substantial Supervision due to<br>Cognitive Impairment |

## ADL's

| | | |
|---|---|---|
| Bathing<br>Dressing<br>Toileting<br>Continence<br>Transferring<br>Eating | Bathing<br>Continence<br>Dressing<br>Eating<br>Toileting<br>Transferring | Bathing<br>Dressing<br>Eating<br>Toileting<br>Transferring<br>Continence |

## Other

| | | |
|---|---|---|
| 20% Spouse Discount<br>100% for Assisted Care Facility<br>100% Home and Comm. Care<br>with Privileged Care Coord<br>Benefit<br>Bed Reservation/Respite Care<br>Waiver of Prem. after NH Elim. | Preferred Rates Available<br>Spouse Discount Available<br>Single Premium Option<br>Bed Res./Care Coordinator<br>Waiver of Prem. when receiving<br>benefits | 20% Spouse Discount Available<br><br>100% for Home and Community<br>based care<br>Bed Reservation<br>Alternate Plan of Care |

## Exhibit II
Husband or Wife
Spouse Discount: Y
Age: 65
Rate Class: Standard

# Long-Term Care Comparison
## Coverage

| Company A | Company B | Company C |
|---|---|---|
| $2232 | $2262  3 Years LTC, | $2112 |
| 3 Years LTC, 50 Day Elimination | 60 Day Elimination | 3 Years LTC, 60 Day Elimination |
| Compound Automatic Increase | Compound Automatic Increase | Compound Automatic Increase |
|  | 60 Day HHC Elimination | $2640 W/Nonforfeiture |
| $150 LTC/100% HHC | $150 LTC/100% HHC | $150 LTC/100% HHC |

## Exhibit III
Husband or Wife
Spouse Discount: Y
Age: 65
Rate Class: Preferred

# Long-Term Care Comparison
## Coverage

| Company A | Company B | Company C |
|---|---|---|
| $3234 | $3320  3 Years LTC, | $3612 |
| Unlimited LTC, 50 Day Elimination | 60 Day Elimination | Lifetime LTC, 60 Day Elimination |
| Compound Automatic Increase | Compound Automatic Increase | Compound Automatic Increase |
| Preferred Rates | 60 Day HHC Elimination | $4515 W/Nonforfeiture |
| $150 LTC/100% HHC | $150 LTC/100% HHC | $150 LTC/100% HHC |

available to this couple in our comparison comes from Company A. Because the shortest elimination period offered by Company A is fifty days, it would have dropped out of contention if the prospects would rather purchase a twenty- or thirty-day elimination period.

It can be stated that an overall comparison of Companies A, B, and C yields benefits and premiums of a comparable nature. Red flags should go up when one's company premiums by comparison seem overly high or unusually low. The actuaries for the company with unusually high premiums may have been too conservative. The concern, however, rests with the company with the unusually low premium. This is especially true if this company accepts health conditions most other carriers would reject or issue with additional premium charges. In this case, cheap may come at a price with the potential for significant future premium increases, especially for older policyholders who may be on fixed incomes. It makes little sense for the insurance industry to condone or for the insuring public to entrust their future to such a carrier regardless of any consumer publications advocating that one can have it all.

The reader may have surmised by now it should be difficult for any long-term care insurance company to lay undisputed claim to having the "best" *and* least expensive long-term care insurance policy. A recent National LTC Network survey asked producers who regularly market long-term care insurance as part of a financial plan to select the most important factors when selling long-term care insurance. From hundreds of responses, the top three factors, ranked by importance, are:

1. Product Benefits
2. Price
3. A.M. Best's Ratings of A- or better

**Long-Term Care Insurance Premium Affordability**

When a person contemplates the purchase of insurance, affordability is a unique personal decision. Before quoting a premium, any conscientious sales agent should first determine if a client needs the coverage and is able to afford it. Properly qualified, the prospect decides to purchase based on factors of his or her perceived need (risk), return (benefit), premium (cost), and love (concern for self and others.) Two people with the same set of circumstances may assign higher or lower priorities to each circumstance, at which point expense becomes a relative term.

Often advocates of socialized long-term care are quoted as saying, "Long-term care insurance is expensive for seasoned citizens." Unfortunately, these statements have created a prejudice among many potential consumers, precluding them from seeking out the true cost of purchasing a policy.

According to data collected and analyzed from the U.S. Census Bureau, household income from 1969 to 1996 revealed a fifty-seven percent rise in real median income for married couples over age 65, compared to a six and two-tenths percent increase for all households. In a survey commissioned by the American Academy of Actuaries, fifty-one percent of retirees say their standard of living has stayed the same since they retired, and sixteen percent say it has improved. In addition, the Academy survey found that twenty percent of retired individuals spend less than sixty percent of their annual income, and fewer than eight percent spent more than their income by invading principal.

Agents and financial planners experienced in counseling older clients on financial matters have learned that overall net worth is a truer measure of financial resources and premium affordability. Many of their clients have chosen to let their IRA accounts or Qualified Tax Sheltered Annuity accounts sit until they must either begin taking minimum distributions at age 70½ or face IRS penalties (Accounts which could be bled for thousands of dollars monthly for the incurred costs of care !). A 1995 report conducted by KPMG Peat Marwick titled *Long-Term Care Insurance Trends and Benchmarks* estimated out of 33 million persons over 65, that 15 million can afford long-term care insurance.

### Long-Term Care Sales in Combination with Life Insurance, Disability Insurance, and Annuities
#### by Harry Stone and Gregory Hill

Long-term care actuaries struggle daily to calculate the morbidity costs. Morbidity cost is "the proportion of sickness or of a specific disease relative to the percentage of deaths resulting from any specific disease, as determined by dividing the number of deaths by the total number of people contracting the disease," and this is essential to producing a long-term care policy for their carrier in today's fast-paced market. Improvements in health care, which extend lives, plus new state and federal government regulations, pose unforeseen complications. Viewing this already difficult marketing arena, a number of companies and actuaries are asking themselves how they might be able to cross-sell clients, through a combined effort of marketing and underwriting, in essence "bundling" products together.

To the knowledge of H. Stone and G. Hill, no one specific carrier to date has captured a large market share by cross-marketing or bundling life insurance with long-term care insurance, individual disability products with long-term care products, and annuities with long-term care products. They do believe that each year more carriers, with the help of their actuaries and marketing staff, will begin to find more success in cross-marketing their respective long-term care products with the other products that they offer.

Whether or not the carriers ever succeed in simplifying the cross-marketing of life insurance, disability products, and annuities with long-term care products, most professional agents believe it is very important that they continue to cross-sell clients, and provide them with this essential protection. By cross-selling, agents protect their relationships with their clients, because if they do not offer them a long-term care policy, someone else could, and the clients may be inclined to replace their original financial advisor.

Underwriting for long-term care policies is based on morbidity. As defined earlier, "morbidity is the proportion of sickness or of a specific disease." The underwriter's main concern in a long-term care policy is related to activities of daily living (ADL's) combined with the likely age of onset and the expected term of specific diseases.

## Cross-Selling Life Insurance and Long-Term Care Policies

Underwriting for life insurance policies is based on mortality, which is defined as "the state or condition of being subject to death or relative frequency of death or death rates." Life insurance actuaries use mortality tables that show the number of persons who die at any given age. These are compiled from specific statistics on selected population groups. Mortality tables have been in existence for well over one hundred years. Although they are not perfect, in general they are very accurate.

There are many conditions in which an underwriter may be able to offer a life insurance policy, even if it is a highly rated policy. But they may not be able to offer a long-term care policy.

Examples of some underwriting conditions under which a carrier may be able to offer a life insurance policy but not a long-term care policy include: Alcoholism, drug or substance abuse, ALS (Lou Gehrig's Disease), Alzheimer's disease, arthritis (if treated with steroids or gold), cerebral vascular disease, chronic obstructive pulmonary disease (COPD), cirrhosis of the liver, confusion/disorientation, congestive heart failure, dementia, diabetes with insulin, Huntington's disease, internal lupus erythematosus, kidney failure, memory loss (recurring), multiple sclerosis, neurogenic bladder, organ transplant (excluding cornea transplant), osteoporosis with fractures, Parkinson's disease, peripheral neuropathy, stroke, and transient ischemic attack (TIA). Cross-selling in today's market varies from insurance carrier to insurance carrier. One major carrier offers a single premium universal life insurance policy in which they claim to have tied three benefits together under one policy. First, you have the benefit of tax-deferred growth on the cash deposited into the policy. Second, you have a death benefit with the policy. The third policy feature contains a long-term care benefit. This is a new concept, so it is difficult to judge whether or not the combination policy will be a marketing success, or whether this type of policy is the right type of policy for a consumer to purchase.

The following is an example of a lump sum premium long-term care policy. The insured is a sixty-five-year-old non-smoking male. It is assumed that he is active and in good health. A lump sum premium of $46,811 would purchase a $91,250 death benefit, income tax free, to beneficiaries if no convalescent care were needed. If convalescent care were required, then a maximum benefit of $182,500 would be paid (at a maximum rate of $125 per day for four years). Assuming that the current investment earnings rate of 5.85% on the universal policy continues for twenty years, the policy would have accumulated a cash value of $91,000 at the end of that period.

For the client that can afford the initial high premium, another alternative may prove to be more beneficial, while accomplishing the same goals. Consider the above example, but using the concept of unbundling the products, as discussed later in this chapter through cross-selling of a separate LTC policy and annuity.

The client would use half of the $50,000 to purchase a single premium whole life policy and use the remaining $25,000 to apply to an investment product returning 5.5% net of taxes. Interest earned on the $25,000 could pay for a LTC policy with a higher benefit and longer benefit period. The life policy has the same death benefit as the bundled policy and, after twenty years, the life policy would have accumulated a cash value of $66,000. The two separate policies would have total benefits of $551,300, more than double the total of the bundled policy.

With the bundled annuity/LTC product, taxation of benefits also needs to be taken into consideration. The monthly benefits paid from the rider could be taxed like any other gain in the annuity.

Another concept adopted by several carriers is to provide a long-term care policy in the form of an Accelerated Death Benefit or Living Needs Rider that is attached to a life insurance policy. These riders pay a part or the entire face amount prior to death under certain conditions. This type of rider may pay a monthly amount for qualified long-term care expenditures up to a maximum percentage of the death benefit. Again, this is a new product offering and it is too early to judge the success of this Accelerated Death Benefit Rider, or whether or not this is the correct policy for a consumer to purchase, in place of a standard stand-alone long-term care policy.

The following is an example of an accelerated benefit payment. The following assumptions are made:

- Five-year no-lapse minimum premium
- Male, age 55, preferred plus non-tobacco user class
- $400,000 base coverage with no loans
- He pays the minimum premium of $4,640 for ten years
- In year eleven, month one he enters a nursing home

- He continues to pay the minimum monthly premium during ninety-day waiting period
- Benefit payments begin in year eleven, month four (benefit equals the expense incurred)
- Daily expense incurred is $125 ($3,750/month) which is a little higher than the national average
- Maximum monthly benefit is $8,000 ($96,000/year) which is 2 percent of the death benefit at time of claim
- The monthly expense incurred is adjusted for 5 percent annual inflation
- 5.75 percent credited interest rate for policy years one to nine and 6.5 percent credited rate for policy years ten and up

| End of Year | Premium | Death Benefit | Maximum Annual LTC Benefit | Actual LTC Expenses Incurred | LTC Accel. Benefit Paid |
|---|---|---|---|---|---|
| 1 | $4,640 | $400,000 | $96,000 | | |
| 2 | $4,640 | $400,000 | $96,000 | | |
| 3 | $4,640 | $400,000 | $96,000 | | |
| 4 | $4,640 | $400,000 | $96,000 | | |
| 5 | $4,640 | $400,000 | $96,000 | | |
| 6 | $4,640 | $400,000 | $96,000 | | |
| 7 | $4,640 | $400,000 | $96,000 | | |
| 8 | $4,640 | $400,000 | $96,000 | | |
| 9 | $4,640 | $400,000 | $96,000 | | |
| 10 | $4,640 | $400,000 | $96,000 | | |
| 11 | $1,160 | $366,250 | $96,000 | $33,750 | $33,750 |
| 12* | $0 | $319,000 | $96,000 | $47,350 | $47,250 |
| 13* | $0 | $269,387 | $96,000 | $49,613 | $49,613 |
| 14* | $0 | $217,294 | $96,000 | $52,093 | $52,093 |
| 15* | $0 | $162,597 | $96,000 | $54,698 | $54,698 |
| 16* | $0 | $105,164 | $96,000 | $57,433 | $57,433 |
| 17* | $0 | $44,860 | $96,000 | $60,304 | $60,304 |
| 18* | $0 | $0 | $0 | $47,490 | $44,854 |

*Ninety-day waiting period, premiums paid for three months, LTC benefits paid for nine months

Since Accelerated and Living Needs Riders are subject to daily or monthly benefits, policy maximums, and elimination periods like traditional plans, it is important for the agent to become familiar with the provisions that govern these. Underwriting for these types of contracts can also have a big impact. As discussed earlier, many conditions that may not affect mortality could cause the insurer to deny approval on acceleration and other LTC benefits.

Because it may be difficult to cancel one part of the combined contracts without eliminating the entire contract, it may hinder the insurance company's ability to alter or change these combined contracts in the future.

A major carrier proposes to offer yet another form of cross-marketing between life insurance and long-term care, within certain age limits and certain underwriting criteria which guarantee long-term care coverage. The carrier proposes to offer a long-term care policy to new or existing life insurance policyholders and make them a conditional offer. Upon delivery of a new long-term care policy, the client must answer a separate questionnaire in regard to activities of daily living. Note: the long-term care policy is an almost guaranteed issue policy.

This, again, is a new concept and may prove successful, but is untested as of now. One advantage to this cross-marketing concept is that a separate long-term care policy is issued with the life insurance policy, so that both contracts will stand on their own merits.

The cross-selling of life insurance with long-term care coverage presents perhaps the best opportunity for cross-marketing sales. But it may be a limited opportunity at best. Some state insurance departments do not allow HIV testing for health insurance products in which long-term care is categorized. Most life insurance carriers will not issue a life insurance policy without an HIV test. Therefore, the cross-referencing of a life application with a long-term care application may be difficult in select states: California,

Colorado, Delaware, Illinois, Indiana, Maryland, North Carolina, and Washington. This could prevent the cross-selling of life insurance and long-term care using the same application in these states.

These are only three marketing concepts that are being tried in this new cross-marketing of life insurance and long-term care, and the outcome for these marketing plans are still uncertain.

### Cross Selling Individual Disability and Long-Term Care Policies

Underwriting for a disability policy does not differ greatly from underwriting of long-term care policy, because both concern themselves with morbidity; however, most disability policies contain different term limits and age restrictions. Most disability policies are not issued after age 65, and it is at this age or older who many carriers write a large percentage of their long-term care business. Term limits on disability policies generally end at age 65, again demonstrating one of the major differences between individual disability and long-term care underwriting.

Morbidity tables for disability policies have been in existence for over forty years, but when applied to long-term care morbidity tables, which have been in existence for less than twenty years, the degrees of accuracy are lessened.

It seems as though only two major carriers have attempted to cross-market individual disability policyholders with long-term care policies. It may be that the reduction in the market in individual disability carriers, combined with the selective limited marketing of individual disability contracts, makes the cross-marketing so limited and so difficult that one might surmise the efforts may not be worth the results.

One large carrier attempted for several years to cross-sell individual disability coverage with long-term care policies but terminated their marketing efforts after minimal success. A second large disability carrier is guaranteeing clients the right to purchase long-term care policies for the same premiums as their individual disability policies, at the age of retirement or up to age 75. In the authors' opinion, this is an excellent benefit to link with an individual policy, especially since there is no charge in the contract for this conversion privilege.

It is the opinion of the authors that the carrier is attempting to transition cash flow from their individual disability book, which will terminate approximately at age 65, to new long-term care premiums. Again, the success of this marketing program is yet to be determined. However, actuarially the morbidity of the book may have changed at age of retirement, possibly to promote adverse selection.

## Cross-Selling Annuities and Long-Term Care Policies

Cross-selling long-term care with annuities is another, altogether different matter. Many of the carriers that offer long-term care policies also offer annuity contracts. Immediate single premium annuities may be the vehicle of choice, but they may not be tax deductible, and they may create a taxable penalty when funding a long-term care policy. Agents and clients should be cautioned to read the fine print when funding a long-term care policy with an annuity. It may work extremely well, or it may not work at all. Please be cautious.

Annuities do not require underwriting but do have issue age restrictions, especially in older ages. Annuities can shelter income on a tax-deferred basis. They can also trigger early distribution taxes and surrender penalties, depending upon the type of annuity purchased, the age at which the annuity is purchased, and the age at which a distribution is elected.

Listed below are two different creative long-term care methods, which utilize annuities to fund the purchase of a long-term care policy:

## I   SPIA REFUND ANNUITY & LTCI COMBO PACKAGE SALE

### The Components

**SPIA Refund Annuity:** A refund annuity is a particular type of SPIA annuity that has a death benefit option attached to it. When the purchaser dies, his or her beneficiary will receive the unused portion of the annuity. To illustrate:

| Total contributions to the annuity | Minus | Payments made under the annuity contract | Equals | Amounts to be paid to beneficiary upon death of lifetime annuitant |
|---|---|---|---|---|

Normally, a regular life annuity, when annualized, will make annuity payments until the purchaser dies. Upon his or her death, the insurance company retains the remainder of the principal.

The Refund (SPIA) Annuity addresses the customer's historical concern about SPIA, for example, "I lose all of my balance of principal if I die." This form of SPIA returns the unused portion of the principal to the purchaser's beneficiary.

**Long-Term Care Insurance Policy:** The long-term care insurance policy would drive the sale of the combo package. Each LTCI policy would be tailored to meet the needs of the applicant. However, for best results in the promotion of the combo package, the following recommendations should routinely be made in the sale.

**Return of Premium Upon Death Rider:** Upon the death of the insured, the ROP Rider returns all premiums paid, less claims, to a beneficiary. The rider would be recommended for each sale. Including this rider in each sale would provide a guarantee that a client would not be throwing away his or money.

**No Waiver of Premium:** The Waiver of Premium rider provides that the carrier will waive premium payments on a monthly basis if the insured is receiving qualifying benefits under the policy. This rider would not be recommended for each sale. Eliminating this rider from the package would free up more money, allowing the client to purchase a more suitable policy, or request less single premium deposit.

## The Combo Package

**SPIA Refund Annuity + (LTCI+ROP-WP) = Combo Package Sale:** The driving force of each combo package will be the long-term care insurance policy, keeping suitability well in mind. The refund annuity rides along as a proposed way to pay for the LTCI while protecting the client's assets.

**How It Works:** The theory behind the combo package is that the client simultaneously purchases a suitable LTCI policy and a Refund Annuity. The total contributions in the annuity are sufficient to produce a guaranteed periodic annuity payment, which is sufficient to meet the premium cost of the LTCI policy.

The concerns of many clients focus on "use it or lose it" (What happens if I don't use the benefits under long-term care insurance? I want to pass along these assets to my heirs). This combo sale addresses these concerns in the following ways:

1. The SPIA refund annuity assures the client that the money will be utilized to pay for LTCI policy premiums during his or her lifetime. Upon the death of the insured, the unused portion of the principal (the balance) will be distributed to his or her beneficiary.
2. The return of premium upon death rider assures the client that upon his or her death all premiums paid into the policy, less claims, will be paid to the insured's beneficiary.

To illustrate:

Richard sets up an SPIA refund annuity/LTCI + ROP – WP combo package. Richard purchases a suitable LTCI policy with premiums of $1,500 annually. Richard invests $50,000 into a refund annuity. The annuity payments of $1,500 per year are applied to the cost of Richard's LTCI policy. Richard dies after ten years of annuity/LTCI premium payments.

If Richard died without using benefits under the LTCI policy...

| The remainder of the Refund Annuity will be distributed to Richard's beneficiary | Plus | The Return of Premium Rider distributes all of Richard's LTCI payments (from the annuity) to his beneficiary | Equals | Richard's contribution into the annuity |
|---|---|---|---|---|
| $35,000 | + | $15,000 | = | Total dollars returned to beneficiary. $50,000 |

## II USING LAZY LIQUID ASSETS TO FUND LTCI BENEFITS, WITH ASSETS RETURNED TO THE ESTATE

**Step 1:**
- Determine appropriate and desired LTCI coverage.
- Calculate annual cost of desired LTCI benefits.

**Step 2:**
- Solve for the lump-sum costs of a SPIA contract, using the income from the SPIA to pay the annual premium for the LTCI policy.
- Use a Life-only, annual pay SPIA design, to minimize the lump-sum cost.

**Step 3:**
- Purchase asset replacement life insurance, with ownership/payment approved to be out of the taxable estate and the beneficiary arrangements to match the client's desired distribution for the lazy liquid assets.
- Amount of the policy to be equal to the assets transferred to the SPIA contract.
- Use a life policy design with a guaranteed death benefit provision.
- Use a policy with a return of premium benefit. This allows the cost of the SPIA/LTCI contract and the life insurance policy to be returned to the estate's heirs.

**Cost/Exposures to Risk:**
- Income from the SPIA is guaranteed.
- Cost for guaranteed death benefit is guaranteed.
- Costs for LTCI coverage are not guaranteed.

**Estate Advantage:**
- If client is in a taxable estate bracket, these lazy assets can be transferred out of the estate, reducing those future liabilities and thereby increasing the assets that flow to the estate, while they are also being protected against depletion from LTC expenses.

**Liquidity Position:**
- Portion of assets transferred to the life insurance policy continue to be available via policy loan provision.

In summary, the cross-marketing and bundling of long-term care products with life insurance, disability insurance, and annuities is a reality. The carriers, the actuaries, agents, and the general public are all learning more about this marketing opportunity.

While these combo products are in their infancy, questions remain as to whose regulation do these products come under: LTCI rules and regulations or life and annuity regulations? The National Association of Insurance Commissions is addressing these very same questions. Most likely the NAIC will need to recommend changes in existing insurance laws to accommodate emerging innovations. In the meantime, experience with consumers tell us LTCI by itself is one of the least understood of insurances in the marketplace!

After careful research, Hill and Stone are not sure if any carrier will succeed with the marketing examples presented or that anyone will be pleased with the final results of the different carriers' marketing efforts. Regardless of the various carriers' marketing successes, agents should continue to seek out successful ways of cross-selling long-term care policies to new or existing policyholders. Careful fact-finding and analyzing of a client's needs and financial situation will help to determine whether separate or bundled products provide greater protection and benefits all around.

## Recommendation for Agents

Two strong recommendations to help agents become successful in marketing long-term care policies: First, agents who are able to represent more than one carrier should find an expert long-term care brokerage firm to help provide them with the contracts, marketing information, and underwriting information that can assist them in becoming proficient with long-term care sales. Agents who are only allowed to represent one carrier should find an expert within that carrier and get as much help as possible. Second, regardless of whether an agent is able to represent more than one carrier or not, if he or she is not comfortable selling long-term care policies, they should form a partnership with a long-term care professional. Agents who have a good relationship with their clients should look for long-term care cross-selling situations, to minimize their client's long-term care risks, as well as eliminate potential errors and omissions liability suits that can arise from a client's unprotected long-term care.

$\sim$

# CHAPTER 6

## Long-Term Care Insurance: Agents Answering the Call

Ask a room full of people for a show of hands to answer the question, "Who believes someone in the room will eventually become a resident in a nursing home?" and everyone will raise a hand. Ask the same group, "Who thinks it will personally happen to them?" and no one raises a hand!

This demonstration confirms the unwillingness of most people to accept the thought of becoming a resident of a nursing facility. Denial can be a barrier to learning about the benefits of long-term care insurance. There are a few nonthreatening ways for the insurance industry to spread the message, since reality directs us to focus on the odds of needing care, the high costs of care, and issues of freedom of choice and access. The nonthreatening ways include public seminars, worksite marketing, and affinity group marketing. Some of these formats may offer advantages of lower premiums and/or underwriting concessions.

Network member Pamela Schmidt of North Dakota, where more residents per capita own LTCI than any other state, begins the chapter with proven tips for members of the insurance community on introducing long-term care insurance to existing clients, one-to-one. Next, Network member Melanie Steele of North Carolina, a state that sponsors LTCI for its employees and retirees, shares her formula for successfully reaching candidates for long-term care insurance through seminars.

Recently, several factors have contributed to establishing the small-employer group market as the most fertile ground in which to market long-term care insurance. Tom Riekse, Sr., the first President of the National LTC Network, describes the various options and advantages available to small business owners to encourage them to adopt a LTCI worksite program.

I will close the chapter with comments on differences in

mass-marketing LTCI to small groups versus large groups, and then address one of the most creative and beneficial aspects to evolve from the mass-marketing of LTCI, the Extended Family.

**"We must build a world, a far better world —
one in which the eternal dignity of man is respected."
— Harry S. Truman**

### Introducing Long-Term Care Insurance
### by Pamela Schmidt

Eternal dignity — such powerful words! — words to carry in your heart and words to build a career on. Let's make that words to build a long-term care insurance career on.

Eternal dignity is that rare gift each of us hopes to receive by virtue of maintaining our freedom of choice and some measure of independence to the very end. Eternal dignity is what every family wishes for a loved one, a chance to make personal health care decisions that ultimately write the final chapters of our lives. In today's world, simply put, that takes money, and money is the precise reason why long-term care insurance is now seen as one of the most important forces shaping the economic future of this country.

What does any of this have to do with marketing, you might ask? It is the foundation upon which to build successful marketing strategies and advertising campaigns! You see, LTCI is first and foremost a personal, emotional sale. Quotes and statistics have their place, of course, but the most effective LTCI ads use prominently positioned pictures of multigenerational families to stir emotions and evoke memories of our own families.

Fear has no place in LTC advertising. In 1980, when I left a broadcasting career to join my husband in building a senior health agency, prevailing wisdom decreed that there were only two ways to sell those first skilled-care-only nursing home policies: fear and gimmicks. Creating fear was done by the use of dire predictions and outright threats if one failed to own a policy. Gimmick pieces promised free gifts or were designed to look like mail from Medicare, with no disclosure that the product was actually nursing home coverage. Neither one has ever made sense to me. Advertising rules and regulations — promulgated with the help of insurance companies and agents — thankfully removed both elements from the marketplace many years ago. I mention them here only because, in the last year, I've seen two companies try to revive these methods. My advice is to stay away from any LTCI company using unethical materials to obtain lead cards. They may try to dazzle you with high rates of return, but don't be fooled. Unqualified leads do not result in high numbers of sales, and even more importantly, they do not create good relationships with satisfied clients. Emotion — love of family — is the common bond that builds rapport and relationships. Use warm, loving family pictures in your LTCI advertising and you'll be pleased with the results.

If you've been blessed with a successful life insurance career, you know all about building relationships. You've earned your client's trust through hard work, service, and dedication. I congratulate you on your success! But I would also suggest that it is now your *personal responsibility* to offer LTCI to those clients. Why would I make such a strong statement? Recent studies estimate that only three to six percent of eligible Americans own a policy. They've all read the newspaper and magazine articles about rising long-term care costs. They've all seen nightly television stories detailing the hardships of caregiving. But not all have been contacted by someone they trust. And the implication may very well be that if they haven't heard from you, they really don't need to worry about it.

So where and how do you begin? First, do a realistic evaluation of how much time you have to devote to a new product line. If the answer is little to none, you must turn to an insurance associate with education, knowledge, and experience in the LTCI market. Strike up an arrangement to split fees based on the amount of time and effort each of you will put into arranging the appointments, making the presentations, and delivering the policies. If you don't know an LTCI specialist you feel comfortable with, contact a well-established organization like the National LTC Network for the names and numbers of reputable agents in your area.

If you have a large number of agents working for you, and an office staff, you may eventually want to develop a marketing plan that includes radio, television, and newspaper advertising, in addition to direct mail. But I never recommend signing a year-long contract with the local paper or rushing out to buy airtime to anyone — regardless of the size of his or her company. Generally speaking, direct mail is still the simplest and most cost-effective way to *begin* a long-term care insurance campaign.

## Letter Writing Tips

When designing a letter for your clients, an important LTCI advertising rule is Never Apologize when making the offer. Some agents worry their clients might feel too young to consider LTC coverage, so their letters and presentations often take on an apologetic tone. To avoid the problem, remember that long-term care insurance is not for everyone — it's only for those with assets and an estate to protect. Your letter, then, should be of a complimentary nature, openly acknowledging their success as the basis for your decision to contact them. The younger they are, the greater the compliment!

If you've chosen to work with an LTCI associate, it's preferable to use photos of both of you in the letter. You want to *transfer* their trust of you to the person you're working with. Using both photos conveys that message instantly through a visual image — the easiest method for the brain to assimilate.

Are you interested in sharing a line or two about an LTC experience within your own family? Give it every consideration, because nothing creates an audience as well as the truth, conveyed in simple heartfelt words.

If you know their birth dates, your letters to clients who are 40-65 years of age should also include a line indicating your willingness to visit with parents, grandparents, in-laws, etc. Some experts now say elder care is rapidly replacing child care as the number one concern of many Americans. Long-term care insurance can help alleviate those concerns.

Explain that you (or your associate) will be calling *within the next week* to see if your clients would like to set up an appointment for more information.

Have your letter approved by one of the LTC carriers you plan to write for, since today's advertising rules and regulations are increasingly difficult to understand. Using the word "will," instead of "may," can be a technical violation inside an otherwise appropriate mailpiece. Your company's compliance department knows the advertising laws in each state. Be patient with any changes! It's their job to protect you and the company.

## Mailing Tips

Eighteen and nineteen years ago, using soft-sell advertising pieces with return cards, our company was able to obtain ten percent returns from direct mail pieces. We stopped using this method entirely in the early 1990s when our rate of return dropped to one-half per cent, and it became painfully apparent the time had come to develop a new, more cost-effective approach. After a few years of trial and error — and carefully tabulated results — we determined that simplicity was the new order of the day.

Here's how it works: Mail only as many households as you are able to call exactly one week after you sent the letter. Seven is the magic number. I can't explain why, but the success ratio declines dramatically for every day you wait past that seventh day. In terms of organizing your work week, it's a simple procedure to look ahead one week for a day when you'll be free to make LTCI calls. Then mail your letters on the current week's corresponding work day.

Hand address your letters. In this day of amazing technology, how important do you regard letters you receive that have a computer-generated label? They're the last ones you open. But a hand addressed letter? It's human nature — and our natural curiosity — that makes us open those first every time!

Be realistic with the number of pieces you mail. Most of our agents make no more than twenty calls per day. Some, who write other lines of insurance as well, make no more than ten LTCI phone calls in a day, yet long-term care insurance has now become a substantial portion of their revenue. Again, your success rate will run parallel with your diligence in making phone calls exactly seven days after you've done your mailing.

If using an LTCI associate, there's no need to give out the names of all your clients. Control the number of names you give out, and ask for a brief statement of each client's response along with the date they were contacted. Our office has developed a client response record, provided free of charge to our agents working on a split-fee arrangement with an LTCI associate, which features boxes to check for the most frequent kinds of client responses. It also provides for a system of tracking call-backs: clients who want to be called again at a later date. This entire procedure is painless: an easy-to-use system that ensures your clients will be contacted in a timely manner and produces results. It also provides written proof that phone calls made on the seventh day are most effective. Take the time to review client responses on a weekly basis

## Phone Call Tips

When placing those calls on the seventh day, your first sentence should refer to the letter you mailed. The idea is to build an immediate connection with that client that says you are not one more long distance company making yet one more irritating-as-can-be call.

Now you've created a forum! The rest is up to you! Effective advertising gains you *the privilege and the opportunity* to meet a potential new client. Your LTCI education, a good product, and your natural talents ultimately lead to success!

Here's one final thought for you: During your presentations, as you cover the necessary statistics and detail your plan's benefits, take just a moment to assure your clients that what awaits you both is surely a wonderful, amazing future! A future where advances in medicine will increase both longevity and quality of life in ways we can't even imagine. A future which fulfills Harry Truman's vision of "a far better world — one in which the eternal dignity of man is respected." Long-term care insurance has a role to play in this future, in this far better world. And so do we.

## Seminar Selling
### by Melanie Steele

One of the most effective ways to market long-term care insurance today is through seminar selling. Whether an agent is looking for sales from a current client base, a local bank, a senior group, or even a small group sale, the seminar gives the agent the opportunity to provide the educational component of the sale, which in long-term care insurance is imperative.

Because the public has considerable interest (but relatively little knowledge) of long-term care and long-term care insurance, seminars are a particularly effective method of disseminating information. This is especially true in targeted demographic groups, for whom a seminar offers a nonthreatening means of establishing rapport with consumers who are not likely to respond to a cold call. Agents who use a well-developed seminar system in many areas of their practice find they result in qualified interested leads for long-term care insurance and other estate-related products.

In addition to the monetary gains generated by the seminar sale, the greatest rewards come in the form of the friendships that are made. The fact that not all attendees will be interested or insurable does not make them less worthy of attention. Some of the best leads may come from people who have heard a presentation and made a referral without purchasing a policy of their own.

What follows are the essential elements of the successful long-term care seminar, possible market places or target markets for long-term care seminars, tips on how to get the most out of every seminar presented by an agent, and the true rewards of the long-term care insurance sale.

### Getting Prospects to Attend a Seminar

Regardless of the market the agent is trying to reach, a dazzling smile, winning way, or spellbinding presentations will have no effect whatsoever if prospects do not attend the seminar.

In my long-term care insurance practice, I have used several means of getting prospects to the seminar. Irrespective of the group or individuals being addressed, I use a pre-approach letter that outlines two or three long-term care statistics about the need for this protection and invites the recipient to an educational, informative discussion on long-term care issues and concerns. If the group is not one where a letter is appropriate, the same information is provided in another format (such as a newsletter or other medium currently being sent to the prospective group). This letter gives the seminar date, time, and location, and an explanation that this program is designed to answer any questions or concerns about the topic. Also included is an invitation and acceptance card asking for the prospect's name, address, telephone number, and birthday. Upon receiving the cards in my office, I hold them until a few days before the seminar. At that point, I call to remind those persons who returned cards of the upcoming date and time, and ask a few qualifying questions about their health when it is appropriate to do so. My office telephone number is also included in the letter in case they prefer to call, whereupon I ask for the information on the cards and perform the health screening.

I also have used ads in local newspapers as another means of inviting prospects to a seminar. This method may be less effective, as it reaches an open market as opposed to a targeted one; however, there are steps that can be taken to streamline this approach in an effort to target a certain group. First of all, the ad should be an insert placed in the paper with the largest circulation in the area. The best time is one week before the seminar on a Monday or Wednesday, which are heavily read yet small enough so that the insert is not lost. Make sure that you let the ad department know that you only want it inserted in the subscribers' papers in certain zip codes, which gives you some control over the market segment you are trying to reach from an income perspective. The ad should be catchy and concise and offer information about the seminar as well as directions on how to get there. It can have a reply card attached and a telephone number to call so that the potential attendees can reserve a place at the upcoming event.

Another place to seek out prospective long-term care insurance seminar attendees is from a referring professional's client base. Since there is already a sense of familiarity with the referring professional, a telephone call to invite prospects or a simple invitation card with an enclosed reply card may be used.

The essential pieces of the puzzle — the name, address, telephone numbers, and birthday — will be delivered by the referring professional. A confirmation call is still essential with this group as well, since seniors, although they may be retired, may be still have very active lifestyles and are as apt to forget as anyone else.

## Hosting a Successful Seminar

Now that you have a means of getting prospects to your seminars, let's look at some essential components of the seminar itself.

The generic seminar, which mentions no long-term care insurance companies or products by name, accomplishes several goals. By not mentioning a specific company or product, the agent can more effectively establish an interest in the audience's needs, and not simply an interest in making a sale. Withholding names also creates an aura of suspense, and piques curiosity about "the rest of the story," which can only be found at a subsequent one-on-one session.

In addition, the non-sales, non threatening appeal of a generic seminar gives one greater accessibility to otherwise closed markets, such as banks, senior clubs, church groups, and so on. It also may be used as a continuing education tool for accountants, tax attorneys, and estate planners, and ultimately could give the agent access to these professionals' clients.

The optimum seminar should last thirty to forty-five minutes, have an audience of twenty-five to fifty people, and focus on the basics (the KISS principle — Keep it simple, stupid — applies here, too). The program should define long-term care, discuss the need for the care, review what to look for in a good long-term care insurance product, and explain how the coverage works. The seminar's objective is threefold: help the participants understand that they are exposed to long-term care risk, show them that there is protection to cover the risk, and demonstrate how the protection works.

In addition to avoiding mention of specific insurance companies or products, try to avoid specific premium levels by quoting a broad range from the podium only if forced. This results partly from my mother's advice to "explain the value before you discuss the price." Quoting an average premium may discourage prospects who would be satisfied with lower benefits at a lower cost.

Professional quality visual aids (either Power Point presentations, slides, or overheads) greatly increase the seminar's effectiveness. A well-designed visual can dramatically emphasize the agent's important points. Visuals also help focus the audience's attention and enable the agent to maintain better continuity in the presentation. An important point to note is that visuals presenting the long-term care story in a lighthearted, somewhat humorous vein get better results than graphs or charts.

Melanie achieves her lighthearted, somewhat humorous view with the use of slides featuring folksy cartoon characters. Some presenters choose to use technical slides, charts, and graphs, making an already emotional subject even more difficult to receive. A word of caution, though; be sensitive to your audience. Jokes about nursing home residents, the elderly and the like, may be humorous to some baby boomers, but may offend someone twenty years older. One of my brokers created a print advertisement balancing the crucial message with a clever touch of humor that is not offensive or demeaning:

## Top 10 Reasons Why You Don't Need Long-Term Care Insurance

10. You never get sick.

9. You just know you would never use it.

8. People in your family live forever.

7. You are so rich that $60,000 per year for the cost of nursing care is just a drop in the bucket.

6. You've always been *real* lucky.

5. You truly believe that the Government will be there to help you and take care of you.

4. You own your own nursing home.

3. You are already protected by an iron-clad trust, drawn up and guaranteed by the world's foremost attorney.

2. Your brother-in-law, mom, dad, sister, brother, friend, teacher, doctor, lawyer, Indian-chief, or psychic told you, you don't need it.

1. You've always been *real* lucky.

**Seriously,** maybe *you* or someone you love will need long-term care someday.

W.A. MACK FINANCIAL GROUP
Reprinted with permission of William A. Mack

### Turning Your Seminars into Sales

Now that the prospects have come to the seminar and listened to the presentation, the agent will want to have a system whereby he or she can turn them into protected policyholders. In order to make the conversion from prospects into policyholders, there must be a means of collecting the names and telephone numbers of those attendees who are interested.

One way in which information can be collected is with a seminar evaluation form, which can be referred to as the speaker's report card. The participants use the evaluation form to grade the speaker's performance along with the convenience of the time and the location of the seminar. They should also be able to choose among several follow-up options: an appointment to discuss their LTC options, a review of a current LTCI policy, or a request for additional information. There should also be a place on the form for the prospect and spouse's name, address, telephone number and birthdays.

The speed with which the agent contacts the attendees is directly correlated to the retention level by most attendees of the facts presented, and the motivation to insure oneself. The agent should contact everyone who attended the seminar within three days of the event and schedule an appointment within two weeks if at all possible. If having fifty seminar attendees does not allow the agent to manage the follow-up list in a timely manner, then he or she should limit the maximum number of participants. There is certainly nothing wrong with letting prospects know a seminar is sold out at a certain point. Reservations can always be taken for a seminar to follow.

The agent must position himself to maximize the time and effort invested; therefore, he must know the magic number he can manage within that three- to four-week cycle. From the invitation to the seminar to follow-up appointments, there should be no lapse in time. Allowing much time to come between the invitation and seminar or between the seminar and the follow-up appointment will result in diminished attendance and sales, and a waste of time on the part of the presenter.

Establishing relationships with those who have attended the seminar never wastes the presenter or agent's time. Even if a sale is not generated, there is the opportunity to obtain referrals from those who have attended. Those attendees who become clients may also offer the opportunity for the agent to experience the true rewards of the LTCI sale.

A case in point is a client of mine who had been in and out of a facility on several occasions, with her husband continuing to bring her home in between. When it eventually became too much for him, he reluctantly left her where she could get better care and spent most of his days there with her. A few months passed and his health began to fail, and he could not get to and from the nursing home on his own. Since they had no children or siblings (the only family member being a niece), he was concerned that the care for him and his wife would be much too demanding on the niece. He took his life so that the niece would have plenty of time to spend supervising the care of his wife. A suicide letter was left, mentioning my name and the relief that he felt as a result of my helping them plan for his wife's long-term care needs. Subsequently, when care at the facility began to be less than adequate, with the permission of the niece I moved this client to a more reputable facility where she lived until the day she died. After her death, the niece called to thank me for the attention and care I took with her aunt and asked if I might be able to help her secure the same type of plan that I sold to her relatives. A sad story to tell, but one that allowed me the opportunity to go beyond the sale and be the best that I could be at the time. And, in addition to the referral of her niece, I received over twelve other referrals as a result of the relationship I had with these lovely people.

## Opportunities for Seminar Presentations

You may find opportunities hiding under some logical and some quite illogical rocks. Certainly, an unprospected client base should be the agent's first target market. Beyond that, he might approach other professionals such as tax attorneys, financial planners, accountants, and trust officers, and ask whether he can assist them in explaining long-term care planning to their clients. By giving clients of these professionals an informative discussion on this timely topic, the agent not only will enhance his professional image as well as theirs, he also will develop direct leads that can result in solving their clients' estate needs.

Within any community, there is a myriad of senior groups functioning within churches and synagogues, hospitals providing community service programs, retirement communities, and other organizations such as service and investment clubs. These groups need speakers and usually are receptive to a presentation on this topic of growing concern. In addition to these groups, most small banks, which have a need to be consumer oriented to compete with the financial giants, have established clubs for their customers over age 50 or 55. Some will take the form of investment clubs, and some will simply offer a monthly meeting with speakers of interest to the group. These are perfect settings which present information on the one event that could wipe out their account at that financial institution one day, if they neglect to plan for it.

The agent involved in either small or large group business can use the seminar as the educational component before taking the application, which will result in reducing the actual enrollment time. By getting an endorsement from the principal of the company and a mandate to attend the long-term care seminars, employees will realize the importance of planning for long-term care needs for themselves and their families. These seminars should be timed according to the workplace, for example, at a hospital or factory during shift changes. At the end of the seminar, the appointments for enrollment can be made, at which time the enroller will not have as many questions to answer or issues to explain. Typically, there is only the application to complete at this point. Since long-term care insurance is primarily an employee-funded benefit, it is imperative that the employee understand the importance of having this protection for which he will be spending his hard-earned dollars.

## Realizing the Power of the Seminar

By keeping an open mind and using the seminar as a tool, the agent can twist and mold it to fit several aspects of his or her business. In doing so, the agent will not have to reinvent the wheel each time he or she is presented with a different opportunity.

Seminar selling can increase the agent's long-term care insurance sales exponentially. The seminar should be viewed as an educational, informative service to younger and older persons alike. The seminar allows the agent to establish rapport and confidence in a nonthreatening environment, and to bring a group of prospects up to a level of understanding that will reduce the time it takes the agent to make the sale.

The agent should never forget the importance of the relationships that are built as a result of the seminar sale. One couple who purchased a policy as a result of attending a long-term care seminar found out several years later that the husband had terminal cancer. The family requested the presence of their LTCI agent at a final planning session with their father's doctor. This agent, though feeling somewhat awkward, was able to add value by explaining the options provided by the coverage as they related to the patient's specific options for care at the time. Payment to the agent came in the form of humanitarianism on that day when the potential hourly rate became immeasurable.

Knowing how to get prospects to the seminar, what to share with them, and how to follow up with a sale, long-term care insurance agents will reap the rewards shared by many knowing that their clients may live out their lives without having their estates potentially destroyed by long-term care costs.

## Joint Seminars

Often jointly held seminars enhance the audience's overall perspective of the evening, and increase the agent's credibility. For example, an agent in a state where a private/public LTC partnership is available gains credibility by having a state official there to explain how the partnership plan works.

Teaming up with a pension specialist who provides strategies for saving and investing is a natural fit and seems to draw well with pre-retirees age 50 and up. The LTCI specialist role is to offer ideas on how to protect pension assets from the high costs of long-term care.

One of the most informative joint seminars for age groups 65 and over involves the LTCI specialist and an attorney. The attorney stresses the importance of having a will, a Power of Attorney, and a Health Care Proxy. Trusts may be discussed, but make damn sure the attorney doesn't make a living primarily from the practice of instituting Medicaid Trusts! A conscientious attorney will advise healthy clients with assets to protect to contact a LTCI agent for information.

## Designing an Informative Long-Term Care Insurance Seminar

Consumer LTCI seminars should include general information on both long-term care and long-term care insurance. In other words, be sure to place the horse before the cart. The following A to Z outline is suggestive of just such a seminar in content and sequence. This seminar takes approximately 40 to 45 minutes, not including time for questions and answers.

A. Factors behind the Age Wave

B. Quantity (of life) vs. Quality (of life)

C. Age-based demographics

D. Samples of media attention on the issues of aging

E. Quote forecasts on the stability of Social Security and Medicare & underlying reasons for the forecast

F. Differentiate between CARE (long-term) and CURE (acute)

G. Explanation of the Activities of Daily Living as they relate to LTCI

H. LTCI — an issue of risk, not age (examples)

I. Life expectancy of a 65-year-old, and odds of needing LTC at ages 65, 70, 75

J. Quote statistics of average stay in a nursing facility and average daily costs in your area

K. Compare the ratio of nursing home care to home health care & ability of policy to pay for HHC

L. Cover issue of family members providing care (Seeing Mom Now vs. Then)

M. Levels of care: Skilled, Intermediate, Custodial

N. Discuss stress on care givers

O. List sources of long-term care financing

P. Medicare — skilled care only

Q. Medicaid — definition/qualification for impoverishment in your state

R. 3 "B's" of LTC Planning: Be rich, Be poor, Be insured

S. Underwriting criteria — reasonable good health

T. HR3103-HIPA — recognition Uncle Sam cannot cover costs of long-term care

U. Individual federal income tax deduction for LTCI premium payment

V. Corporate tax deduction for LTCI premium payment

W. Self-Employed tax deduction for LTCI premium payment

X. Your state's long-term care insurance premium tax deduction/credit, if available

Y. Your state's LTCI Private/Public Partnership, if available (New York, Connecticut., Indiana, California)

Z. Why people buy long-term care insurance

Some invitations to speak on the topic of long-term care

insurance must be limited to 15 or 20 minutes. This may be especially true of service clubs who meet at breakfast or lunch time. In these situations, it's best to focus the audiences' attention on long-term care insurance benefits.

Many of the benefits can be summed up through the ensuing nine points.

1. Freedom of access and freedom of choice for private payers.
2. Care coordination for guidance and peace of mind.
3. Minimizes disputes between siblings over location and costs associated with parents' care.
4. Respite care providing relief for caregivers to visit or vacation with children, grandchildren, brothers and/ or sisters.
5. Allows the well spouse an opportunity to maintain physical and emotional balance.
6. Extended asset protection in public/private partnership long-term care insurance states.
7. Now vs. Then. Enlightening baby boomers to the aftermath of aging parents' inability to do the activities of daily living. The devil is in the details.
8. Affordability and value. Odds of total property damage claims under auto or homeowners insurance. Odds of needing nursing facility care at ages 65, 70, 75, and average life expectancy of 65-year-old.
9. Tax benefits associated with tax-qualified long-term care insurance premium payments and paid claims.

### Group Long-Term Care Insurance (Rieksie):

Long-term care insurance, thought of by many as elder insurance, ironically has been labeled the baby of the life and health insurance industry. Long-term care insurance also shares a similar distinction in the world of employee benefits, based on 1999 Group LTCI Sales and In Force figures released by LIMRA (Life Insurance Marketing and Research Association). However, premium revenue from new group long-term care insurance sales in 1999 grew 121 percent, and the LTCI industry begins the new millennium with just over 3,000 employer sponsor plans, insuring some 800,000 participants, with premiums exceeding $357,000,000.

Just as all signs point to a burgeoning LTCI market, so too will LTCI take its place among the more popular employee benefits. In addition to the demographics of aging, with their attendant cause and effect, recent surveys among employers and employees bear witness to increasing interest in LTCI as an employee benefit. The question remains how to convince employers that adding LTCI to their benefits list, sooner rather than later, is good business. On July 6, 1999, an article appeared in *The Wall Street Journal* touting new CEO benefits. Leading the list is company-paid long-term care insurance. In some instances, companies pay LTCI premiums for their executives as long as the executive remains in office. A growing list of companies are agreeing to pay LTCI premiums over their executive's lifetime.

One impetus to offer LTCI as an employee benefit comes from companies known for sponsoring cutting-edge benefits. Some corporations whose chief executive officers or human resource directors were placed in a position of caring for a loved one have been personally influenced to install a group LTCI plan. However, the big picture has eluded the attention of most of corporate America. As soon as corporate America awakens to the costly effects that long-term care has on their bottom line, the sooner they will shift from being prospects to becoming buyers.

**Why Employers Need to Be Concerned About the Effects of Long-Term Care**

- 40% of those who need long-term care are working-age adults who need care because of stroke, trauma, heart disease, disabling injuries, or mental impairments.
- Primary caregivers spend an average of 4.2 hours a day caring for the impaired. For the most impaired, many average 8 hours of care per day or more.

- 52% of impaired people need help eating, bathing, dressing, and using the bathroom; 25% need help with nutrition and intravenous devices; 60% with cooking, housework, and transportation.
- Absenteeism caused by inadequate elder care can cost a company $2,500 per year for each caregiving employee, plus the drain on productivity from co-workers.
- About half of all caregivers are employed. Of those, many take a leave of absence from work; the majority are often late for work, engage in window staring, leave early, or take unpaid leave to provide care.
- One-third of employees working and caring for family members work less effectively due to stress and loss of sleep.
- Most caregivers tending to their parent's needs view caregiving as a higher responsibility than work, a spouse, or children.
- An increasing concern of employees who have been asked to relocate is their family ties.
- Elder care is beginning to replace child care as a leading employee dilemma. Many boomers are caught taking care of parents and children.
- Every day employees quit to take care of their families. Replacing them is far more costly than sponsoring a long-term care insurance plan, whereby employees are given the opportunity to shift the risk of care coordination and the costs of professional long-term care for their loved ones to an insurance company.

The 1999 MetLife Juggling Act Study, produced in conjunction with the National Alliance for Caregiving and the National Center for Women and Aging at Brandeis University for Metropolitan Life Insurance Company's Mature Market

Institute, revealed some troublesome statistics about working caregivers.

Eighty-four percent of the caregivers studied made adjustments to their work load through one of the following actions:

64% used sick leave or vacation time.

33% decreased their hours on the job.

22% took leaves of absence.

20% elected to work part-time instead of full-time.

16% quit their jobs.

13% took early retirement.

According to the MetLife study, employees should be just as concerned abut the issue of caregiving as their employers. Actions of employee caregivers cost these employees significant dollars over their lifetimes in lost wages, lost retirement contributions, and lost Social Security benefits.

Another MetLife study demonstrates that employers can empower employees to insure for the risks of long-term care by offering long-term care insurance as a voluntary employee benefit. This conclusion was born out in a mid-1998 MetLife commissioned Roper Starch Worldwide survey about the financial concerns of American workers to explore their attitudes and purchase behavior regarding voluntary benefits.

## I. The Worksite Advantage

### To the Employer/Employee:

The purpose of offering long-term care coverage through an employer is to give the employees of a company a better deal than they can get on their own. Some of the advantages are:

- Saving the employees time and effort by having the employer's broker screen LTCI companies and select the best carrier;
- More premium discounts;
- Underwriting concessions;
- Ease of enrollment;

- Tax advantages to the employee with the
employer paying all or part of the premium.

**To the Employer's Insurance Representative:**
The most important advantage to the agent is that he or she
can maximize their selling time rather than prospecting and
selling one policy at a time. Other advantages include:
- Offering a solution to the employer who wants
to provide a new and much needed benefit to
his or her employees;
- Providing value-added service to the employees
who are interested in LTCI and who can receive
a premium discount and/or underwriting
concessions at their worksite;
- Effective way to prospect in the LTCI market;
- Higher compensation levels available than
through traditional group health and other
voluntary insurance coverages;
- The renewal commissions on individual LTCI
policies are more meaningful because of a
history of high persistency and because most
LTCI companies refuse to recognize Agent of
Record letters.

# II.  Tax Laws for Long-Term Care Insurance

**C-Corporations (Plus Spouses & Retirees):**
- LTCI premiums are deductible to the
corporation.
- Not considered income to the employee
- Benefits are tax-free.
- Employer can pick and choose. Eligibility can
be defined by occupation, salary levels, tenure,
or other factors at the employer's discretion (do
not use Stockholders as the qualification.)

## III.  S-Corporations Principals, Partnerships & Individual Proprietors (Plus Spouses & Retirees):

- Schedule for deductibility as a business expense:

| | |
|---|---|
| 2000-2001 | 60% |
| 2002 | 70% |
| 2003 and after | 100% |

- Deductibility limitations:

| Age | Premium |
|---|---|
| 40 or less | $220.00 |
| 41-50 | $410.00 |
| 51-60 | $820.00 |
| 61-70 | $2,200.00 |
| 71 & Older | $2,750.00 |

- 2000 per diem limitations:

Indemnity Plans — $190.00

Reimbursement — No Limit

### Individual 1040 Taxpayer:

- LTC Premiums deductible subject to the 7.5% AGI rule.
- Deductibility limitations:

| | |
|---|---|
| Age 40 or Below | $220.00 |
| 41 through 50 | $410.00 |
| 51 through 60 | $820.00 |
| 61 through 70 | $2,200.00 |
| 71 and above | $2,750.00 |

- Benefits are tax free.

### Individual Policies vs. Group Master Policies:

LTCI sold at the worksite is delivered either with an individual policy or a certificate/master policy approach. Generally, the master policy approach is used with quite large cases, while smaller employers use the individual policy approach.

It is important to recognize that underwriting, ERISA, and separation rights can be treated alike with either approach.

**Individual Policy Approach:**

Each participating employee is issued an individual policy. The policy will have rates for that employee's age. The employee's spouse will receive a separate individual policy.

Underwriting — there are many approaches:

- Full Underwriting: Each employee is underwritten as though they were an individual purchaser.
- Simplified Issue: This approach offers a company more liberal underwriting than an individual buyer could get, yet sill underwrites the major conditions such as stroke.
- Guaranteed Minimum Offer: The insurance company makes every eligible employee the offer of a minimum long-term care insurance plan. Sometimes this involves a higher premium and/or a lower benefit plan than initially applied for.
- Modified Guaranteed Issue: This is typically an almost guaranteed issue plan involving one or more simple health questions. For example: Can you perform all of the activities of daily living? Sometimes this approach is used for spouses of employees in large firms where the employee has been granted guaranteed issue.
- Guaranteed Issue: The employee who is actively at work is guaranteed to receive the benefits applied for, because the underwriting is waived.

Rates: The common approach is to make the rates lower than the street rates. This usually entails a 5% or 10% discount. The most recent trend is to combine the discounted rate with some simplified underwriting. The rates are guaranteed renewable and rest on the claims experience of the LTCI company, rather than the experience of a particular employer or industry.

**Master Policy/Certificate Approach:**

The employer is issued a master policy with certificates for each employee.

Underwriting: Same approaches as the Individual Policy Approach.

Rates: The rates can be different for each group. Experience is generally pooled; however, very large cases can be experience rated on their own.

Portability: The rules are the same for either approach. LTCI must be fully portable.

# IV. Affinity Group/Association LTCI Plan

**Eligible Insured:**

- Persons having a membership in an association or other organization, their spouses, and sometimes their extended family.

**Eligible Groups:**

- The group must be formed for purposes other than obtaining long-term care insurance.
- There must be by-laws and a formal organization structure.
- The affinity group must endorse the plan.

**Uses:**

In return for the endorsement, many LTCI companies grant a premium discount for enrolling members. Typical examples of affinity groups are:

- Credit Unions
- Chambers of Commerce
- College Alumni Groups
- Professional Associations
- Trade Associations

Note: Some insurance companies may exclude one or more of these groups from their program.

**Advantages of Affinity Group/Association LTCI Plan**

- Members of the affinity group or association can receive a premium reduction.

- The endorsement is recognized as a value-added membership benefit, a good third-party introduction of the agent to members at large.
- It allows the LTCI agent the ability to work with groups of prospects.

Note: There are usually no underwriting concessions applied to these plans.

## V. Employer-Based Voluntary LTCI Plan

Employer-based voluntary LTCI plans are available for groups of two or more. Some state exceptions may apply. Generally, the smaller plans allow a premium discount, whereas the larger plans allow underwriting concessions.

Rate Discounts: Generally 5% or 10% (sometimes referred to as List Bill Discounts).

### Advantages of Employer-Based Voluntary LTCI Plans:

- The employee gets a special premium discount which also applies to their family.
- The employee receives the advantages of the employer's research through the broker in selecting a reputable LTCI carrier.
- The broker receives entrée to the employer's employees.

### Disadvantages of Employer-Based Voluntary LTCI Plans:

- If the plan is not properly implemented and results in poor enrollment, it can cause embarrassment for the employer, agent, and benefits person at the company.
- The employer may be hesitant to send employees to enrollment meetings.
- (Agent Only) Most LTCI companies require the agent to participate in the premium discount by reducing commissions.

Underwriting Concessions: Voluntary LTCI plans can give a wide range of underwriting options from no concessions at all to full guaranteed issue for the employee and his or her spouse. Almost always, the concessions are based on the size of the group.

**Advantages of Underwriting Concessions:**
- The employer is hesitant to deny coverage to handicapped employees.
- Enrollment percentages are helped due to simplicity.
- The proposed plan is more appealing to the employer because most employers expect underwriting concessions with their voluntary benefit plans.

**Disadvantages of Underwriting Concessions:**
- Carrier selection can be limited.

## VI. Core Benefit LTCI Plan

Definition: The employer agrees to pay all or a portion of the premium for a base benefit LTCI plan for eligible employees and, if desired, the employee's spouse.

Uses: The use of the word "core" means that the employer provides the basic benefit and the employee can choose to purchase extra benefit (or "fruit") to enhance the core. There are two ways for the employer to provide the core benefit:

1. Defined Contribution Plan: The employer selects a monthly contribution amount to be made available to each employee who participates. The amount of the contribution is usually enough for the younger employees to purchase a minimum plan. It will usually never cover the costs for a minimum plan for the older employees.
2. Defined Benefit Plan: The employer selects a minimum benefit plan and pays the premium for all eligible employees.

Under either approach, the employee can buy up to a higher benefit.

Underwriting: The core benefits are usually issued on a guaranteed basis. The buy-up amounts are available either on an evidence basis or with no underwriting evidence if the employee stays within certain defined classes. Typically, the larger the group, the more liberal the underwriting. Eligible spouses and extended family are usually subject to full underwriting.

**Advantages of the Core Benefit LTCI Plan:**

- The employer is assured of a good enrollment since most employees will take advantage of the employer's offer to pay all or a large part of the premium.
- Employer costs are held to a minimum, since the core benefit is usually quite modest.
- The employer's employees receive liberal underwriting because of the high enrollment percentages.

**Disadvantages of the Core Benefit LTCI Plan:**

- This type of plan does not maximize the LTCI tax advantages if the employer pays $25 per month. For example, if the employee, with $150 of monthly premium (employee and spouse) is paying $150 per month with after-tax dollars, the net $125 paid by the employee will probably not qualify for a medical deduction under Form 1040 since the employee most likely will not exceed the 7.5% of adjusted gross income needed for the medical deduction under the current tax code
- Currently these plans do not qualify for Section 125 plans.
- The employer is contributing and this is an expense not existing under the non-contributory plan.

## VII. Executive Benefit LTCI Plan

Definition: The employer selects who will participate and pays the premium for those employees and, if desired, for the employee's spouse.

Tax Effects:
  1. If C-Corporation:
  • Deductible to the corporation.
  • Premium not attributable to the employee's income
  • Benefits are tax free.
  2. If Partnership, Sole Proprietor, or Sub S shareholder (over 2%):
  • 60%* of premium is deductible in 2000 as a business expense.
  • The amount paid by the employer is income to the employee.
  • Benefits are tax free.

| *Deductibility | Schedule | Age | Premium |
|---|---|---|---|
| 2000-2001 | 60% | 40 or Less | $220.00 |
| 2002 | 70% | 41-50 | $410.00 |
| 2003 and after | 100% | 51-60 | $820.00 |
| | | 61-70 | $2,200.00 |
| | | 71 & Older | $2,750.00 |

**Advantages of the Executive Benefit LTCI Plan:**
  • The employer can "pick and choose" those eligible.
  • Best way for the "owner(s)" to use corporate dollars for personal benefit.
  • Can shop for premium discounts and, if big enough, underwriting concessions.

(A specimen long-term insurance plan document follows in the appendix.)

**Disadvantages of the Executive Benefit LTCI Plan:**
  • Possible resentment from those employees not included.

- Others in the company who might be interested on a voluntary basis are not given a chance to participate unless the employer agrees to a voluntary enrollment.

Note: Professional corporations are excellent candidates for Executive Benefit LTCI Plans. A Professional Corporation (PC) can be either a C-Corporation or a Sub S Corporation. In regard to treatment of LTCI premium tax deductibility and owner/employees, the C-corporation enjoys a 100% tax deduction. A C-corporation files Form 1120, whereas a Sub S files Form 1120S.

## VIII. The Executive Limited Pay LTCI Plan

The amount of premium an employer pays for LTCI for an employee and the employee's spouse is not limited for a C-Corporation. This has created a wonderful new executive benefit whereby the corporation can pay more than a normal annual premium and deduct the higher premium. Since the premium paid is not attributable to the employee, this idea leverages high economic benefit to the employee and employee's spouse.

Plan Types: Typically, the employer has three ways of purchasing a limited pay plan:

- Single Premium — one very large premium.
- 10-Pay — 10 payments.
- To age 65 — Premiums are increased so that the plan is fully paid at the employee's age 65.

And, of course, once the policy is fully paid up, the LTCI company cannot implement a rate increase on that policy. It is, in effect, a noncancelable long-term care insurance policy.

A 65-year-old executive who is retiring is an excellent example of this concept. One LTCI company charges 19 times the annual premium for a 65-year-old. The single premium for a $2,000 annual premium plan is then $38,000. If a 65-year-old spouse is included in the plan, the single premium is $76,000. The company deducts the premium in full under IRC section 162 and the $76,000 is not considered income to the executive!

The company and the employee need to follow a few rules:

- Make certain the corporation has not retained any interest in the TQ LTC policy (for example: no return of premium to the corporation nor any residual rights to such premium).
- The employee must be a bona fide employee of the corporation.
- The amount of the single premium must be reasonable compensation.

### Advantages of the Executive Limited Pay LTCI Plan:

- No future premium payment.
- No future rate increases.
- Wonderful new executive compensation idea to discuss with large clients.

### Disadvantages of the Executive Limited Pay LTCI Plan:

- Premium is expensive relative to an annual premium plan.
- Limited number of LTCI carriers marketing this benefit.

Note: For companies wishing to include members of their Boards of Directors in the long-term care insurance benefit program, the following rules need to be kept in mind. A board of Director is an independent contractor and not an employee, at least when acting in the capacity as director. As a non-employee he or she is not covered by the tax-favored health benefit plan rules for employees under Sec. 105-106. Premiums could be deductible to the corporation as compensation paid to the director, however, directors will have taxable compensation on any long-term care insurance premium paid on their behalf. The IRC imposes nondiscrimination coverage requirements on employers who adopt Self-Insured Medical Reimbursement Plans under IRC Section 105.

**Worksite Prospecting**

To most people in sales, the Law of Large Numbers can be an intoxicating proposition. I would urge members of MDRT to weigh the pros and cons of engaging a large employer or association group long-term care insurance plan in favor of small employer plans. The first order of your worksite prospecting should be to define the size of the target market you want to serve, and why and how you can maximize your efforts.

A rule of thumb for categorizing by size is:
- Small Employer/Association — 3 to 999 employees/members
- Employer/Association — 1,000 to 4,999 employees/members
- Large Employer/Association — 5,000 to 49,999 employees/members
- Very Large Employer/Association — 50,000 + employees/members

Large and very large groups involve a great deal of time, energy, politics, and expense. At this point in time, the rewards for putting all your eggs in one basket may be too risky, as long as LTCI plans are based on voluntary participation. Results from Large and Very Large plan offerings can be broken down by percentage of employees/members enrolled.

Poor enrollment — 2% to 5%

Average enrollment — 4% to 6%

Good enrollment — 8% to 9%

Excellent enrollment — 10% to 12%

Enrollees typically receive kits through the mail with toll-free numbers to call, or sometimes are exposed to enrollment teams. Large employers deal directly with insurance company hierarchy or through a consultant. Deals are made to set up separate reserve accounts subject to termination agreements. These cases usually begin with lengthy Requests for Information proposals and/or Requests for Proposal. When long-term care insurance reaches the status of an employee benefit paid for by the employer, these cases will be worth fighting tooth and nail for.

In the meantime, don't ever shy away from the chance to talk to an employee or association member about their large group long-term care insurance plan to educate and hand-hold. Let these plans spread the word and raise the consciousness level of long-term care insurance in the workplace and general public. The odds are an independent agent will be able to compete against the large group long-term care insurance plan very effectively. These plans cannot effectively imitate, substitute, or replace an agent, and with an average enrollment of 4% to 6%, there is a large void left for the independent agent to fill.

On the other hand, smaller employer groups offering LTCI to employees and family members, allow agents to reach groups of prospects more efficiently during their working years when premiums can be more affordable. With approximately 24 million small businesses in the U.S., there are plenty of opportunities. To get plan approvals, decision makers in small groups are more accessible and can make unilateral decisions. If the plan is properly implemented, sign ups of 15% to 30% are very achievable. If an employer is only willing to give lip service to the LTCI plan, agents should cease involvement as failure is certain.

Employee education is the key to a successful LTCI program. Twenty years ago, employers faced a major challenge educating employees to understand the necessity to plan for retirement and to capitalize on the value of participating in their 401(k) plan. LTCI represents the new employee benefit education frontier.

**Employer Presentation**
1. Explain the consequences of long-term care to business in general.
2. Establish the need for long-term care in an aging society.
3. Explain how long-term care insurance helps pay for long-term care by professional caregivers.

4. Present proposal of benefits and costs.
5. Secure employer's commitment to support plan implementation:
   a. Employer letter to employees endorsing plan.
   b. Several weeks allowed for the dissemination of educational materials regarding LTC.
   c. Employees allowed and encouraged to take time during the work day to attend worksite meetings.

## Employee Presentation
1. Introductory letters.
2. Payroll stuffers.
3. Table tents placed in common areas.
4. Posters announcing date, time, and place of employee meetings.
5. Worksite meeting:
   a. Introduction of agent or enroller.
   b. Educational video.
   c. Employee enrollment kits.

The National LTC Network worked in excess of two years developing a state-of-the-art small group LTCI plan with guaranteed insurability underwritten by a national carrier. One of the more interesting insights gained in marketing the plan is how broad based a small business can be. With modern technology and the ease of communicating via miniature portable telephones, computers, faxes, satellites, etc., a business can operate from anywhere on the continent. Add to these developments global expansions, mergers, acquisitions, and buy-outs, and a "small" business can be located in several states across the country or grow overnight.

## Extended Family Members: A Unique Benefit

Mass-marketed long-term care insurance holds a unique position in the world of Employer/Association sponsored benefits. Unlike traditional health or life insurance benefits, which are only offered to employees and their immediate family members, LTCI plans can be purchased by extended family members. Depending on the insurance carrier's definition, extended family members can include parents, in-laws, grandparents, brothers, and sisters.

The prime advantage of this extended offering is that any discounts negotiated by the employer on behalf of employees pass on to extended family members. Full underwriting review is applied to this class of business. It's easy to see how benefits return to the employee when a parent who purchased long-term care insurance is about to enter a nursing facility under this option, rather than becoming dependent upon the employee for care or support. That said, have you ever tried talking to your parents about sex, long-term care, or money? In the early 1990s, a son or daughter's concern for their parents' future care could easily have been misunderstood. For example, if the son said, "Mom and Dad, have you thought about nursing home insurance?" Mom heard, "So you want to put me in a nursing home!" and Dad heard, "So you want my money!"

Today, parents are much more aware of the issues surrounding long-term care, which helps when children initiate the afore-mentioned conversation. But one of the best ways to eliminate the stigma attached to such a conversation is when a son or daughter can say, "Mom and Dad, my employer is sponsoring a long-term care insurance plan to all employees at a 10% premium discount, and guess what? The discount is available to our parents also! I brought some of the brochures that were handed out at the employee information meetings for you to review."

This is a wonderful means of opening a dialogue with parents on the subject of long-term care. Who knows, the son or daughter might be relieved to learn their parents have already purchased policies! The relief would be especially welcomed in situations where parents live hundreds of miles away or in distant states.

Because we live in a mobile society, it might be a challenge for an agent to represent an employee's extended family member. However, members of the National LTC Network are able to solve this challenge through regional offices. Members of MDRT have developed universal relationships during annual meetings that may also prove to be of assistance.

Expanding the marketing of long-term care insurance into the worksite will extend coverage to actively at-work employees, spreading the risk over a generally younger and healthier population. The federal government and several states have begun, or are in the process of, offering private, nonsubsidized long-term care insurance to their employees. In addition to shifting funding for the cost of care from public sources to private insurance, government hopes to serve as a "model employer," and spur private employers to follow suit.

**LTCI Via the Internet**

Most of the major insurance companies now have Web sites for their agents and consumers. These Web sites provide information on a company's history, financial ratings, product portfolio, and style of distribution. The sales of insurance products over the computer are in a developmental mode for most insurance companies. Insurance lines that are considered commodities, such as automobile insurance and Medicare Supplement insurance, are more adaptable to internet purchasing. Certain lines of insurance are more easily sold than bought. People generally tend to shy away from the subject of their own mortality or morbidity. Most people, for instance would substitute, "If I die" for "When I die."

Denial often makes it more difficult for an insurance agent or financial planner to focus on the harsher risks in life as they pertain to one's state of being, family, or business. The planner assists the prospect in verbalizing and visualizing the financial and psychological implications of these risks and suggests solutions to lessen the impact. It's unlikely that computers can be effectively utilized to focus attention on these difficulties. But we are undeniably part of what's being hailed as the Information Age, and change is not only certain, but rapid. The more informed society becomes, the more decisions will be made independently.

Close to 30% of Internet users are age 45 and older. Almost 30% of the seniors using the Internet have purchased over-the-counter drugs online. Some purchases have created growing controversy around issues of safety. There is also increasing debate over the necessity of laws to regulate Internet marketing.

The passage of the Electronic Signatures in Global & National Commerce Act has granted legal status to e-signatures, as a written signature on a legal document. In addition, a requirement specific to insurance mandates insurance companies to send premium lapse notices by U.S. Mail in paper form.

There is general agreement among insurers that rules and regulations need to be established for handling the following issues:

- Passwords used in communicating.
- Security of records.
- Privacy of personal and medical information.
- History of insurance purchases.
- Response to consumer requests.

Life insurance policies have withstood the test of time. How the insurance industry reaches this goal over policy language requiring "certificates," "seals," "notaries," "in writing,"etc., in regard to Internet business remains to be seen. The debates represent several points of view. What is to become the point of view acceptable to all is still to be determined.

The National Association of Insurance Commissioners is studying the new Act seeking to determine its suitability for insurance matters under the McCarren Ferguson Act that stipulates "states shall regulate the business of insurance." Meanwhile, California incorporates some of the Act's provisions in its laws, and the New York State Department of Insurance has drafted its own Internet regulations, as well as fifteen other states in between.

**Marketing LTCI Over the Internet at the Worksite**

A growing number of employers are communicating with their employees over the Internet, especially in the area of employee benefits. This method of communication, education, and solicitation at the worksite can be very efficient and productive when dealing with large employers or associations. When an employer/association has chosen a LTCI company for its employees/members, as well as one, two, or three core benefit plans, the person targeted at the other end of the computer screen is able to focus on making informed decisions and execute them quickly.

∽

# CHAPTER 7

## Do Not Abandon the Uninsurable!

Usually, people with enough money can afford most anything their hearts and pocketbooks desire. Insurance involves risk, and for some forms of insurance, no matter how high the risk, insurance companies can establish a commensurate premium.

Take, for example, people with poor driving records who need automobile insurance. Points may have been assigned to their driver's license records for reckless driving, moving violations, or accidents. As long as the state hasn't lifted their licenses, insurance is available in a special high premium program. I am reminded of the time when the wife of a policyholder came to the agency one day to pay her husband's auto insurance premium. She stated she didn't remember the insurance company's name, but she knew her husband "was in the cess-pool," when what she should have said was, "he is in the assigned risk pool."

Some people cannot buy long-term care insurance, or for that matter, life or disability income insurance, regardless of how much money they have. They can't because, with the exception of receiving a guaranteed issue policy under an employee benefit, insurance companies use application responses to determine if certain pre-existing health conditions disqualify an applicant from purchasing coverage. Obviously, in the eyes of underwriters, there are people more disposed to going on claim because of their health history. Some people are born with uninsurable conditions. Others may develop one or more of these during their lifetimes. This chapter will address options that may provide resources to care for uninsurable individuals, or a mechanism for preserving assets for spouses. First, Ruth Hallenbeck, of CFK LIFE Plans, addresses the issues of insurability and underwriting.

Being uninsurable, individuals or couples become self insureds by default. Eventually, many self-insured persons will exhaust their ability to pay for care. In the process, among married couples, the remaining spouse is unable to maintain his or her standard of living. It may be difficult to tell who the biggest loser is. When assets are depleted, the spouse in need of care loses freedom of choice and freedom of access. A study conducted by Harvard University reveals that 80% of single people and 55% of married people become impoverished within one year of entering a nursing home.

One of the biggest challenges to face an agent or financial planner who assists clients with long-term care planning is dealing with a couple where only one spouse is insurable. Agents in this situation might recommend a team approach and have their client engage the services of an Elder Law attorney. In general, Elder Law attorneys concentrate on specialized issues, such as preserving spousal assets to cover nursing home care. In the absence of long-term care insurance for one who is uninsurable, an Elder Law attorney may be the next line of defense. Ideally, look for an ELA who, for the past three years, has devoted a great percentage of their practice to Medicare and Medicaid cases. Following Ruth's discourse on underwriting, she will also share her insight on the relationship between uninsured long-term care, Medicaid, and the Medicaid Trust.

Uninsureds faced with paying for long-term care learn soon enough that their C.D.'s, stocks, bonds, mutual funds, and life insurance remain vulnerable to spending down. This chapter discusses methods for converting some of these assets to benefit the spouse who is well and/or the person in need of care.

**Underwriting for Long-Term Care Insurance (Hallenbeck):**

**ADL's and IADL's**

An applicant for long-term care insurance must have the ability to function independently without assistance from another person or mechanical device in the performance of the Activities of Daily Living (ADL's) and the Instrumental

Activities of Daily Living (IADL's) to be considered for long-term care insurance. The activities of daily living are such things as bathing, dressing, toileting, transferring, continence, mobility, and eating. The instrumental activities of daily living are such things as housekeeping, meal preparation, shopping, handling finances, getting to and from a doctor, and taking medications. The applicant also must be cognitively sound, without signs of forgetfulness, confusion, or memory loss.

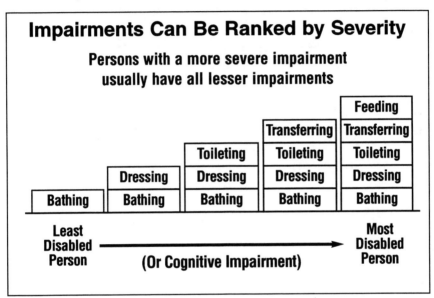

## Misconceptions

There are many misconceptions about the underwriting of individuals applying for long-term care insurance. All too often, people have told their agents that they could never qualify for long-term care insurance because of some medical condition. While there are pre-existing conditions that are uninsurable, there are many others that still can be considered. If the condition is stabilized and is not expected to progressively deteriorate, or in the case of certain surgeries, if the condition has been corrected, repaired, or removed, and a specified period of time for adjustment has elapsed with full recovery, there is a good chance for a favorable underwriting outcome. If surgery is recommended or pending, the application must be postponed until after the surgery is completed with full recovery and the appropriate adjustment period met. Insurers realize that people in the middle and later years of life may not have a perfect medical history, but they do require that the people they insure be in *relatively good* health. Lifestyle also plays an important part in an underwriting decision. People with chronic conditions who maintain a physically and socially active life are often more determined and able to overcome physical impairments and continue to be active and productive, as opposed to those who are less active, more isolated, and less inclined to rise above their afflictions. Positive consideration is often given to an active lifestyle which can sometimes offset other adverse factors. Activities could include working regularly at a job, engaging in gardening, golfing, skiing, hiking, artistic, and/or theatrical endeavors, or involvement with church or volunteer programs.

Conversely, many people, and agents, think that a person is a good candidate for long-term care insurance because they have just been favorably underwritten for life insurance. Underwriting for long-term care insurance differs considerably from the traditional underwriting criteria used in the life insurance industry with which we have all become familiar. Where life insurance underwriters are concerned about *mortality*, long-term care insurance underwriters are concerned about *morbidity*. Because someone has just been issued a life insurance policy with a preferred risk classification does not necessarily mean that the same person can qualify for long-term care insurance. For instance, a person who has crippling arthritis but is otherwise in good health may have a normal life expectancy, but may live the later years of life in a nursing facility, needing assistance with the activities of daily living. The arthritic condition would adversely affect morbidity but not mortality.

### The Agent as Underwriter

The agent, in many ways, becomes a field underwriter for long-term care insurance. Applications must be taken in person. At the outset, the agent must evaluate whether the insurance is appropriate for the client. Does the client have enough assets to protect or enough income to afford the premium? If there are valuable assets but low income, are there children who could pay the premium and protect their inheritance, as well as provide for good long-term care for their parents? Is the client in relatively good health?

The agent needs to observe the client and be aware of any condition that could affect underwriting. Does the client's build fall within acceptable limits for height and weight? Does the client have difficulty moving around; use a cane, walker, wheelchair, or other aid; have difficulty with speech, attention, or understanding; or exhibit any signs that might indicate a rateable or uninsurable condition? Since medical exams and blood tests are not routinely required, and, in fact, are rarely requested by an underwriter, it is necessary for agents to question their clients thoroughly about their medical history and record all pertinent medical information on the application. Be sure to include the 4 "D's" for each condition:

Diagnosis: name of the condition;

Dates: of the diagnosis and treatment;

Dosage: names, amounts, and frequency of any medication prescribed and taken;

Doctors: names, addresses, and phone numbers of all physicians involved.

Underwriting guides are available from all companies that market long-term care insurance. These guides usually contain a height and weight chart. They also list an array of medical conditions and medications with instructions on how to determine the probable underwriting outcome for each. By consulting the underwriting guide, the agent is better able to determine the insurability of the client and to provide pertinent information to assist the underwriter in assessing the risk.

The exception to this would be an employee group contract where there may be an open enrollment period with guaranteed issue for the employee. Other family members may be eligible to apply under the group plan, but they will be fully underwritten with no guaranteed issue.

**Underwriting Procedures**

We have already stated that medical exams and blood tests are rarely required. What are the tools that an underwriter uses to evaluate the insurability of an applicant? After reviewing the information supplied by the agent on the application, the underwriter decides whether additional information needs to be ordered. This is accomplished by several means:

**Personal History Interview (PHI):** This is a telephone interview of the applicant to verify and clarify information on the application. The interviewer also will be listening for clarity of thought and any indication of confusion or memory loss. Some companies require these routinely and others, at the discretion of the underwriter.

**Attending Physician's Statement (APS):** Medical records and office notes are supplied by the primary care physician and sometimes by hospitals and specialists who may have more complete or detailed information. Some companies require these routinely and others, at the discretion of the underwriter.

**Face to Face Assessment:** This is a personal (face to face) interview conducted by a trained professional. The interviewer observes the applicant for ability to function independently, gathers information on medical history and prescribed medications, and conducts a simple cognitive and memory test. This test consists of the ability to recall the names of family members and well-known people in the news or in history, such as George Washington or President Clinton, as well as the ability to use a list of words, such as "house" or "car" or "flower," in sentences and then to remember the words later in the interview. These assessments are required routinely for people over a specific age, but may be ordered for any applicant.

After all information has been gathered and the risk assessed, the underwriter makes the decision to accept or decline the applicant for insurance. At this point, the importance of a cover letter from the agent may play a part in the decision. If the agent can provide information attesting to a physically and socially active lifestyle, the balance may be tipped in favor of a positive decision.

**Underwriting Philosophies**

There are different underwriting philosophies employed by the various companies which market long-term care insurance. Some offer discounted (preferred) rates to nonsmoking people who are in exceptionally good health. Some companies underwrite strictly on an accept or decline basis, while others may accept substandard risks by limiting benefits and/or by charging a higher than standard premium. Most companies offer spousal discounts, assuming that married partners care for each other as long as possible, thus delaying the need for formal or professional care. Some will even offer discounts to nonmarried people living together in a committed relationship or to related adults, such as brothers and sisters, sharing a home. While all companies take into consideration overall health, age, build, past and present medical conditions, cognitive ability, use of medications, functional capacity, and lifestyle, the weighting given these various factors in the underwriting decision differs from one company to another.

Pre-existing conditions such as Alzheimer's disease, Parkinson's disease, AIDS, multiple sclerosis, severe arthritis, or osteoporosis, or certain combinations of conditions such as diabetes and circulatory problems would not be insurable by **any** company.

However, there are some applicants who cannot meet the underwriting criteria of some companies but would be accepted by others, perhaps with a rated and/or limited policy. Many companies require that the modal premium be paid with the application. When the full modal premium is submitted with the application, the application date is the date on which the applicant is eligible for coverage unless otherwise requested on the application. If it is determined by underwriting that the applicant was insurable on that date, then the insurance protection will take effect as of that date. Should the applicant become uninsurable one day after the date they become eligible and approved, their coverage will be in force and remain so for as long as premiums are paid. When amounts less than the full modal premium or no money is submitted with the application, then there is no insurance coverage until after underwriting approval and full modal premium has been paid.

Underwriting for long-term care insurance is not an exact science. There is little historical data to rely on for claims experience and pricing. Companies have analyzed the available data. Through simulations and actuarial formulas, they have determined criteria that they believe will be accurate in determining their risk in providing long-term care insurance to their policyholders. Major carriers expect their pricing projections on each plan offered to be accurate for approximately twenty years.

Although medical exams are not routinely required, there are always exceptions to that rule. Over an eight-year period, we have had two exceptions. In one case, a gentleman applicant stated that he was in good health and, except for getting annual flu shots from a senior center, had not seen a doctor in over forty years, since he was discharged from the army. The insurer decided that after forty years, it was high time this man had a complete physical check up and declared he would not be considered for long-term care insurance unless he agreed to have a doctor's exam at the insurer's expense. The gentleman complied. The applicant not only passed the exam with flying colors, but he liked the doctor so much that he decided to get regular checkups from then on with the doctor.

In another situation where a medical exam was required by the insurer, a woman who was taking medication for a heart condition was having her prescriptions renewed but had not been given regular monitoring checkups, and in fact, had not seen her doctor in several years. The underwriter required a checkup, this time at the applicant's expense. The doctor found that her blood pressure was extremely and dangerously elevated and her medications needed to be changed. In this case, satisfying an underwriting requirement may have prevented a serious problem and prolonged this woman's life.

The importance of submitting premium with the application for long-term care insurance was demonstrated by a situation we encountered several years ago. A husband and wife in their early 50s applied for long-term care insurance and paid the full modal premium with the application. They were both in superb health, and after full underwriting were issued preferred policies about four weeks after the application was taken. Upon delivery of the policies to the insureds, the agent learned that the husband had suddenly had a stroke, just a few days before, without any detectable previous warning signs. Fortunately, he made a quick and full recovery without any residual impairments, but if he had required assistance with two activities of daily living and rehabilitation over a long period of time, his long-term care policy was in force to pay for his home care or nursing facility care. If no money had been submitted with the application, the policy would not have been put into force and chances are remote that he would be able to purchase a long-term care insurance policy, at least until a period of time had passed and the stability of his condition had been determined.

## Medicaid Trusts

### What is a Trust?

What is a Trust? By definition, a Trust is a legal instrument holding title to property placed in the Trust by one party (the grantor) to be administered by another (trustee) for the benefit of another (the beneficiary). Trusts are very useful legal tools and are widely used in estate and tax planning, to protect the interests of minors and the disabled, and for a variety of other private and business applications.

In recent years, a whole new area of law practice known as Elder Law has emerged. This practice has spawned the creative use of Irrevocable Trusts to qualify people for Medicaid benefits in the event they should require nursing facility care in the future. Informational seminars for the aging and elderly population have become the norm. These address the necessity to prepare for participant's final days with properly drawn wills, health care proxies, and durable powers of attorney. Elder Law attorneys also advise their clients on preparing themselves for the possibility of needing long-term care and protecting their assets from depletion by the high costs of this care.

## Costs of Nursing Facility and Home Care

The costs for care in a skilled nursing facility can range anywhere from $90 to $400 per day depending upon geographic location and an array of other factors. That is an annual range of $33,000 to $140,000. This may cover room, board, and basic nursing services. Medications, therapies, physicians, special equipment, services, and transportation incur additional charges. Alternate care facilities such as assisted living, board and care homes, Alzheimer's facilities, etc., usually charge a somewhat lower daily rate but primarily provide custodial and social environments. They also have higher staff-to-patient ratios and are not equipped or staffed to care for residents who require higher levels of care.

Costs for receiving care at home have an even broader range than facility care, again depending upon the level and amount of care required and its geographic location. A Certified Home Health Aide may cost $10 to $20 per hour, while a registered nurse or therapist may cost $45 to $75 per hour or more. An aide providing intermittent care for 8 hours per week could cost about $5,000 annually, while a registered nurse providing round the clock care, seven days a week, could cost $400,000 annually.

## Who Pays?

Currently, only 7% to 10% of eligible Americans carry long-term care insurance that pays for these services. More policies are being purchased daily, but in the meantime, 93% of our population must pay for long-term care costs with their own resources. If they are without resources, then Medicaid, the jointly funded federal/state program that provides health care to the indigent, will pay nursing facility and related expenses. Given the high cost of long-term care and the fact that 50% of people who reach age 70 will need care, it's no wonder seniors seek ways to protect their hard-earned retirement nest eggs from being devoured by a long-term care event in their own lives.

This chapter is dedicated to people whose health renders them uninsurable and others who depend on Medicaid Trust planning strategies because they cannot afford premiums. When a Medicaid Trust is implemented, clients will want an attorney who is experienced in Elder Law and is well versed in the drafting of trusts, so that the client's strategies conform to rules interpretations in their specific jurisdictions.

A great number of prosperous Americans are putting the burden of the cost of their long-term care on our publicly financed welfare system by making themselves Medicaid eligible when they could afford to pay their own way or afford the LTCI premiums. The very funds they have saved to guarantee quality of life and a comfortable environment in later years become no longer available to them if those later years include the need for long-term care.

**When the Payer of Last Resort Becomes the Payer of First Choice**

Many people who become convinced that transferring wealth to become eligible for Medicaid is a good idea ultimately discover that, by protecting their assets for someone else, they have drastically limited their own options and choices for long-term care. For instance, the level of Medicaid reimbursement for Assisted Living facilities and Alzheimer's centers is so low that these types of institutions seldom accept Medicaid residents. Most skilled nursing facilities accept Medicaid recipients now, but may have a limited number of Medicaid beds and may have long waiting lists of people ready to fill them. Those facilities with large numbers of Medicaid residents find they cannot provide an optimum quality of care on Medicaid funding, which is far lower than private pay rates. This often drives privately paying patients to the better facilities where larger numbers of privately paying residents provide funding for better quality care. Sometimes the only Medicaid openings available are some distance from relatives and friends with whom the resident would like to maintain contact. Home care, which is preferred by most people when possible, is difficult to get via our overburdened welfare system. If the cost of providing home care approaches 90% of the cost of a residential facility, then a facility must be used. All in all, much of the freedom to choose how and where you will be cared for is lost to people on Medicaid. Medicaid was designed to be a safety net for those who lack the means to provide long-term care for themselves. It was never intended to be an entitlement for a prosperous middle class.

## Applying for Medicaid

Applying for Medicaid can be an exercise in research and perseverance. Records of all assets, purchases, and financial transactions (going back at least three years) must be provided. Some of the documents required are birth certificates, marriage certificates, death certificates of spouses, deeds to all properties owned including cemetery lots, automobile registrations, driver's licenses, social security cards, bank statements for every account going back every month for at least the last three years, records of stocks, bonds, annuities, notes, etc. Just when you think you have provided every private document you own, there always seems to be something else that's needed. This process has to be updated annually with new documentation. To complicate matters, one often does not deal with the same caseworker in the Medicaid agency. Alongside lessons in humility, frustration can be the name of the game when applying for Medicaid.

## The Future of Government Funded Programs

How sure can we be of what Medicaid laws will look like in the future? With budgetary pressures to make cuts in our welfare costs, and with the added burden of an aging baby boomer population, it seems highly likely that there will be changes in Medicaid availability. One researcher predicts that, over the next twenty-five years, the nursing home population will increase by two-thirds, and we know that for every person receiving care in a nursing facility, there are four others receiving care at home. How long can we, the taxpayers, continue to pay the escalating costs of a government program designed for the poor and being used indiscriminately by the financially comfortable and wealthy? It seems certain that people who are making themselves eligible for Medicaid under today's rules may find themselves under much different rules in the future, when they actually need care. If eligibility for benefits is made more stringent or if benefits are reduced, curtailed, or otherwise restricted, this would be tragic for people who had the means to provide quality care for themselves but gave that up to depend on a government-funded welfare program. On the other hand, if healthy, financially responsible persons insure for their own freedom of choice and freedom of access, a system of adequate care can be preserved for people of lesser means, or for those who find themselves in an uninsurable state.

The crusade to campaign for preservation of limited long-term care government resources for the most needy, while at the same time encouraging fiscal long-term care responsibility from those who are young, healthy, and affluent enough, has no greater champion than Stephan A. Moses, President of The Center for Long-Term Care Financing. Those wishing to combine the emotional and practical aspects of long-term care and long-term care insurance planning for the immediate events in our lives, advanced in this book, with a scholarly approach of alarming LTC statistical projections into the future, are encouraged to contact the Center for Long-Term Care Financing, 11418 North East 19th Street, Bellevue, WA 98006, (425) 467-6840, or at htpp://www.centerltc.com.

## A Personal Note
### by S. Larry Feldman

My dad Leo spent his entire career in the insurance business, retiring in 1974 to enjoy the fruits of his labor. Soon after his retirement, my mother's health deteriorated and Dad became her caregiver. He was chief cook and bottlewasher, and a hell of a cook at that! For 18 years, he provided her care until 1992, when Mother suffered a severe stroke. She was totally paralyzed on her left side, lost the sight in one eye and had only partial hearing. Mom was 5' 2" tall and weighed 230 lbs. It took uncommon effort to move her. As much as she wanted to go home, and as much as Dad wanted her home, it was an impossible situation from either a practical or financial standpoint.

The cost of Mom's semiprivate nursing home care in April 1992 was $185 per day for room and board. In simple math terms, that adds up to $5,600 per month or $67,000 per year, not counting the costs of prescription drugs and therapy. After coming to terms with the cost of Mother's care, Dad asked me if there was any way to stop the financial bleeding. I told him, at this point in time, he needed to meet with an Elder Law attorney to discuss the feasibility of a Medicaid Trust. The attorney told Dad he would draft a Medicaid Trust for him, but Dad would have to pay Mother's nursing home bill out of pocket for the next thirty months to get by the "look-back period." Dad's last asset was placed in the Medicaid Trust the final week of June, 1992, when the clock started ticking off the days to get past the "look-back period."

When we left the attorney's office that day, we stopped for coffee and to talk. Even though he had considered all his options and chose the Medicaid Trust, naming me as Trustee, I felt the need to review the trust one more time. Scanning a list of the assets placed in the Irrevocable Medicaid Trust, I pointed out the monthly income generated by the assets he would receive for life. He looked at me and asked, "Is that the allowance you will give me for the rest of my life?"

During my mother's stay, the look-back period for the Medicaid Trust went from thirty months to thirty-six months. Fortunately, our family's trust was grandfathered under the old 30 month rule. On April 1, 1995, my mother was eligible to apply for Medicaid. From April 1992 to March 1995, Dad had paid out over $200,000 of their life savings for Mother's care. (He had devoted a career of helping others to shift their risks to an insurance company. Unfortunately, Mother became uninsurable before she had the option to purchase a meaningful long-term care insurance policy.)

I scheduled an appointment with the Welfare Department to apply for Medicaid on the first business day of April 1995. I informed my father of the appointment and offered to go with him, or go myself. He said he had a dentist appointment at 8:30 that morning and he would appreciate it if I went alone. Thank God he couldn't go. At the Welfare Department, I had to pass through a metal detector at a security checkpoint manned by an armed deputy sheriff. Standing inside the waiting room with many other people applying for Welfare, I could sense I looked out of place. I could only speculate what my father's reaction would have been had he been with me. Probably he would have grabbed me by the arm and said "Let's leave!"

The application was approved by mid-May, retroactive to April 1st. Dad and I try to meet every Thursday morning at a local diner for breakfast. At our first breakfast following Medicaid's approval Dad said, "I can't sleep, I don't feel right". I froze and said, "What's the matter, Dad?" He repeated "I can't sleep, I don't feel right." "They know!" "Who knows what?" I asked. "When I go to the nursing home and walk down the halls, they know we are on welfare," he said. After spending over $200,000 for his wife's long-term care, the trust that allowed him to hold onto his remaining assets was now causing him to feel a great loss of dignity. What seemed helpful thirty months before now left him feeling helpless.

There is an old Jewish saying, "When a father helps his son, they both smile. When a son has to help his father, they both cry." At that moment, I wanted to cry. Since the laws affecting Medicaid Trusts have changed again to a sixty-month look-back period, there will be many tears shed by many families. My mother passed away in the nursing home December 3, 1995, a full twelve months longer than the national average of two and a half years.

During Mother's Medicaid qualification period, my father purchased a long-term care insurance policy after he satisfied a waiting period due to some pre-existing health history. Some financial advisors might have asked, "Leo, you've taken steps to qualify for Medicaid, why would you buy a long-term care insurance policy?"

The answer to that question can best be answered by an event that took place during August 1999. Dad was lying in a hospital bed too weak to walk and hardly able to talk when he mustered enough energy to ask, "Is that long-term disability (his words at the moment for LTC) policy current?" I responded "Do you mean is the premium paid to date?" He replied, "Yes." "Dad, the premium is paid." Then he said, "That means if I'm going to a nursing home I get to choose which one I'm going to." "Right again, Dad." At one of the most significant crossroads of our lives, for the next minute or so, neither one of us spoke another word.

## Next Best Options

### Pre-Paid Home Care Services

A survey of insurance carriers reveals that 20% to 30% of the applications for long-term care insurance are not approved. Other than poor health, some factors which influence this percentile include lack of agents' knowledge when completing an application, conservative underwriting, and aggressive tactics within the sales branches of some insurance companies.

Some companies, whether insurance related or not, are courting people who have been rejected for long-term care insurance. The pitch is to provide pre-paid services for home care, as long as these people do not have a terminal illness at the time of application, or reside in a hospital or nursing home. The services are nonmedical, and performed by someone other than a doctor, hospital, or therapist. Pre-existing conditions are covered after the waiting period and subscriber's services are based on a plan of care issued by a doctor, RN, LPN, or medical social worker. Services are purchased in blocks of days from thirty to 360, and in bands of hours, from four to twenty-four.

Services likely to be provided in the home are:

| | | |
|---|---|---|
| Cooking | Eating | Bathing |
| Dressing | Toileting | Grooming |
| Shopping | Laundry | Cleaning |
| Taking Medication | Mobility | Transportation |
| Care for pets | Make phone calls | Read to subscribers |

On its face, this program appears to be a viable alternative for those refused long-term care insurance. The companies representing the pre-paid home care service program have designs on marketing them through insurance agents. A word of caution to agents: Even though the programs have been conceived as pre-paid home care services and NOT filed as a plan of insurance, some state insurance departments may look askance at this perception.

**Annuities**

In the mid 1990s, the Health Care Financing Administration (HCFA) apparently granted certain annuity transactions immunity, as assets which are not subject to Medicaid spend-down rules. When an uninsured client who has assets and needs long-term care is faced with admission to a nursing home, an annuity may help to protect a portion of those assets from Medicaid. The strategy is to convert assets which are subject to Medicaid "spend down," and use them to create an income stream for the community spouse. I have dubbed this strategy the "Medicaid Annuity Fire Drill." The uninsured couple is faced with the question of which assets Medicaid views as "exempt" and which are "non-exempt." Exempt assets are the assets a couple is allowed to keep, i.e., residence, car, personal belongings, a small paid-up life insurance policy and burial fund. Medicaid considers all other assets as non-exempt and available to spend down for the care of the spouse in a nursing facility. Sometimes (the key word being time), with a great deal of knowledge about the Medicaid system, a non-exempt asset can be converted to an "unavailable" asset. This may be the case with the purchase of a single premium immediate annuity, converting liquid assets into a stream of income.

The goal is to have the community spouse buy an immediate annuity, prior to when the institutionalized spouse enters the nursing facility. The annuity must be irrevocable and non-assignable with regular or periodic payments of principal and interest extending to the actuarial life expectancy of the person covered. If done properly, the purchase of an immediate annuity by the owner of the policy does not constitute a transfer for value. The window of opportunity for this method of planning is always very narrow, coming at a time of high emotional, financial, and mental stress. The period for dotting the "i's" is fraught with minefields.

Following are several minefields of which to be aware:

- Life expectancy tables established by Social Security Administration (SSA), under Kassebaum/Kennedy and OBRA '93 Act must be used. These tables are different than the payout table of many insurers.
- The standard insurer annuity contract is assignable. If the annuity contains a "free look" period and the "free look" period rolls into the period of institutionalization or during the Medicaid application process, Medicaid would consider the asset available and demand that it be cashed in. The annuity is disqualified and benefits are recoverable if the annuity contains any rights of joint ownership or survivorship. Federal guidelines to qualify for Medicaid are implemented differently by the states. Social workers within a state interpret state's guidelines differently from county to county.

Note: As this book went to print, word was received of a HCFA letter from the Region IX office to the California Department of Health Services, allowing for recovery of annuity proceeds from a Medicaid recipient's estate at time of death. This information is not intended for Medicaid planning or tax advice. A professional Medicaid planner or tax advisor should be consulted.

### Life Insurance: Viatical Settlements/Accelerated Death Benefits

An uninsured, on account of their uninsurability, also may be terminally ill, and in need of long-term care. If this person owned a life insurance policy and is in the throes of Medicaid spend down, their life insurance policy is in jeopardy of being reduced to a $1,500 paid-up death benefit, and stripped of its cash value by Medicaid. Instead of subjecting the life insurance to spend-down rules, mileage may be gained through a viatical settlement. A viatical settlement occurs when a person who faces life-threatening illness sells his or her life insurance policy's future death benefit to a third party for a cash settlement.

Cash proceeds from viatical settlements may defer or delay Medicaid eligibility. The viatical proceeds can be used to pay for care at home, or equally important, to gain access to a nursing facility of one's choice. The cash released by converting "non-exempt assets" to "exempt assets" could be used to pay off a mortgage, pay medical bills, prepay tax, buy care, etc. The proceeds could also be used to fund the purchase of a long-term care insurance policy for the healthy spouse. In certain cases, lump-sum cash proceeds from a viatical settlement can be placed in a Supplemental Needs Trust to retain Medicaid benefits. Monthly payments of viatical proceeds, matched to the insured's spending needs, can keep cash from accumulating and preserve Medicaid eligibility. Installment payments are not permissible unless the viatical settlement company is a licensed insurance company or a bank, or the viatical settlement company has affected the purchase of an annuity or similar financial instrument issued by a licensed insurance company or bank.

The viatical settlement process typically takes between four and six weeks. A viatical settlement payment ranges between 50% (terminal diagnosis greater than twenty-four months life expectancy) to 90% of the face amount of the policy sold (for terminal diagnosis of less than three months life expectancy.)

The settlement payment is calculated by using a combination of the medical information, and insurance information as well as current interest rates.

The Health Insurance Portability and Accountability Act of 1996 has a provision that declares certain viatical settlement payments free from federal income taxes. Coincidentally, tax form 1099 LTC required by the federal government for recording viatical settlements is the very same form required for recording payment of long-term care insurance benefits. (See Chapter 4.) Some states also have exempted viatical settlement proceeds from state tax liability.

Anyone considering this method of planning should also inquire as to whether or not their life insurance company offers an accelerated death benefit option. Although the accelerated death benefit option is similar to a viatical settlement, there are some distinct differences.

**Viatical Settlements Compared to Accelerated Death Benefits**

| VS | ADB |
|---|---|
| • No risk of lapsed policies | • Policies can lapse |
| • Rapid payment | • Hard to administer |
| • Payout generally 50% to 90% | • Payout generally 50% or less |
| • May cover life expectancies of up to seven years | • Generally covers life expectancies of one year or less |
| • Policies from any life insurance qualify | • Only a limited number of policies qualify |
| • Viatical settlement involve a 3rd party | • ADB between insured and insurer, therefore no additional costs |
| • Viatical settlement involves a third party | • ADB's estimated to be on less than 5% of policies in force |

### Reverse Mortgages

Reverse mortgages, also known as home equity conversions, can be a source of necessary cash to finance uninsured long-term home care expenses. To qualify, homeowners must be at least 62 years of age and have more equity than debt in their residence. In general, larger monthly loan advances are paid to older homeowners. Factors in addition to age are the value of the house and the prevailing interest rate. Reverse mortgages are not practical for seniors who are going to remain in their home for only a short period of time. Seniors entering into a reverse mortgage convert home equity into cash, retaining the right to maintain residency until death or when they make a permanent move from the premises. The loan is repaid when the house is sold. Cash is available in several options: lump sum, monthly payments, a line of credit, or any combination. Homeowners who execute a reverse mortgage retain title to their home. As a result, they are still responsible for taxes, repairs, and maintenance.

On April 6, 2000, the House of Representatives passed a housing bill (H.R. 1776) that will allow elderly homeowners who take out reverse mortgages on their homes to waive the upfront financing fees if they use the money to buy long-term care insurance. If a similar bill is passed in the Senate and signed by the President, this bill may mean a great deal to healthy insurable spouses.

## Long-Term Care Insurance Planning for Parents with Disabled Children

### Supplemental Security Income

Supplemental Security Income and Medicaid are available for disabled children or grandchildren. When healthcare for disabled children can't be gotten elsewhere, Medicaid provides free health care. Money and assets willed to a disabled child can cause loss of SSI and Medicaid benefits.

## Supplemental Needs Trust

Willing an inheritance to a SSI dependent child permits the government to seize assets to pay for current or past board, food, and medical expenses. Instead, consider creating a Supplemental Needs Trust to provide income for the purchase of extras. With proper drafting of either a viatical settlement or a reverse mortgage, eligibility or retention of SSI and Medicaid benefits can be preserved.

Attorneys familiar with OBRA '93 legislation and the Foster Care Independence Act of 1999 should be consulted.

Parents of disabled children need to recognize that these offspring won't be able to care for Mom or Dad when they become elderly, because of their son's or daughter's physical or mental handicap. Neither will the parents be able to buy long-term care insurance for their disabled children. But, if parents aim to keep assets to make them available to meet their disabled children's needs in old age, the parents will be wise to shift the risk for the costs of their own care to a long-term care insurance company, thus preserving assets for the disabled children's use. If the long-term care insurance policy pays benefits for both facility and home care, it may be possible for the parent to remain at home, with the added benefit of not dislodging the disabled child from his or her own familiar surroundings.

## Computer Web Sites, Internet Resources and Newsletters Related to Care Giving

The following resources may be useful for people who need care and/or caregivers.

National Families Caregivers Association (www.nfcacares.org) offers educational materials, resource guides, and newsletters.

Care Guide.com (www.careguide.com) answers questions about caregiving on its website and maintains nationwide lists of child and elder care facilities.

Elder Web (www.elderweb.com) offers information on home and day care. Also provides information broken down by regions and states on hospice programs and shared housing.

Parent Care Advisor addresses a multitude of parent care issues and is published monthly by LPR Publications, 747 Dresher Road, PO Box 980, Horsham, PA 19044-0980. Telephone: (215) 784-0860.

Finally, in a situation where one spouse of a couple is uninsurable, LTCI may still play an important role in the uninsurable's favor. This can be accomplished by the insurable spouse applying for an indemnity policy for more than actual average daily costs of NF care in the area. The strategy is to capitalize on the indemnity policy feature of paying out whatever the stated scheduled daily benefit in the policy is, regardless of actual changes. For example, if area nursing facilities charge $120 a day for care and the insurable spouse applies for $180 in daily benefits, $180 will be paid out if the insurable spouse enters a facility. If the unhealthy spouse has to follow, 50% of that spouse's facility costs will be covered, or money may be applied toward the potential costs of home care for the uninsured.

# CHAPTER 8

## Going On Claim

With thirty-eight years of experience in the insurance business, and holding licenses for all forms of insurance, I have experienced just about every type of claim covered by insurance. Most agents view a claim as their moment to rise to the occasion. It's a time to validate your purpose, wed a client to you forever, and gain referrals.

Insurance policies are legal documents that spell out what is a covered loss and what is not a covered loss. On several occasions, we have challenged a company's handling of a property claim and won reversal or settled on a compromise. Some of the reasons might have been because the adjuster misinterpreted the policy language, or their point of reference was an old policy form, or they didn't read beyond a few initial clauses. When it comes to property and casualty claims, it's more likely the agent will be in a reactive role rather than play a proactive role.

As they say, there are exceptions to the rule. Take for example when my father received a telephone call at home on a Sunday morning from the owner of the Town Tavern. "Hi, Leo, this is Ginger, how are you?" "Fine." "How's Belle and Larry?" "Fine." " Ginger, why are you calling?" "Well, I came in to start cooking sauces and there's a fire down in the boiler room. I called to ask you what should I do?" "Ginger, HANG UP AND CALL THE FIRE DEPARTMENT!!!!!" That's one way a proactive role in a P&C claim.

The long-term care insurance agent is truly in a position to be proactive, and long-term care insurance companies encourage their clients and agents to use a claims hotline. A major advantage to owning a long-term care insurance policy is the assistance a policyholder should expect from their LTCI company at the beginning stages of the inability to perform the ADL's or cognitive impairment. For the average family, unprepared and hard-pressed to deal with the issues of long-term care, this assistance is a wonderful value-added benefit. Many times this advice will permit the insured to stay in their own home longer than they would have without it.

Susan Palla's report on Care Coordinators titled "Understanding Care Management Is First and Foremost" illustrates how seriously the companies view their opportunity to be proactive on behalf of their insureds. Susan, Chairperson of the National LTC Network's Education Committee, originally put together this information for the May 1999 issue of *Broker World* magazine.

National LTC Network member Gene Tapper, MS, NHA, offers advice on what to look for in a nursing home at time of claim. Gene's roles as a former nursing home administrator, a son responsible for selecting his mother's nursing home, and the agent answerable for his mother's long-term care insurance policy, imparts a unique perspective.

This is not a perfect world, and not all situations meet policyholders expectations. Should a claim be denied, most companies will entertain an appeal with a written explanation for the appeal. Every state insurance department has a consumer complaint division. Complaints are taken very seriously and no insurance company wants to be on top of a state's complaint list.

One of the minimum standards of the New York State Private/Public LTCI Partnership is that all denied claims for benefits based on disability are reviewed by the Partnership's Joint Technical Review Board and are subject to Partnership-sponsored binding arbitration. Gregory Belardi, Ph.D., Director of the New York Partnership for Long-Term Care Insurance, said out of the 23,000 active policies, approximately 150 claims have been filed, and none have had to go before the Technical Review Board. According to an industry wide long-term care claimant study by LifePlans, Inc., presented at the 13th Private Long-Term Care Insurance

Conference by Marc A. Cohen, Ph.D., more than 17,000 LTC claims have been filed, from the more than 5 million LTC policies sold.[1] To file a claim, the basic information required is the claimant's diagnosis, a written plan of care by a professional describing the treatment needed, and a list of providers. Claim payments begin following the elimination period, and future premiums will be waived, depending on the definition of Waiver of Premium clause in the contract.

Depending on the nature of the assessment, the insurance company may require that a Supplemental Form be completed as often as monthly by the nursing facility. The insurance company will pay benefits to the insured, unless it receives an assignment of benefits to the nursing facility, signed by the insured.

The firm of AUL Reinsurance Management Services, LLC, has compiled long-term care insurance claims histories from forty-four insurance companies globally, spanning the years 1981 through 1998, examining close to 20,000 claims in the process. From a layman's point of view, some of the more interesting facts and figures are summarized here:

- Leading Causes of Claims:
    - Alzheimer's     – Diabetes         – Nervous System
    - Arthritis         – Hypertension     – Other
    - Cancer           – Injury            – Respiratory
    - Circulatory      – Mental            – Stroke
- Claims with the shortest duration come from cancer. Claims with the longest history are a result of Alzheimer's and central nervous system disorders.
- The most prevalent cause of claims was due to injury from dizziness and osteoporosis, and the least prevalent cause was hypertension.
- Men experienced more claims days for at-home care, while women experienced more claims days in nursing facilities.
- The states noted for the highest incidence of long-term care insurance claims were Connecticut, Illinois, Maine, Missouri, Ohio, and North and South Dakota. The five states with the

greatest average length of claims were Iowa, Kansas, Minnesota, Nebraska, and North Dakota.

• The month with the least incidence of long-term care insurance claims is November. The month that should be designated "Long-Term Care Month" is January.

Typical forms required by LTC insurance companies to submit a claim for benefits:

a. Claimant's Statement (completed by insured or Power of Attorney).

b. Authorization Clause.

c. Plan of Care (completed by physician/licensed health care practitioner). For claims on policies issued after January 1, 1997, be aware of terms "substantial assistance," "2 of 6 ADL's," "period of 90 days," and "substantial supervision for cognitive impairment."

d. Provider's Statement (completed by the nursing facility).

To date, the leading cause of claims in the long-term care insurance industry are from cognitive disorders as shown by frequency, dollars paid, and duration. These claims can last a long time, especially when they begin under the age of 60, as experienced by several carriers.

---

## SAMPLE INDIVIDUAL LONG-TERM CARE PROVIDER'S STATEMENT

You must complete this form in full.
Please print or type all information except where signature is required.
Please return the completed form to the insured or authorized representative.

| Name of Insured | Policy Number | Social Security # |
|---|---|---|

| Name of Provider | Taxpayer ID # | |
|---|---|---|

Address

| Telephone Number | Fax Number |
|---|---|

1. Is your agency licensed by your state to provide care?  ☐ Yes  ☐ No

2. What is your level of licensure?  ☐ Skilled  ☐ Intermediate  ☐ Custodial/Personal

   Other: _____

3. Date Services/Confinement Began: _____

4. Date Services/Confinement Ended: _____

5. Has the patient been absent anytime, including overnight, during this admission?　☐ Yes　☐ No

6. Please indicate the level of assistance your patient needs with the activities of daily living.

| | Independent | Supervision/ Cueing | Physical Assistance | Totally Dependent |
|---|---|---|---|---|
| Eating | | | | |
| Bathing | | | | |
| Dressing | | | | |
| Toileting | | | | |
| Transferring | | | | |
| Continence | | | | |
| Ambulating | | | | |
| Managing Meds | | | | |
| Housekeeping | | | | |
| Meal Preparation | | | | |

7. Indicate the services received by the patient that must be performed by an RN/LPN/LVN:

☐ Oxygen　　☐ Tube Feeding　　☐ Lab Tests　　☐ Catheter Care

☐ Suctioning　☐ Dressings　　　☐ IV　　　　☐ Other: _____

8. Is the patient receiving any of the following services?

☐ Physical Therapy　　　　　☐ Speech Therapy

☐ Occupational Therapy　　　☐ Respiratory Therapy

To be completed by the representative of the facility/home care agency completing this form.

_____

Name (print)　　　　　　　　　Title (print)

_____

Signature　　　　　　　　　　Title　　　　　　　　Date

_____

Comments: _____

_____

_____

Having money available from a long-term care insurance policy to pay for nursing facility care if and when an event strikes can be measured in several ways:

1. Freedom of Choice: be it the nicest, nearest, neatest, most nutritious, etc.
2. Freedom of Access: avoid being on Medicaid waiting list. Medicaid reimbursements are discounted dollars. What nursing home administrator wouldn't welcome a resident at the full private pay rate?
3. The mindset of the insured, who after paying premiums for several years, feels entitled to enter a facility of their choosing.
4. Family members who can discuss placement with dignity.
5. Preparing for the right moment to employ the services of a nursing facility is an emotional and financial turning point in the lives of those involved. When long-term care insurance is in place, the financial stress is peeled away and all considerations turn to locating the most appropriate care.

### Understanding Care Management Is First and Foremost
### by Susan Palla

Care management helps to assure that insureds actually get the level and type of care they need, minimizing the influence of the cost of care decisions.

There are two types of care management. One is basic eligibility assessment, which provides a plan of action or treatment plans. The other is care coordination, which is intended to assist the policyholder and the family with various types of care that are available in the client's area. This insures patient needs are being met. Such services can include finding volunteer care, Meals on Wheels, and helping the client through the red tape. Agents and consumers must be aware that some carriers charge the consumer for this service.

Hadley Reivich, claims manager of Transamerica Occidental Life Insurance Company's long-term care division, states, "At

Transamerica, we believe in the value of care coordination for our long-term care insurance policyholders. Care coordination offers a unique personal service by providing our policyholders with a knowledgeable resource on the difficult questions that arise when long-term care is needed. Our care coordinators help guide the policyholders through the maze of complex options. The key word is coordination. Care coordination is not managed care. This service is intended to help the policyholder and his or her family to make informed decisions. With Transamerica, the care coordinator will assist the policyholder and their physician to develop a service plan. The care coordinator does not restrict a policyholder's access to care, nor do they mandate the use of specific providers or facilities. If for some reason the policyholder is not eligible for benefits in accordance with the terms of the policy, the care coordinator can still act as a resource by locating alternative resources that can be of assistance at the policyholder's own cost."

Ms. Reivich continues, "Care coordination is a beacon to guide the policyholder. After establishing the service plan, the care coordinators will help as little or as much as requested — from setting up appointments to troubleshooting problems. We do not charge the policyholder for care coordination and total policy benefits are not reduced for this service. The policyholder can make the final decision about the care preferred."

Timothy M. Kelly, AIG director of marketing, states his carrier's philosophy as follows: "AIG views care management as an optional benefit to our policyholders that can enable them to preserve their pool of money. Our personal care specialists (PCS) can assist our clients with making decisions regarding care. The use of the personal care specialists is not only optional, but it is free! Charges for the PCS do not come out of the client's pool of money."

Mr. Kelly continues, "The PCS can help to save a policyholder's money. By using the services of a PCS, a client may be able to identify less expensive ways of receiving the care that is needed and preserving their pool of money."

At Fortis Long-Term Care, Gretchen S. Schaefer, personal

relations coordinator, looks upon care management as "a critical part of the service we provide to our policyholders when they turn to us for long-term care assistance. This function assures our policyholders of receiving essential services, advocates for policyholders, which is especially critical when they have no immediate family involved in their care, and educates family/personal caregivers."

Ms. Schaefer goes further, "Care management is not new, but we have seen an increase in intensity of care management to help ensure that policyholders and companies are not paying more for services than they should be paying." Fortis explains care management in layman's terms with a heart. "Care management is a term that encompasses a broad spectrum of activities. Included in care management are such services as assisting a policyholder in finding an appropriate health care provider in their community, working with the policyholder's physician to ensure they receive all of the health care services necessary for optimizing their rehabilitative potential, encouraging the policyholder to regain their independence, and educating families and caregivers to enhance their abilities to be helpful and supportive during this time of rehabilitation."

Ms. Schaefer made an excellent point, that most laymen miss. She said, "Cost is not the issue as much as appropriateness of care services, setting, and time. Care management provides the policyholder with the best opportunity to receive the appropriate care, in the appropriate setting, for the appropriate amount of time for the appropriate cost. The impact of claim cost is variable. Care management may identify the need for an increased level of services for a policyholder, which would result in increased claim costs. Care management may identify situations of overutilization of services, which may result in lower initial claim cost and an extended period of time over which a policyholder could receive these services."

A discussion with Shareen Kobus, RN, care manager for CNA Long-Term Care Insurance Company, is similar to our talks with the other carriers. She says, "Traditionally, care management is a process that targets the most appropriate, highest quality, and most cost effective services to meet the assessed needs and expressed wishes of the claimant and their family. Our care management team realizes that the policyholder's choice of long-term care provider is a personal decision made by the client and his family."

"We have found that every claim does not need care management. Many policyholders have already selected a service provider and have begun receiving care before notifying the claims department. Experience has shown that many prefer to locate their own providers. The following factors are considered in care management: provider availability in their area, availability of community resources, cost of care versus the available benefits, the desires of the policyholder, the mental status of the individual, and/or the level of family involvement. Care management is a service provided to our clients at no cost to them or a decrease of benefits," mentioned Ms. Kobus.

Shareen Kobus explains a very important factor that all brokers selling long-term care insurance should know. "Long-term care management is fundamentally different from acute medical or disability care management. Evaluate a benefit-eligible individual's need for services. We cannot recommend care or a provider of care. For care management to function effectively, we must know the requirements of the policy, listen closely to the policyholder's concerns, and assist him within the scope of the product."

The carriers that responded to Susan's inquiry had honest heartfelt concerns and want to work to create the perfect product, making sure that the consumer as well as the family gets the care that is needed without loopholes and red tape.

## What to Look for in a Nursing Home
### by Gene Tapper

In 1985, my mother required nursing home care. Fortunately, my background as a nursing home administrator allowed my brother and me to be very selective as to what facility we would allow to provide her care. No one really wants to stay in a nursing home or be dependent upon help at home or in an assisted living facility, but that doesn't change the facts. Facts make it clear that no one is immune from the jarring effects of long-term care. We know from *The Wall Street Journal* that more than half the women and almost one-third of the men turning age 65 will spend time in a nursing home during their lifetime.[2] Seven out of ten couples can expect one partner to use a nursing home after age 65.[3] Women generally outlive men and are twice as likely to need long-term care.[4] When it is needed, it's nice to know there is a way to avoid paying the entire cost yourself and having to lose everything you've worked your life to save.

All the knowledge in the world about LTCI, Medicare, Medicaid, and nursing home operations doesn't totally prepare you when it comes to admitting your mother into a nursing home. Like everyone else you begin by asking, "What do I do? What do I look for?"

Check out the facility of your choice about 11:00 in the morning. All nonbedridden patients should be up and dressed by that time of day, either in wheelchairs, chairs, or walking around the facility. Look to see they are clean, dressed, hair combed, and have their make-up on for ladies, or the men are shaved and are generally up for the day. Expect to see patients at various levels of physical ability. There may be some who are slumped over due to physical or cognitive conditions — are they up to the best of their ability?

By that time of day, all the beds should be made, the rooms should be clean, and general activities such as beauty shop and group activities should be taking place. The facility should be odor free, except for the uncontrollable bowel and bladder accidents that do happen in nursing homes. If you observe something of that nature happening, observe how the staff responds to the patient's needs — is the reaction timely and performed in a kind manner?

Regarding the facility staff, how are you treated as you walk through the facility? Are you greeted with a "How may I help you?" attitude, or are you greeted with a "What do you want?" attitude? Attitude and a caring philosophy are important indicators to consider when looking for a nursing home.

If you are still in the facility at lunchtime, check out the lunch. Compare it with the posted menu for the day — does what is delivered to the patient follow the menu? And observe how the meals are delivered to the patients. Are the trays delivered in a timely manner so the food is still hot by the time the tray reaches the patient? Are feeder patients who need supervision brought together as a group? Are patients who are ambulatory or able to feed themselves allowed to eat on their own (with supervision for safety reasons)? Overall, does the facility have a pleasing environment to live in and does it have a staff you can feel comfortable to communicate with during your visits with loved ones?

Let the facility personnel be an extension of your family. That will allow you to focus on visiting with your loved ones, which is what they want *and* need. With this approach, you can leave the heavy and continuous care to the nursing home staff. As you visit frequently, you will get to know how well the facility staff provides for your loved one. Choose a facility that will allow you to visit according to *your* schedule rather than at the demands of the patient or the facility.

By using this screening process, you may select the facility of *your* choice and feel good that the care you are providing is right for your loved one. Obviously, check the facility's patient contract, but overall look at the staff, its reputation in the community, its attitude toward patients and the facility's environment. This will be important for your peace of mind and for the patient's safety.

## Managed Care
### by S. Larry Feldman

Some people will want to confuse Care Coordination with Managed Care. There is a world of difference. The effect of managed care on LTCI would place an emphasis on controlling costs for the insurance carrier, unlike the services previously mentioned for care coordinators to assist policyholders.

Cost containment is becoming a priority to federal and state government budgets imploding to cover the costs of long-term care through a welfare dependency system. All too often, government's answer to containing costs is to cut back Medicare and Medicaid funding, creating a crisis in the delivery system of care. Managed care is a staple of the acute care community in the form of Health Maintenance Organizations (HMO.) However, as HMO's go about their business of managing costs, more and more insureds are appealing to their legislators to force HMOs to abdicate their original mission and primary responsibility.

Does managed care have a place in the lexicon of private long-term care insurance? I remain skeptical, unless someone can show me an HMO-model LTCI plan with a proven track record for managing services, a.k.a. containing costs, and client satisfaction. In terms of healthy aging, the needs for long-term care usually involve a downward spiral due to the natural effects of aging, which at face value appears to contradict HMO's mandate for health maintenance. One possible benefit would be for managed care to act as a bridge for those entering a cycle of long-term care in disease management and in the prevention of acute illness. Otherwise, would managed care in long-term care encourage inappropriate lower levels of care to achieve cost savings? How much leaner can nursing facilities operate? Currently, nursing home employees already receive low wages for their services, and few benefits, despite working in difficult circumstances.

**Preferred Provider Organizations (PPO)**

Long-term care insurance companies are forging alliances with LTC providers as a method of cost containment. These alliances are a positive step and offer a win-win-win situation. There is no penalty for not using a LTC company's PPO, however, when the insured (claimant) agrees to use a carrier's Preferred Provider, the insurance company may reward the insured. There are several methods of reward or incentive:

1. Waiving or reducing the elimination period.

2. Increase coverage percentage from 80% to 100%.
3. Increase the benefit period, by adding savings to the "pool"or "pot" of money.
4. Accelerating the time element to qualify for waiver of premium.
5. Guaranteed access to care.
6. Network provider discounts of up to 15% for insured and uninsured goods and services.

The insured benefits, the insurance company has built in accountability and cost control, and the provider has a steady source of new business.

## Alternative Plan of Care

If a claimant would otherwise require confinement in a nursing facility, the insurance company may pay for medically appropriate services and supplies in another setting. The extra payments for such things as wheelchairs, wheelchair ramps, door widening, in-home safety devices, and additional supportive equipment may allow an insured to remain at home. It is not the intent of the insurance company to deny a policyholder from accessing facility care when it is more appropriate. Given a choice, most insureds would rather remain at home where surroundings are familiar, they receive one-on-one assistance if available, and they get to sleep in their own beds. The insured is happier and the benefit for home care most likely costs less than the nursing facility benefit. Again, a win-win situation!

Nothing in life is perfect, therefore, we must look for the best solution at the time of our decision. Also, what consumers hear and want may not always be in their best interests. For example, if you ask a prospect for long-term care insurance if he or she needed care, would they prefer to have their care provided by a family member or close friend, they would probably respond by saying, "Yes." To that end, some LTCI companies market plans that pay benefits while the insured is being cared for by informal family caregivers.

Most LTCI plans will reimburse a policyholder for expenses within policy limits, up to an agreed daily amount, for billed expenses on an approved claim, which does not recognize informal caregivers. I personally believe in the reimbursement type policy over the per-diem type for the safety of the insured and the sanity of the family members.

### The Safety of the Insured

Plans that pay benefits on a per-diem basis pay a stated dollar amount per day regardless of actual incurred expenses. One per-diem carrier in particular compares its LTCI claim paying procedure to that of a disability income claim. When an insurance carrier does so without demanding periodic review by a care coordinator, the seeds for potential abuse of the insured have been planted.

The aging of society is producing some very nasty risks outside the box of our conception of aging. These risks fall under the heading of homicide, suicide, and abuse. As difficult as it is to associate these terms with images of grandma or grandpa, recent studies have brought these revelations to light. One study conducted by Professor Donna Cohen, from the University of South Florida, sheds light on the fact, those 65 and over have the highest suicide rate in the U.S. Tracking acts of homicide and suicide among the elderly, the study concluded these violent acts were predominantly committed by males despondent over poor health, imminent separation, or exhaustion from providing care to an ill spouse.

Stories of elder abuse are frightening, as well as sickening, since they almost always are attributable to children, with the root cause being money. Close to forty years in the financial services business has taught me that money can do bad things to good people. The problem is nationwide, as substantiated on the west coast by the San Francisco Consortium for Elder Abuse Prevention at the Goldman Institutes on Aging, and by the National Center on Elder Abuse. Data from state agencies, shows that the majority of abuse comes at the hands of relatives who are caring for the elderly.

According to a *20/20* television report aired March 17, 1999, "Neglect and abuse of the elderly may be the fastest-growing family crime in America." Diane Sawyer, a host of *20/20*, interviewed several law enforcement officials across the country who were just beginning to come to terms over the magnitude of the problem.

In an unrelated story, the head of the Los Angeles County Sheriff's Department Elder Abuse Unit, Sgt. Barbara White, has stated police must realize that physical abuse often comes in an effort to get money from the elderly. Her experiences lead to the belief physical abuse is the symptom and financial abuse is the motivation. To get to the money, perpetrators have been guilty of neglect, isolation, starvation, and ultimately death.

One of the newest services to emerge from the aspect of the aging phenomenon occurred in Calgary, Canada, in May 1999, with the opening of a shelter for abused seniors, the first of its kind in North America, with a similar shelter being built in New York City. Eligibility begins at age 60 for seniors wishing to escape an abusive situation, usually emotional and/or financial, who are able to care for themselves. Shelter can be provided in the center for up the three months.

Being physically and mentally able to recognize an abuse situation and having an option to voluntarily remove yourself from it is wonderful. But what about neglected parents who lack the physical and mental wherewithal to seek assistance with the daily activities of living, or who fear the unknown as a result of their complaining?

Using the claims handling format of a long-term care insurer, who isn't listed in the top twenty LTCI companies by total assets, to illustrate a potentially abusive scenario and to demonstrate a point may upset a few colleagues. However, carriers with this or similar marketing philosophies can institute measures to protect insured claimants by initiating periodic reviews from care coordinators.

## The Sanity of Family Members

The prospect that thinks he or she would prefer to have care provided by a family member can only imagine themselves in normal daily circumstances: the usual, "Honey, can you lend a hand?," "Got a minute?" "When you get a chance?" and so on. Long-term care can be demanding, time consuming, energy draining, and mentally fatiguing.

For those not up to the task, what does the claimant (who hired the informal caregiver who is cashing the claim checks) do to get appropriate care? How demanding can the claimant be, and who does he or she turn to, to resolve disputes? The most effective use of LTCI claims payments is the employment of qualified caregivers, trained to perform whatever care best suits the insured's needs.

And what of the personal needs, health, and sanity informal caregivers require to spell them of the rigors of being a full time caregiver?

## Senior Sposal Relationships
### by S. Larry Feldman

According to health care officials, this story about my mother-in-law and father-in-law, is sadly commonplace in senior spousal relationships.

Fran and Ethel raised three children: David, my wife Nancy, and her sister Gretchen. David was born with severe Downs Syndrome. Dave had very little capacity to communicate, but was always very considerate of other people and was helpful doing chores asked of him. When David turned age 56, it was a milestone for a Down's Syndrome person. Science tells us that for his age and condition, his mind and body were equivalent to a man in his late 70s. David developed Alzheimer's disease, but he is not the focus of my tale.

Mom was the epitome of a woman of the '50s, and then some. When most families were hiding or institutionalizing children born like David, Mom kept him at home and in the community. Active in her community and church, dutiful to her children, a wonderful homemaker, gardener, and wife, she was loved and admired by all who knew her. My father-in-law, Francis, possessed a brilliant mind in the subjects of math, chemistry, and science, all of which helped him survive at sea during World War II. Standing a trim 5'10", he was a handsome sailor. He chose a career in education, mentoring to others first as a teacher, then a principal, and finally as the first Director of Eastern Maine Vocational and Technical College, all while serving on many boards of industry, commerce, and education. It wasn't easy to witness Fran's loss of good health. His sight was declining, his memory was failing. He was on five or six medications four times a day, prolonging his decline. It was difficult for Mom to care for him, especially because he dozed much of the day and then he stayed awake half the hours of the night demanding attention. During the day, he was sensitive to light, requiring shades to be drawn, and most of the time he was cold, when in fact everyone else felt warm, or because of his demands for heat, hot.

Mom was a short 5'2" and it was difficult for her to assist Fran in getting around. The scariest times were when Fran fell down the stairs. Taking care of Fran and David would wear anyone down, especially a woman in her late 70s, but Mom never complained, and she tried not to show the strain. One daughter, Gretchen, who lived over an hour's drive away, spent more than her share of time commuting to her parent's home to provide assistance. As time passed, these trips became more frequent. When extra help was needed, my wife Nancy, who lives eight hours away by car, would make the drive from our home in New York to her parents' home in Maine. Sometimes Nancy could tell when her sister Gretchen, who has her own family, was running on empty. On a few occasions, Nancy even felt the urgency of catching a flight to Bangor.

Obviously, at this time, my father-in-law was uninsurable, but my mother-in-law, at age 78, was still a good risk. Her annual long-term care insurance premium was $3,000. Mom paid $1,000, my sister-in-law and brother-in-law paid $1,000, and Nancy and I paid $1,000. Mom's long-term care policy provided nursing home care and home health care, bringing peace of mind to all of us, and for Nancy and I, who lived 400 miles away, it added an extra dimension of sleep insurance.

Fran's health continually declined and he passed away at age 80. Mom grieved at the loss of her partner of 55 years, but this gritty woman also looked forward to regaining some of life's rewarding experiences, such as paying a visit to our new townhouse. Plans were made to visit, but soon after Fran's death, Mom seemed to be experiencing some uncharacteristic health problems. Health care providers see these changes as all too common in cases where spouses have been in charge of providing round-the-clock care for their mates over an extended period of time. The person providing care becomes so focused on the spouse with the more serious need for care that he or she turns off or ignores his or her own body signals of distress and pain. Once left on their own, the problems become exacerbated and more pronounced. If symptoms have gone unattended over a long period of time, the damage is often irreparable. I remember thinking when Mom entered the hospital that it would be a short stay. She should be out soon, but would need a couple of months of nursing home care or several months of home care before she would be able to resume daily activities and take care of David. It was comforting to know her long-term care insurance policy was there to provide the cash for the best professional care available.

Mom's physical condition, which had been ignored for too long, came crashing down on her. Mom never did leave the hospital alive. Following Mom's death, Gretchen brought David into her home. She and her husband, Tom, provided David with loving care until the Alzheimer's robbed David of the opportunity to remain at home, requiring more care than one or two informal caregivers were capable of providing. I truly believe if my father-in-law had long-term care insurance, providing him a care coordinator and the dollars for professional care, allowing Ethel time to accommodate her own physical, mental, spiritual, and recreational needs she would have been able to make that visit to our new townhouse.

## Faith and Hope (Without Charity!)

Long-term care insurance in the new millennium is much like health insurance was in the early 1960s. Not everyone then was covered by health insurance and, indeed, it was a risk that most assumed personally, whether they chose to insure for it or not.

Often, I would receive a call from a hospital or doctor's office to verify a client's in-force policy status. Following verification, many would ask, "What is the dollar amount of the daily benefit?" "Can you tell me how long is the waiting period?" or "What is the surgical schedule for an XYZ operation?" As bills for claims were presented, invariably they matched the schedule of benefits I quoted from the client's policy.

As the years passed, the schedule of daily benefits for hospital stays has been replaced by the clause "semi-private room costs," and the cost of most other services are recognized for reimbursement as "reasonable and customary." In today's aura of negotiated fees, Preferred Provider Organizations, discounted fees through Health Maintenance Organizations, etc., determining charges for acute care is no longer a simple exercise. It's also no secret that private health insurance is being used to subsidize medical costs for society at large.

It's to be hoped that the long-term care industry will, to some extent, avoid the temptation to follow suit and instead provide value-added recognition to clients who have chosen to insure for their costs of long-term care.

If the average time it takes to spend down to the poverty level for uninsured residents of a nursing facility is thirteen weeks, and if a nursing facility receives less than two-thirds of the privately billed rate for the costs of long-term care from Medicaid, wouldn't it be accommodating if policyholders received some sign of appreciation for their decision to insure, from their provider?

If you owned a nursing facility and received the $150 a day private pay rate from your insured resident (opposed to the reduced $120 Medicaid reimbursement for twenty-four, thirty-six, or sixty months) would you consider recognizing or rewarding your financially responsible client? Providing no federal or state regulations were violated, it would take simple acts such as providing complimentary issues of a daily newspaper for those who wished it, a computer hook-up line for a personal computer, flowers in the resident's room, etc. Sure, there are many excuses why such endeavors may not be feasible, but now is a good time for providers to begin thinking outside the box.

## LTCI: WHEN "THANK YOU'S" ARE NEVER BELATED

Following a sale of long-term care insurance and delivery of the policy to a new policyholder, people eventually thank their LTCI agent. This may seem odd to those who only perceive the agent as benefiting at that moment. Unless one has experienced an LTCI interview with an agent and learned of the odds of needing long-term care and the costs they will incur, the casual observer may not understand the value of owning a policy. The cost of LTCI peace of mind or "sleep" insurance is the premium. But, some of the most heartfelt thanks an insurance agent or financial planner will ever receive comes from spouses and children of LTCI policyholders who have had to file a claim.

# CHAPTER 9

## Complete the Circle

Financial Planning, Retirement Planning, and Estate Planning are not exact sciences. Given the same set of client circumstances, a roomful of planners may develop more than one recommendation to achieve a client's objective. We must also keep in mind that, like a floating target, clients' needs are subject to change, requiring us periodically to refocus on a previously drawn plan design. The three mechanisms — financial, retirement, and estate planning — are all subject to failure without consideration of long-term care planning.

Eskimos once were known to have an uncomplicated way of dealing with old age. When elders no longer felt useful and able to carry their own weight, they would gather their parkas and blankets and settle on ice floes without paddles, setting out to sea to be carried from their earthly homeland to the spirit world. In today's world, we've come to realize that our elderly are deserving of better and more enlightened treatment from their communities. Even our practical sense dictates that if their social and physical needs are adequately met, they can still make useful and meaningful contributions to society.

Native Americans place great emphasis on the meaning of circles. Everything has a beginning and an end, coming full circle. We can transpose the Circle of Life with the Circle of Planning, which would be incomplete without long-term care planning. After all, how many plans can withstand the pressure of the costs of an average two and a half years stay in a nursing facility, ranging from $150,000 to $300,000?

The logistical cost of providing necessary care for the world's aging population is poised to become a huge financial burden. The most immediate threat is to the baby boom generation, fast becoming known as the Sandwich Generation.

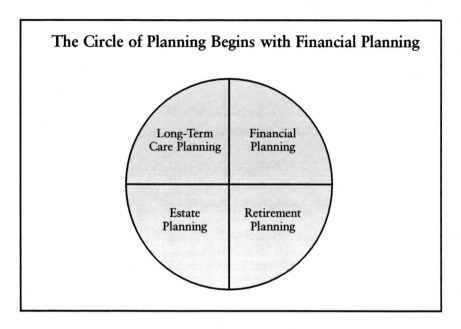

**The Circle of Planning Begins with Financial Planning**

| Long-Term Care Planning | Financial Planning |
| Estate Planning | Retirement Planning |

As I began writing this chapter, the irony of the moment could not escape me. I was on a ski holiday working my way toward a quarterly meeting of the National LTC Network. I had the good fortune of being a guest of friends who moved from New York state to Breckenridge, Colorado. My hostess, Marcia, informed me that day she wouldn't be skiing because she was also hosting a support group who meet periodically. The group consists of fourteen women who have moved to Colorado from various communities throughout the U.S. The "newcomers" were going to discuss caring for elderly parents from afar. At dinner, Marcia shared some of the stories and frustrations expressed by the women that afternoon. I wish I could have been a spectator, although I did have one burning question, "Was long-term care insurance discussed at any time during the group's conversations?" Marcia's answer was "No."

Had the topic centered around parents with cancer, or heart disease, it is almost inconceivable that remarks about the adequacy of their parents' health insurance would not have surfaced. My heart of hearts tells me that, within five to ten years, similar conversations will almost certainly include comments about parents' long-term care insurance.

One of the support group women recited a prose poem she had written about the dilemma of families acting as care givers.

## OBSERVATIONS AT 3:00 AM

### MY MOM

*I see an old, tired and lonely woman. A tiny shadow of the woman she used to be, huddled under her covers. She sleeps, because she takes a pill to make her sleep. She awakens to another day of making herself eat. There is no joy in anticipating what yummy delight it might be fun to cook and eat today. She awakens to another day of angling the skin and bones of her feet into positions higher than her head on her tiny love seat. There is no joy of looking forward to feeling strong enough to spruce herself up or her home up. She awakes to another day of feeling lonely. There is no joy in any social activity — there is none. The only person she talks to daily is one loyal friend. She doesn't even know why no others (friends or family) come sit with her and talk with her. There is no joy in conversation because she has forgotten how to have one. She can't hear and will not listen. She feels badgered and blameless. She is childish and defensive and does not know she is anything but sad, tired and lonely.*

### MY SISTER-IN-LAW

*I see a strong-willed, well meaning woman. She has many interests, many talents and a great deal of love. She feels trapped by the old woman next door. She tries to help her eat right — she even shares her good food with the old woman from time to time. She takes her to the doctor, shopping, for haircuts, and much, much more. She is frustrated by the old woman's resistance to her suggestions. She thinks she knows what is best for the old woman, who thinks she can run her own life. She sees that the old woman needs her. The old woman sees her as an intruder — someone who corrects her too often and in embarrassing places.*

## MY BROTHER

*I see a man in the middle. A man who cared enough to bring his parents onto his property so that he could care for them in their later years. I see a man so full of love and compassion that he can't bear to hurt someone. Can this man see, feel and hear the tension building? Yes, he can — but what can he do. He can't take the side of the well meaning younger woman or the fragile old woman. The pain for either of them or himself would be too much to bear. They both desire his love and respect. He deserves to be at peace and out of the middle. Please, wonderful man — give yourself the break you deserve. Keep these two wonderful but not compatible women as far away from each other as possible!!!*

## The Sandwich Generation

"The Sandwich Generation." What an appropriate phrase! A lot of us today and many more tomorrow will begin to experience this strange phenomenon. Even those of us who have already gone through this at times turbulent, at times wonderful adventure, the best advice we could collectively give to the next group of inductees would be to "fasten your seatbelts."

You are about to experience a roller coaster ride. When it's completed, you will hopefully feel an inner peace and exhilaration for surviving it all. Until then, a possible emptiness within you can only be resolved by taking the time to be good to yourself and your spouse.

Though we may feel there is no way to emotionally ready yourself for this experience, there are some vital steps to be taken to prepare for it, on multiple levels: physical, emotional, and, at least as important, financial.

Who is part of this so-called "Sandwich Generation?" Anyone who has both children (minor or not) and parents and/or grandparents who are still alive (in particular those who are bearing all or a part of the responsibilities for these folks) would certainly qualify as a "Sandwich Generation" member.

Many who are part of the baby boom generation (those born between 1946 and 1964) will find ourselves belonging to both groups! A significant number turning 50 are finding kids still at home or in college, getting engaged or married who still require considerable assistance, emotionally and physically, but in particular financially.

At the same time, 80% of this same group have at least one living parent as well as spouse's parents who are still alive. In a *Heinz Family Philanthropies/Newsweek* poll of baby boomers, 62% of the boomers polled expressed concern about having to care for an aging parent or relative. (For the complete *Heinz Family Philanthropies/Newsweek* poll on boomers, log on to newsweek.com). The problem, or challenge, can be dramatically exacerbated if either you or your spouse also needs some type of assistance.

This is how we are, sandwiched in between three or four generations of people we love and care about and find ourselves responsible for. I've "been there and done that" as the popular phrase goes. I've titled this portion of the chapter, **"The Gelbwaks Family Long-Term Care Dilemma: Will It Be Your Family's Story?"**

I'm not going to teach you about why one long-term care insurance company is better than the other, or why one long-term care insurance product is better than the next. You will not be reading about premium comparisons, tax benefits, or benefit provisions. It's not the name of the company or the lowest premium! Those are not the items driving long-term care insurance or the future of the business. Believe it or not, the future of this vitally important activity is going to be determined by the ability or lack of ability of those in the business to relate. People caught in the eye of the long-term care storm know caring doesn't always spell relief for the care giver or the person in need of care.

The "Sandwich Generation" occupies a unique place in the history of aging. Many are going back to college, possibly alongside their children, or even with their own parents. Some can be found participating in marathons and other sporting activities with their 70-year-old folks. Others find it hard to believe they are standing up for 80-year-old widowed moms and dads who are marrying 80-year-old widowed high school sweethearts!

Since 1996, the baby boom generation has included over ten thousand new people reaching the age of 50 each day. This phenomenon will continue throughout the first decade of this new millennium. "Original" baby boomers like President Bill Clinton, started this group by being born in 1946, just after the end of World War II. The problem is that many in this group and their loved ones will be living longer, whether or not they or their families are prepared for the risks that accompany aging.

Mine is a story about a family from Brooklyn, New York. A story not just of financial hardships or of physical pain but also one of togetherness. A story of many, many struggles, and of some great successes.

My parents, Jack and Lea, are both gone now. Mom died five years ago and dad fourteen years ago. Three years ago, my oldest daughter, Julie, gave birth to beautiful twin girls and named them both after my mom. According to Julie's logic, it would take two people to replace her grandmother. Lauren and Lindsey are off to a pretty good start.

In 1996, I turned 50 and became the grandfather of two. A pretty traumatic year. Now I'm the aging parent in that sandwich! A little depressing maybe, but based on all those statistics, I have thirty, forty, or even possibly fifty more years to enjoy...assuming proper planning.

My mom was the typical American housewife and homemaker of the 1950s, looking after a husband, who was out working two jobs, for seven days a week, with three kids to take care of. In other words, she was a full-time wife, mother, housekeeper. We were a healthy, happy, relatively financially comfortable, middle class American family — until our first tragedy hit!

In 1962, my dad had a major heart attack at 50 years of age. Until that time, he hadn't taken a day off work in over a decade. Now, he was in intensive care for a week and then seven more weeks in a private hospital room with round-the-clock nurses at his side. The good news is he survived! The bad news: the private room and nurses were not covered by his insurance. An

$8,000 bill was big money in 1962. It wiped out our entire savings. Of course today, it's more like eight days, not eight weeks in the hospital for heart problems, and it's more like $80,000 rather than $8,000! All the more reason to face up to some of these realities.

My mom was a real trooper. She hung in there, caring for dad when he came home from the hospital and meeting all his needs: special diet, medications, etc. My brothers and I were still in school, and mom also had concerns and issues about her own parents. Wow, talk about the "Sandwich Generation," here was a woman in the '60s nurturing and caring for all of the most important people in her life, long before such a category was created by the demographics of aging. My brothers and I went to work and that, combined with Social Security disability allowed us to just scrape by. You see, though my dad was a wonderful guy and a good provider, a loving husband and father, he just didn't have the vision to set aside money for disability insurance. Besides, it wasn't going to happen to him! He was never sick a day in his life until this happened and there were much more important items to spend those "extra" premium dollars on. Isn't all this beginning to sound familiar? It's NEVER going to happen to you, right?

Dad stayed out of work for two years and the doctor then recommended sunny Florida instead of that small upstate town in New York we had moved to, to get out of the city. The winters there were just too cold.

So, we arrived in Coral Gables, Florida, and my dad went to work at the Doral Beach Hotel and Country Club. Then tragedy #2 struck. After only two weeks on the job, he had another heart attack. Again my father survived, but now he really needed my mother's full-time attention.

At the outset, I said this was a story of many struggles and some great successes. Well, my dad and mom struggled together for thirteen more years, until at age 65 my father decided to celebrate that birthday by doing just the opposite of what his contemporaries were doing. He went back to work! He'd been disabled for fifteen years minus two weeks. He just had had enough! For ten years, up until his death, he managed to become a success in his community and in his second career.

Mom had been the primary caregiver for my dad for fifteen years, pretty much without a break. When he took the big chance and went back to work, she went into a major depression for ten years, at the end of which she lost her spouse of fifty years. She had gone from caregiver to long-term care patient. Along the way, we got some rude awakenings! By the time my dad passed away, mom had already developed both mental and physical problems. We learned that in this country, if you're both mentally and physically impaired there is no place for you.

You see, if you have manic depression and you break your hip, the hospitals of America cannot effectively deal with you. How do I know this? My mother had five broken hips, all surgically repaired, and during all that time was suffering from manic depression. This was a pretty tough period, but we didn't know how tough it was going to become.

We went to Medicare for help. Most of you by now are well informed about what Medicare can and cannot do. That wasn't very much. Each time she went into the hospital and then the rehab center, she did qualify for the first twenty days of skilled care and even got some additional days from her Medicare supplement. She was one of the lucky ones. Here is my summary of Medicare: chronic and custodial conditions need not apply. When you have long-term illnesses, one hundred days of coverage is a joke. We needed help for years, not days!

By this time, we were getting pretty desperate. My mom had fourteen different surgeries and sixty different hospital stays, as a result of a heart condition, cancer, and severe osteoporosis requiring five hip surgeries. In addition to her manic depression, she now also developed emphysema, even though she had quit smoking many years before.

Now it's time to talk about the financial part of this dilemma. When my dad died in 1986, he left my mom with $100,000 in savings and insurance. He qualified for his state pension the day he died, so between his pension and Social Security, which totaled about $20,000 a year, and the $100,000 in the bank, mom could have managed very nicely, if she'd stayed healthy. But all during my adult life, my mom had illnesses. Even when she was caring for dad. She could never qualify for long-term care insurance! She had all the multiple conditions that insurance carriers would not insure, and they are right not to do so, but this didn't help us any.

Mom's conditions were developing more into custodial and chronic care, than they were acute care. These are very important words for you to know. Medicare was never designed to pay for chronic or custodial conditions. It was designed for immediate, acute conditions requiring skilled treatment. That is still the case today, and probably will be so in the foreseeable future.

At this juncture, mom needed round-the-clock care. I'd made her a promise that, as long as it was in my power, she would not have to go to a nursing home. Does this sound familiar? She also flatly refused to live with us, so we set up her apartment like a mini hospital/nursing home. Hospital bed, oxygen tank, special equipment in the bathroom, and round-the-clock nurses, aides, therapists, whatever she needed. It even went as far as bringing her to doctor's visits in wheelchair vans. If necessary, ambulances would bring her to the doctor on stretchers. Her physical ailments were making her so depressed there were times she wouldn't even sit up. After two years at home, we had spent the $100,000 my dad had left mom and her overall conditions were not getting better. They were worsening. This is a simple reality of aging that we need to accept and recognize. As we age we tend not to get healthier. At very best, we stay the same and often we deteriorate.

At this point mom was broke. She didn't hide her assets, she didn't transfer her assets to a trust, and she didn't give her assets away. We spent them on her care. Medicaid seemed the natural way to go. The first problem we encountered was that mom was still at home and therefore ineligible for any services or benefits from that system. She also didn't qualify financially. Though she was flat broke, no car, no home (she was in a rental apartment), no savings account, no investments, she still didn't qualify for Florida Medicaid. Here's why: Florida has two tests, an income test and an asset test. Mom had no assets but she had income, fixed and guaranteed income: state pension plan and a Social Security check that totaled about $1,400 a month. But because of that $1,400 a month, she didn't qualify for any assistance. Today there is a program for people in that situation. It's called the "Income Cap" Trust or the Miller Trust, but she was out in the cold with Medicare and out in the cold with Medicaid, and of course she was still always ineligible for long-term care insurance. Falling through all the cracks in the system!

Allowing mom to stay at her home just was not working. She was firing aides in the middle of the night and then sustaining injuries. An assisted living facility was our next best try. A beautiful place costing about $2,700 a month, but after only six months there, she just couldn't make it. Every time she got up to go eat, she was so out of breath from the emphysema that she couldn't eat or even breathe. Rescue squads were visiting her almost daily. She became totally bedridden and decided to sign on to the hospice program. Her diagnosis was terminal. She was expected to live thirty days or less. After thirty days in hospice and on 120 milligrams a day of morphine for pain, she had become incontinent and totally bedridden. One day she sat up in bed and said, "Peter, where am I?" I reminded her that she was in hospice. She replied, "How long have I been here?" I said, "Thirty days." She said, "Well then get me the hell out of here because I guess I'm not dying yet!" She was a lady with unbelievable spirit!!!

At this point, we had her transferred to a local, superior rated nursing home just behind my office in North Miami Beach. Still not eligible for Medicare or Medicaid assistance, but totally and completely dependent. My mom was expected to live another few weeks or a month at best. I insisted on a private room for her since she had no cognitive impairments, and we didn't want to add to her anguish or ours.

Now comes the shocker of this story. Mom didn't survive thirty more days, she survived 1,300 more days. That's right, three and a half years. During that time she was one of only three residents in the entire facility to get a daily newspaper delivered. In fact, she got two, one of which was *The Wall Street Journal*. She watched CNN round the clock. I used to go there just to get my local and world news updates from her. On mom's 80th birthday, I went to her bedside and said, "Well mom, you made it to 80. Did you ever expect to make it to 80? After all, at 50 you had a 107 fever and the doctors said you would never survive. At 65 you had an emergency appendectomy and peritonitis set in and the doctors said you wouldn't survive. Now you have outlived two of your doctors. Did you ever think you could make it to 80?" She said, "No, I guess I never did." "Well what do you have to say now?" I asked. Here she was, down to about sixty-five or seventy pounds, not even able to feed herself. She looked up at me and replied, "I look at it this way...As long as I made it to 80, I might as well shoot for 90!" Wow, what a lady! What an inspiration! My mom had a drive to survive that was just unparalleled in my experience.

It cost us over $250,000 to take care of her in a way we had never expected or desired. You see, she was never going to a nursing home, none of us are, and yet, most of the superior rated nursing homes in this country have waiting lists that are filled and the better ones don't need Medicaid patients.

During the time of attending to my mother's needs for care, Sharon and I were raising two beautiful daughters who needed our attention as much as my mother. Sandwiched as I was, obviously there was a need to continue to make a living and keep everyone's ship afloat. Insurance agents do not live by the clock. Nine-to-fivers need not apply. On the other hand, those involved in an insurance sales career work as long and as hard as they please. Fortunately, this freedom allowed me to successfully schedule appointments around my family obligations. Not many bosses would have tolerated my coming and going. Even as my own boss, I couldn't have expected anyone to work the hours I had to put in.

Bad things can and do happen to good people. But state-of-the-art, long-term care insurance is now available and most people can medically qualify for this coverage. The physical, emotional, and financial devastation that accompany long-term care can be alleviated by shifting the risk to an insurance company.

Sharon and I do not want Julie and Marjorie to become a "Gelbwaks Triple-Decker Sandwiched Generation." We want our daughters, sons-in-law, and grandchildren to care about us, not care for us. No juggling family ties, sacrificing career opportunities, jeopardizing personal health and well-being to be our long-term care providers. That should be left to professional caregivers in our choice of settings.

In addition to our own personal dignity, we wish to leave a financial legacy to those we love. We've taken many steps to insure our goals are met, including buying our own long-term care insurance policies. In order to usher in feast and not famine, we pay an annual premium to an insurance company. The premium is not the problem, the premium is the solution to the problem.

## DO YOU NEED LONG TERM CARE INSURANCE? A CONSUMER'S QUESTIONNAIRE

It is suggested that an individual who is contemplating the purchase of long-term care insurance take sufficient time to review all aspects of their potential long-term care needs. Long-term care insurance can be an integral part of the protection of one's total financial portfolio. In this regard, it is highly recommended that the individual obtain the services of a qualified long-term care insurance professional. The following questionnaire is not a substitute for such professional services. The questionnaire is offered only as a

GUIDE to help clarify one's POSSIBLE need for long-term care insurance. For a more effective evaluation of your nursing care needs, contact a long-term care insurance professional.

1. While everyone is at risk for the services provided by long-term care professionals, not all people have the ability to pay for these services or pay for the premium of a long-term care insurance policy. The following questions will help determine your financial risks and premium paying ability.

   Q. If you are single, do you have over $75,000 of assets?      Yes ☐ No ☐

   Q. If you are single, is your annual income from ALL sources over $24,000?      Yes ☐ No ☐

   Q. If you are married, do you have over $75,000 of assets excluding your home?      Yes ☐ No ☐

   Q. If you are married, is your annual income from ALL sources over $40,000?      Yes ☐ No ☐

   Q. If you have children, would they be able to share in the costs of your LTC insurance policy?      Yes ☐ No ☐

2. Some people might consider self-insuring. If you have a large amount of assets, you may prefer to pay for the cost of nursing care out of your savings.

   Q. For example, the cost of nursing homes in the Northeast can range from $55,000 to $100,000 per year. If you (or your spouse) needed nursing home care, would spending this much per year for Long-Term Care cause a significant change in your lifestyle?      Yes ☐ No ☐

   Q. If married, is it of significant importance that your spouse retain most of your assets?      Yes ☐ No ☐

Q. Is it of significant importance
that you leave an inheritance
for your children or heirs?                    Yes ☐ No ☐

3. Informal care, provided by your family or friends, can
postpone and possibly eliminate the need of paid care.

Q. Do you have family or friends living
with you or close to you who
would provide assistance?                      Yes ☐ No ☐

Q. Would you feel comfortable having
to ask them for assistance?
(Examples: Managing medications,
dressing, meal preparation, feeding,
toileting, etc.)                               Yes ☐ No ☐

Q. Could they afford to take time away
from work in order to provide you
assistance?                                    Yes ☐ No ☐

Q. Could they afford to take time away
from their family in order to provide
you assistance?                                Yes ☐ No ☐

Q. Could you move in with them?                Yes ☐ No ☐

Q. Would you want to move in with them?  Yes ☐ No ☐

Q. Could they bathe you?                       Yes ☐ No ☐

Q. Could they lift you up from
a chair or bed?                                Yes ☐ No ☐

Q. Could they carry you out of the house?   Yes ☐ No ☐

4. How you feel about "Choice" will also determine
if long-term care insurance is right for you.

Q. Welfare (Medicaid) was designed as the last
resort for widows and children with no other
place to turn. Yet, some people hide their
assets in an Irrevocable Trust to qualify for
welfare. (1993 Medicaid rules for trusts created
a 60-month look-back period and possible longer

penalty periods, for transfers.) Do you feel
people with means have an obligation to
pay for their own nursing care costs?      Yes ☐  No ☐

Q. In order to qualify for welfare, one must
spend down all their assets to the poverty
level and relinquish most of their
income. Would this matter to you?      Yes ☐  No ☐

Q. On welfare (Medicaid), nursing home care
can be rendered up to a 50-mile radius from
your home. Would this matter to you?    Yes ☐  No ☐

## REQUEST FOR LONG-TERM CARE INSURANCE INFORMATION

The answers given to the following questions will assist a Long-Term Care Insurance agent to provide a complete and accurate proposal(s) with estimated premium cost. They assist the agent with the three major elements in drafting a policy recommendation. They are:

• Suitability      • Insurability      • Benefit-Structure

Name _____Date of Birth  _____

Name of Spouse _____Date of Birth  _____

Address  _____

Telephone Number  _____

Best Time to Call _____Today's Date _____

Employer _____

Occupation_____Retired? Yes ☐  No ☐

Spouse's Employer _____

Occupation_____Retired? Yes ☐  No ☐

Health history is an important factor in qualifying for LTC insurance. Although insurance companies do not expect you to have the health of a 20-year-old, they do want you to be in "fairly" good health for your age.

Q. Are you dependent on the use of a walker or wheelchair or confined to bed or home?                Yes ☐  No ☐

Q. Is your spouse dependent on the use of a walker or wheelchair or confined to bed or home?                Yes ☐  No ☐

Q. Do you use any medical appliance such as a catheter, oxygen, respirator, or dialysis machine?                Yes ☐  No ☐

Q. Does your spouse use any medical appliance such as a catheter, oxygen, respirator, or dialysis machine?                Yes ☐  No ☐

Q. In the past TEN years, have you, (or your spouse), been hospitalized for any reason?                Yes ☐  No ☐

If "YES", list the name of the person who had the hospital stay, the reason for the hospital stay and the date of the hospital stay(s).

NAME: _____

REASON FOR STAY: _____

_____

DATE OF STAY: _____

Q. In the past TEN years, have you (or your spouse), taken a prescribed medication?                Yes ☐  No ☐

If "YES," list the name of the person taking the medication, the complete name of the medication, the amount taken per day, and the purpose for taking the medication.

NAME: _____

MEDICATION: _____

AMOUNT: _____

PURPOSE: _____

Q. In the past FIVE years, have you
(or your spouse), seen a medical doctor? Yes ☐ No ☐

If "YES," list the name of the person who saw the
doctor and reason for seeing the doctor.

NAME: _____

REASON: _____

_____

Q. In the past FIVE years, have you
(or your spouse), used any tobacco
products, including cigarettes, pipe,
cigar, or chewing tobacco?        Yes ☐ No ☐

If "YES," please list who used or uses
tobacco products _____

Q. What is your height & weight? _____
Your spouse's height & weight? _____

Q. The dollar value of the assets you
wish to protect: _____
Household income: _____

❧

## C H A P T E R 1 0

# Bringing the Ghost Out of the Closet
## by Paul Elisha

Too often, the simplest wisdom is the hardest to perceive. But writers, we're told, are supposed to be perceptive. This one thought he was until a forest of circumstances, too close for objective scrutiny of its trees, proved otherwise. Thoreau wrote that independence means to breathe after your own fashion; to live after your own nature. But Thoreau was lucky enough to die before he'd reached a point where he might have to depend on others for survival. Many of us, indeed most of us, in these technologically driven times, will not be as lucky as he was.

This writer was blest with a genetic bequest of longevity, from both maternal and paternal limbs of his family tree. Add to this a strong dose of innate self-sufficiency, and you have a fairly workable formula for independence. But it's one thing to spend nearly five decades of one's adult life becoming a capable curmudgeon. It's another to learn, in an eye-blink, that the effort has been in vain. That's what befell this writer when — less than a month after my 74th birthday – I tripped over an unmarked curb at a just-opened shopping center and arced onto unforgiving pavement, battering a kneecap into several disparate shards.

Random misadventure replaced a chunk of my (for the most part) carefree life, at a time when one comes to expect that, with eighteen months of unforeseen physical and mental agony. This stint of hellish existence transposed simple survival into a struggle with constant frustration. Even more significant, postponing the purchase of a long-term care insurance policy may have needlessly confounded and disarrayed the lives of my wife, two grown children residing in distant venues, and even upset our family dog's daily routine, dependent on supervised exercise.

In the OR, the orthopedic surgeon turned from a pair of back-lit X-rays and aimed his most sanguine and reassuring smile down at me. "We have to do a little surgery here," he said. "Physically, you're in excellent shape, for your age. We'll wire you up and have you back on your feet in no time." "In no time," I learned, is a generic phrase in the doctor-patient lexicon, subject to extensive and highly uncertain interpretation. In my case, it meant weeks of confinement to a bed in the upstairs portion of our three-story townhouse, with brief excursions to the nearby bathroom by way of a walker, three more months on crutches, and for several months after that, hobbling about with the help of an adjustable cane. Add to this, thereafter, countless days of difficulty in driving, stair climbing, simple acts of bending and stiffening, pain with each change in climate and temperature.

One of the most disturbing problems of living in a society geared to the communications revolution results from the disparity between what is promised (or expected) and the reality of what is delivered...or the lack of it. Whether or not our organizational efficiency has benefited from technological advancement is moot. One area of certainty, though, derives from a noticeable boost in consultants, who oblige any and every entrepreneurial need; also a disturbing change in the use of language...not to inform, but to deflect persistent and probing questions. And even more alarming, to absolve responsible service providers and their representatives from accountability.

So, it was that an amiable and reassuring "Discharge Planner" was sent by the hospital to organize my release and put me at ease (a more accurate description would be to relax my natural skepticism). Not to worry, she asserted (while furiously scribbling in the blocks of an impressive chart-pad), everything's being arranged in advance: transportation from hospital to home (since my immobilized leg precluded our own compact automobile); physical assistance once I arrive there; aides for home care during hours my wife must be away at work; and regular visits by a physical therapist.

Somewhere, between the blocks on her chart-pad and the Medi-Transport, Visiting Nurses Association, home care agency, etc., the lines of communication either were crossed or cut. On the day of my discharge, no Medi-Tran showed up. Ditto the home care person. We finally called a locally advertised taxi company whose driver had no experience with my type of injury. He did, however, know an ambulance driver who moonlighted with a helper. After three failed attempts to negotiate our townhouse stairway, with me strapped to a vertical litter and the straps seriously suggesting castration, they left me on a couch in our living room. A visiting nurse did show up, took copious notes, but we never saw her again. A local hospital supply firm delivered a walker (ordered by the doctor and covered by my insurance, they said). This turned out to be sized for a person much shorter than I, invoking visions of further falls and injuries. On calling the provider, we were told the size was standard. For anything larger, we were responsible (out-of-pocket) for any cost differential, which — in this case — came to one hundred and thirty dollars. Fearing the envisioned alternative, we of course paid it.

As the ghost writer of this book, I've become much more aware of how valuable it would have been, if my own long-term care insurance policy was in force at the time of this accident. How much different to have had a care coordinator appointed as my own advocate, and home health care benefit dollars to meet the need for my care and alternate Plan of Care flexibility, suited to my requirements.

If a picture of incredible chaos emerges here, for the reader, this is the writer's intent. But as one perceptive philosopher has observed, fact is something established by at least several good testimonies. So, here are some additional accounts which should convince readers — as they convinced us — that while long-term care insurance may be an arguable option for some, for those with a modicum of financial wherewithal, it's a virtual necessity.

Take, for instance, this case involving the client of a caring insurance broker, a horror tale that only proves that true stories can be more graphic than fiction.

Mary's clients, a husband and wife in their forties with two teenage children, enjoyed a comfortable lifestyle. They were both employed, he by a major Fortune 500 company. One evening as they left a social gathering and were on their way to their car, he complained of a sharp pain in his left shoulder and arm. The pain appeared to be intensifying and the wife suggested she drive her husband to the hospital. At first he declined her offer; men know the old macho anthem "It's nothing, I'll be okay." When it became obvious the pain was something more significant, the wife demanded he give her the keys so she could drive.

Once inside the hospital emergency room, this seemingly healthy man of 44 was struck down by a severe stroke. On the twelfth day of his hospitalization, the head nurse informed his wife the hospital could do no more for her husband, and she needed to find a nursing home for his ongoing care. After several futile attempts to obtain the care her husband needed, one more call was placed to her friend and insurance agent, Mary. The wife began by telling Mary there was a terrible mistake which she knew Mary could correct. She described a conversation she had with her husband's Human Resource Department at the General Electric Co. They had informed her the company's medical insurance plan does not cover nursing home care. "Surely, Mary, there must be some mistake. You are my friend, as well as my insurance agent. HELP ME!"

An astute insurance agent experienced in the areas of long-term care and health insurance, Mary could only swallow hard and tell her friend there was no mistake. Her client's medical insurance did not cover long-term care. Her friend responded in disbelief, "But Mary, we can't afford a nursing home. I'll be destitute before the year is over. We will have to go on welfare. We've been saving for the children's college education. How will they ever be able to go to college?"

Before a nursing home could be found, the husband's condition worsened. Sixteen months passed and, as Mary tells it, doctors informed the wife that her husband's situation was hopeless. They implied they could let him "go" with her consent. After several days of agonizing over this life or death decision, the wife scheduled one last appointment with the doctor. Incredibly, just as the wife and doctor were to meet, the husband awoke from his coma! Since that day, this man has been at home. The effects of the stroke at age 44 robbed him of all faculties with the exception of very limited use of his right hand. About the only thing he is able to do is raise food to his mouth. By the time he finishes this task, he is as covered with food as a two-year-old might be.

The family is grateful for the group disability income insurance benefit they receive monthly. Of course, the monthly benefit they currently receive is for the same amount they received back in 1992. While her husband remains a prisoner in his own body, the wife is a prisoner too, unable to leave his side during the day, lying sleepless at night trying to figure out how to make ends meet.

The lesson here is this: Traditional health insurance does not pay for long-term care!

Die-hard cynics who still need convincing may be interested in the incredible tale of one of this writer's acquaintances, who married a successful dental surgeon, had two young daughters and, when the eldest was midway through high school, her husband was stricken with a fatal heart attack. His life insurance coverage at the time was typically generous for a well-to-do professional. But it was nowhere near enough for a self-fancied yet inept investment wizard, who also was less-than-sufficiently attentive to his accounting responsibilities. After medical and funeral expenses (plus payment to all his creditors), this writer's friend was forced to seek employment to meet her family's most basic needs for food, shelter, and the expenses of two school-age daughters.

At this juncture, experienced insurance professionals will riddle the narrator with interruptions, questioning the failure of an apparently intelligent family to forearm itself against catastrophe. Points well taken, yet typical of eventualities known by many. But the story doesn't end here. After years of struggle as a single working-parent, just as she was beginning to enjoy hard-won success with both daughters out of college and gainfully employed, the older daughter was diagnosed with an inoperable cancerous tumor of the brain. The ensuing agony (for the stricken young woman, as well as her suffering family) endured for nearly two years. Its tragic conclusion left the mother drained of savings and faced with an unbelievable aggregate of new debt...much of it the result of long-term hospice care, a need neither foreseen by most who initiate conventional insurance plans nor covered in plans proposed by most insurance carriers.

Enough of woeful tales. Experienced script writers tell us successful stories should always end on notes of hope. For those whose career histories are bound up with efforts to erect family defenses against times of trouble, here's something to think about. The American writer Elbert Hubbard has noted that fellowship means helping oneself by helping others. It's true, ours has been a national psyche of progress based on individual initiative. But in things that mattered essentially the same to all of us, fellowship was key to our response. Like the pioneers who drove the frontier westward, circling the wagons against adversity. Or the farmers who were fiercely independent, but came together for barn-raisings. Ranchers were perhaps the most independent of all, yet rode together on cattle drives and against rustlers. Laborers found bargaining strength in unions and employers bucked unfair competitions with trade consortiums.

If every insurance sales agent views his or her mission as helping in a cooperative effort to preserve the independence of America's infirm and aging citizens, including members of their own families, long-term care insurance can soon become a workable and attainable reality. With a large enough client roster, long-term care can also become the means to a profitable insurance product for providers, with a fair return on resources invested. One might honestly say that long-term care insurance is an American requisite, because it reflects a typical American way of providing care, when just caring doesn't go far enough. The facts and viewpoints in this book are provided by some of the most knowledgeable and experienced analysts in the field of insurance planning. They've created an invaluable compendium, for providers and consumers, at a time of critical necessity. For this writer, that's enough said.

> When is the "best" time to purchase a long-term care insurance policy? Paul Elisha wasn't the first person to ever pose that question. The ideal answer is: "in enough time for your coverage to be in effect one day before you become uninsurable or one day before you enter a nursing facility, whichever happens first." Not living in an ideal world, we must prepare for events beyond our control that have the power to alter physical and mental well-being and to inflict difficulties on those to whom we look for our care.

# Long-Term Care Insurance Around the World

Seniors around the world are beginning to have an impact on society as a whole. Their notoriety is evidenced through such acts as the United Nations designating 1999 the International Year of Older Persons, and through a new project examining the cross-national effects of the simultaneous aging of major industrial nations, called the Center for Strategic and International Studies (CSIS).

The United Nations draft resolution enumerated twenty-one principles, of which items three and four dealt with the issues of seniors in need of help and the increased demand for care and support.

The CSIS project is led by a commission of international leaders in health sciences, economics, and finance, who through the Global Aging Initiative (GAI) will attempt to put aging policies on the diplomatic agenda.

As the Million Dollar Round Table is an international organization representing nearly 23,000 members, with close to 36% of the membership coming from countries outside the United States and its territories, this book would not be complete without addressing the issues of long-term care globally. It is with deep appreciation the author acknowledges Terri Haugen, RHU, CLU, HIA, REBC, AIM, Assistant Vice President of AUL Reinsurance Management Services, LLC, for her participation.

Long-term care insurance is slowly being introduced into developed countries, as many of these countries struggle to balance socialized medicine for acute and chronic care with the burgeoning need for long-term care. Developing countries, on the other hand, are on the cusp of dealing with the Age Wave and the need to discover a solution for paying for long-term care. As nations join the ranks of developed countries, two scenarios will manifest themselves:

1. Women will enter the workforce, removing themselves from traditional caregiving roles.

263

2. As standards of living rise, demand for health care services available in developed countries should also rise.

Because members of the Million Dollar Round Table are leaders who are able to effectuate change, both in their respective communities and throughout the insurance industry, information on how to prevail in the international market should be of utmost interest to them.

National LTC Network member, J. Eugene Tapper, MS, NHA, having pioneered long-term care insurance in Latin America, is well qualified to lead MDRT members in this direction.

On St. Patrick's Day, March 17, 1999, and I was in Syracuse, New York, to present a Continuing Education credit class on long-term care and long-term care insurance to the Upstate New York Chapter of International Association of Financial Planning. As is my custom, I will scan current magazines and newspapers for articles dealing with aging to enhance key points of my presentation. I've never failed to find something relative to my message, be it an article on aging, Medicare, Medicaid, Social Security, long-term care, genetic breakthroughs, or the dread diseases of aging. That day's issue of *U.S.A. Today* was a bonanza! The cover story is titled "Longevity Is Global Sleeping Giant," and it contains a bar chart illustrating the median age in Europe, North America, Asia, South America, and Africa, for the years 1950, 1998, and 2050. According to this article, the Age Wave is sweeping the globe, and "Every upward tick in life span has an even larger impact on society and the economy." There's also a three-page special report on Extending Life —the promise and perils, titled, "Forever Young?" In my presentation, I display a photo of Jeanne Louise Calment of Arles, France, who lived longer than any human on record. She was 122 years old when she passed away in 1997. Her picture is on the front page of the special report, under the banner "SCIENCE FINDS NO LIMIT ON LIFE SPAN." That day was blessed with the "Luck of the Irish."

Our world is undergoing a demographic revolution. For the first time, more of humanity is growing older. In 1900, there were ten to seventeen million people aged 65 or older, less than one percent of the total global population. By 1992, there were 342 million people in that age group, making up 6.2 percent of the population. By 2050, the number of people 65 years or older will expand to at least 2.5 billion people — about one-fifth of the world's projected population (*Scientific American,* April 1993).

The post-World War II baby boom, and its attendant improvement in medical care in most parts of the world, has created history's largest aging population. With an older society come new and varied challenges. One is increased longevity. But living longer does not always mean living a better or healthier life. In reality, it means increased probability of the mental or physical frailties that accompany an older body. These frailties demand a change in today's medical and social attitudes. Health care for the aged does not necessarily mean "making repairs" for acute impairments. Instead, it means helping the elderly and some younger persons retain function and independence despite chronic conditions.

In the United States and many other countries, concerns about costs are a key factor driving changes in long-term care financing and service delivery. The attempt to substitute home- and community-based services for institutional care is the most visible response to cost concerns. Other cost-control strategies include limits on nursing home beds, capping budgets, controls on provider fees, and case management. In the U.S., the lead in this shift has been taken by various states, hoping to contain welfare system costs while responding to the desire of disabled people to avoid institutionalization. Other countries faced with high and rising public demand and costs for long-term care are pursuing similar strategies. To contain expenditures, many countries are applying global or capped budgets to long-term care outlays. They have also strengthened other controls such as cost sharing, fee negotiation, the setting of rates, and management of nursing home bed supply.

The problems of aging are universal, but the medical and social solutions for meeting the needs of the elderly are as different and varied as there are cultures in our world. With strained economies and the sheer size of populations increasing pressure on current support systems, the insurance industry worldwide is responding to rising costs for long-term care and governments' inability to expand entitlement programs with a common solution: long-term care insurance.

In this section, we will outline the existing or developing markets for long-term care insurance around the world, analyzing each country where information is available.

**LTC Insurance Around the World:** The number of elderly people around the world is growing, and many of them at some stage will be disabled or simply too frail to care for themselves. Nursing care is far from cheap, and few can afford it from savings or pensions. Options open to those without some sort of insurance protection are to forego care, rely on relatives to care for them, sell their family homes to pay for care, or fall back on the state. Even the most devoted children are unable to invest the necessary time and attention to care for elderly relatives, although evidence suggests that many do give up their social life and suffer financial hardship to do so. As people live longer, the children of elderly parents may themselves become retired and need care. This is not unusual. Many people who live to the age of 90 and beyond have children who are 70 years old.

In developed countries, there is an increasing awareness of the hardships people may suffer in old age as their need for long-term care services increases. In some countries, the concept of state care is ingrained, but governments have realized that the working population will continue to shrink, while an increasing number of the population will need care.

In many countries that face continuing or impending financial/budgetary crises, the issue is attracting the attention of political parties and governments, for whom solutions are the subject of much discussion. Critics of the American health care system often point to health care systems in other developed nations as better, citing universal access and delivery and lower cost as innate to those systems. Most of these systems are a part of social insurance programs, with government control and tax funding the norm.

Universal coverage, however, often applies only to basic health services and not to comprehensive long-term care. Most countries, for example, require patients to share in the costs of either institutional and/or home care services, with the amount of co-payments usually based on income levels. Global budgets often impose daily, weekly, or monthly caps on the number of services provided, with little flexibility for buying additional services.

**Defining Chronic Care:** National health insurance coverage of chronic care in most countries is limited to medical care and nursing home care. Coverage of long-term care services depends on how such services are classified. If considered medical services, they usually will be covered by social insurance; if classified as social services, coverage often is excluded.

Social services usually are means tested and often require a co-payment based on ability to pay. The only noninstitutional chronic care service covered by most countries is medical day care. Nonskilled home care services fall into the social service category. Many of these are funded through local or regional governments and may be eligible for national matching funds in some countries. Some countries such as Australia, Germany, the Netherlands, and Sweden have programs that will pay families cash benefits to care for their elderly relatives. In some cases, these benefits are paid to families only if formal caregivers are unavailable and family income is below a specified level.

**Means Testing:** Most countries use some type of means testing to determine benefit eligibility and cost sharing based on ability to pay. For example, Canada and Australia set co-payments in relation to social security income benefits. In Scandinavian countries, nursing home residents contribute their social security pensions plus 60 to 80 percent of their private incomes.

Most European countries offer home care services on a sliding scale, with assistance completely phased out at higher income levels. In the U.K. and Canada, fees for home care services are determined at the local level. Some municipalities and provinces charge sliding-scale fees; others provide services free of charge.[1]

**Institutional vs. Home Care:** One misconception about long-term care systems in other countries is that home care coverage as a means of reducing public institutional expenses is more prevalent than in the U.S. Interestingly, the U.S. has one of the lowest rates of institutional care for the elderly among developed countries, with only 5 percent of the over-age-65 population living in nursing homes at any given time. Only the rates in Great Britain and Germany parallel the U.S., at 4.1 percent and 4.5 percent, respectively. The rates of other countries are higher, with Australia at almost 7 percent, Canada at 8 percent, and the Netherlands at 11 percent.

Social programs in France and Germany are biased toward institutional services. Programs in other countries, such as Great Britain, strongly emphasize community-based care. According to the U.S. Department of Health and Human Services, however, social insurance programs for home health services have not appreciably reduced expenditures for institutional care. In fact, the opposite appears to be true. Countries with the greatest availability of home care also have the largest nursing home bed supply.

Because long-term care services of a personal, custodial nature are not part of the social or national health insurance programs of most countries, financing and delivery of these services are not well integrated with acute care systems.

As a result of changes in population composition, the old-age dependency ratio is changing. The old-age dependency ratio (defined as the ratio of the population aged 65 and over to those aged 15 to 64) is expected to increase in every major world region, with the most dramatic increases occurring among the more developed regions and in East Asia. As people live longer, and as demands for income support and for a range of social services increase, the difficulties of supporting comprehensive social security schemes will be felt. Countries will face growing fiscal burdens as expenditures increase and the working-age population shrinks.[2]

Growing problems of social responsibility for huge aging populations are forcing the world to confront the issues of the elderly. Traditionally, different cultures have assigned the elderly varying levels of respect and importance in society. In the Bible, the Jews were strictly commanded to take care of their aged parents. Some cultures, particularly in Asia, for example, have revered older people, making their needs a priority. The question of who would care for you in your twilight years was easy to answer your family.

In recent years, however, in the United States, where numerous cultures diverge and health care costs are high, a quandary has arisen over how to take care of a rapidly aging population. It's a dilemma other industrialized nations are beginning to face as well.

In the U.S. in the mid-1970s, private insurers came up with an answer to the tangled problem of caring for the elderly: long-term care insurance. Indeed, recent surveys have demonstrated that long-term care is ranked by Americans as one of their greatest financial planning concerns.

That concern is now shared by consumers in other countries. Private insurers began selling long- term-care policies in Germany, France, and Israel about eight years ago, and insurers in England in 1991 jumped into this evolving market.

Although the market for long-term care insurance in other countries is not as well developed as it is in the U.S., interest is high, as we share many factors that drive our markets:

- Younger adults have lower birth rates, while older ones with ever-larger numbers and post-war baby boomers among them find their longer life expectancy accompanied by greater health care needs.

269

- The cost of acute health care is increasing dramatically because of the increased use of acute care services by the aging population; access to care is becoming more difficult, with government programs straining to handle costs of acute care and never fully covering long-term care costs.
- Government resources are dwindling as social pension programs head into difficult times, there are fewer workers to pay taxes, and tax rates already considered too high are making it politically risky to raise taxes further.

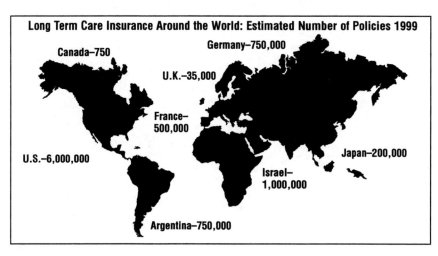

Long Term Care Insurance Around the World: Estimated Number of Policies 1999
Germany–750,000
Canada–750
U.K.–35,000
France–500,000
U.S.–6,000,000
Israel–1,000,000
Japan–200,000
Argentina–750,000

## Asia

Early in the next century, two-thirds of the world population aged 60 or more years will live in developing countries, especially in Asia.[3]

Cultural differences between the East and the West are well documented, but in the process of aging, these differences are less marked. A case in point:

ADL-assessment scales commonly accepted in developed countries in the West — the Barthel ADL Index in England, the Katz in the U.S. — were found by three Thai physicians to be lacking when applied to Asians; specifically in a study conducted on 703 Thai elderly people. Many ADLs are performed in different ways in Asian countries, which may lead to differences in the meaning of ADL scores in different countries. For instance, Thai people eat using either a short spoon or their hands; they take a bath by using a bowl to scoop and pour water over the body; they use a squat lavatory. Therefore, the relative ease of ADLs applied in Asian countries will differ from Western countries and the underlying dimensions of ADLs may also vary. Early pioneering studies of between-country differences in disability used Western ADL items without any adjustment for cultural factors, and the levels of disability appeared to be high. The physicians felt that assessment of variation in disability between populations and over time required the development of more culturally independent ADL scales. Thus, an extended ADL index — the Chula ADL Index — suitable for use in developing countries was designed.[4]

Other differences will no doubt emerge as the issues of long-term care and LTC and LTCI are studied in Asia.

**Japan:** Japan's aging population is growing faster than any nation in the world. The seeds of aging in Japan's future were sown long ago. Following a brief postwar baby boom after World War II, the average number of children born to Japanese women between 1947 and 1957 dropped from 4.5 to 2.07, below the rate of 2.1 needed to stabilize the population over time. Together with impressive life expectancy — 75.5 years for Japanese men and 81.3 years for women (about four years longer than for Americans) the plunging birth rate has triggered near hysteria in Japan.[5]

Currently, 41 percent of the national income goes to fund Japan's universal health insurance and pension systems. Policy makers estimate the national burden will rise to just below 50 percent in 2020, but projections by private Japanese economists show the national burden headed to 60 percent or higher, driven mainly by exploding costs. One measure proposed: raising the age at which Japanese become eligible for public pensions from the current 60 to 65. Most Japanese firms still force nonmanagement workers to retire by age 60 or 62. If the pension eligibility age is raised, these firms fear that they also will have to hike their retirement age, saddling them with costly older workers as a result.[6]

Roughly 11 percent of Japan's 124 million people are now 65 or older. With a plunging birth rate and the world's longest life expectancy, Japan's share of aged will rise to 17 percent by the year 2000 and to 21 percent by 2010, — making the powerhouse that was once the youngest of all industrialized nations into the oldest by far.[7]

A prime reason for Japanese policy makers to think they can get by with a lower level of services for the aged is Japan's tradition of multigenerational families living together, also the Confucian-based doctrine of obligation to parents. In fact, more than 60 percent of Japan's elderly live with their children or extended families, compared with fewer than 10 percent in the U.S.[8]

Critics complain that the government is underestimating cataclysmic shifts in Japan's family structure. Not only is the number of multigenerational households dropping but the ratio of adult children in their 40s (caregivers) to people aged 65 to 79 is now about 3:4 and this will decline by almost half over the next 15 years.[9] In the past, care of the elderly was traditionally provided by the family. Today, it is no longer an unquestioned duty of Japanese children to care for their aged parents, so increasing number of people will need to make use of more costly, professional care services.

Japan's welfare institutions for the aged are divided into three categories: "home with moderate fee," "home for the aged," and "special nursing home for the aged." The first two have strict income restrictions for admission and provide basic living accommodations. The third type is a long-term care facility for the bedridden elderly and provides care and nursing services, with only limited medical supervision. In this third category there are no income restrictions for admission; patients are charged monthly fees in proportion to their or their legal supporters' income (averaging Y20,000 and up to

Y160,000 per month). The rate of nursing home residents in Japan was about 10 per 1,000 elderly in 1988, much lower than in the U. S (46.2 per 1,000 in 1985). Japan's nursing homes are operated by public organizations or by nonprofit private organizations, with local government welfare offices primarily responsible for deciding eligibility for admission. Demand for nursing home beds far exceeds supply, and applicants commonly wait for more than a year. In 1988, the government established an institutional category halfway between nursing homes and hospitals for the aged, called "Health Institutions for the Aged." The new institutions provide more caregiving than a hospital and more medical supervision than a nursing home. Home health care services are not as well established in Japan as in some Western nations.

Japan has developed a controversial long-term care system that went into effect in April 2000. The plan mandates contributions from everyone over the age of 40. Contributions for services for citizens between 40 and 65 will require less yen per month than contributions from citizens over 65. When the program was implemented, citizens residing in care facilities were subject to new evaluations to see if they may continue living in a residential care setting. At-home services previously available at no charge now require some out-of-pocket expense.

LTC funding products were first offered by the Japanese life insurance industry in the mid-1980s. These products, which use a much-restricted ADL model (requiring the insured to be bedridden and unable to perform at least four ADLs), are life insurance policies with varying combinations of other features (such as survivor benefits) and varying levels of benefits payable in the event of disability, in the form of an annuity. As many as thirty Japanese insurers market this type of product (Life Insurance Association of Japan).

The largest Japanese life insurer in 1988 developed a product which seems to mirror what in the U.S. might be called an accelerated death benefit plan. It is a paid-up whole life policy which gives the insured three options at the end of the premium payment period: to continue the life insurance protection, to annuitize the benefits, or to pay for long-term care.

While there is no current knowledge of LTC insurance products in Indonesia, Malaysia, Philippines, Singapore, South Korea, or Thailand, in the year 2000 South Korea was introduced to professional home care services, which if successful, could lead to incentive for a private insurance product.

## Australia

Today Australia, with 12 percent of its population over age 65, is relatively young compared with many industrialized countries. Large-scale immigration at the end of World War II delayed the aging of the population. Substantial numbers of postwar immigrants are now reaching old age.

In 1994, the average life expectancy of men was age 74; of women, 80. Eighty-five percent of Australians live in urban areas.[10] By 2020, men can expect to live another nineteen years after they reach age 60; women another twenty-seven years.[11]

All but a very few older people currently live independently. Only 7 percent live in any kind of institution, including boarding houses, hospitals, and nursing homes. Fewer than 5 percent of them live in their children's homes.

Elderly nursing home residents must contribute 87.5 percent of their social security benefits to pay for nursing home care. Individuals who do not receive full pensions must contribute 87.5 percent of their private pensions or supplementary assistance to meet this minimum contribution. The Commonwealth government provides subsidies for low-income elderly who live in hostels and require personal care services. Hostels provide supportive services for individuals requiring assistance with activities of daily living, but not medical services.

Federal financial incentives have served to shift the balance of care from nursing homes to less intensive service providers, such as hostels and services funded by the Home and Community Care Program. Although nursing homes remain the major item of expenditure in long-term care, expenditure on nursing homes declined between 1985/1986 and 1990/1991 from 81 percent of the total to 69 percent, while expenditure on hostels increased from 5 percent to 10 percent. (Hostels in Australia provide accommodation to people who need help with daily living tasks. They typically provide a single room with either private or shared bath. Staff are available on a twenty-four-hour basis to provide a wide range of nonmedical care.)[12]

In an effort to encourage families to assist with the care of older relatives, the Commonwealth introduced the Domiciliary Care Benefit in 1974. Through this benefit, a family member who cares for an aging relative receives a monetary subsidy. Despite public recognition that caring for an older family member can be a financial and emotional burden, the program has not been particularly successful and is not widely publicized. Payments have not kept up with the Consumer Price Index and are not sufficient to induce potential caregivers to forgo other employment. Furthermore, for those people age 65 and older, or others who care for an older relative, the payment is deducted from their pension.[13]

Some long-term care insurance products were available in Australia until 1990, but the company providing this interest sold it. There has been increased discussion about long-term care-type products within several carrier organizations.

## Europe

### Socialist European Countries

**Denmark:** With a population totaling just 5.2 million, Denmark's aging population is sizeable 832,000 (16 percent over age 65). The average life expectancy of men is 73; of women, 78. A full 85 percent of Danes live in urban areas.[14]

Danish social policies for older people are typical of the social democratic model of welfare. There is a large public sector, comprehensive social services and a free or subsidized benefit system, financed largely through personal taxation. The state takes direct responsibility for the care of older people, leaving the family with only a minimal role to play.[15]

All persons in Denmark are covered by public health security. This entitles the individual to free medical treatment in a hospital or by a general practitioner or specialist. Medical drugs and dental treatment are not free, but are heavily subsidized.[16]

Today, most nursing homes are municipal institutions for the very frail elderly or persons with dementia. Municipalities decide who will be accepted as residents. Nursing homes provide a separate room for each resident with a bathroom, but no separate kitchen. Residents can have their own furniture. Residents pay for food and housing with their pension money. Nursing services are financed by the county.[17]

The home help service is the mainstay of home care policy in Denmark. Local municipalities decide who receives home help and how many hours of help are to be provided. The main criteria for receiving a service is impaired functional ability and lack of relatives who can provide help and care.[18]

Nursing home residents in Denmark must contribute their social security pensions plus between 60 and 80 percent of other private income, including that from interest, toward the cost of care. However, they are not required to tap the principal of investment assets, liquidate investments, or sell their homes.[19]

Unlike the U.S., where means testing usually limits access to publicly supported homemaker and personal care services to the poor or near poor, Denmark offers these types of home help to all citizens on a sliding scale, income-related fee basis.[20]

Nothing is known currently about the existence of long-term-care insurance products in Denmark.

**The Netherlands:** With a population totaling 15.4 million, a full 13 percent of the Dutch are over age 65. This figure is expected to increase to 14.1 percent by 2000. The average life expectancy of men is 74; of women, 80.[21, 22] The Dutch national statistical office has estimated that in 2010, 15 percent of the population will be older than 65 years.[23] For the first time in history, the Netherlands is being confronted with a society made up of four generations.

Various experiments are underway. There are so-called kangaroo houses, in which an aging parent lives downstairs and the adult child and his or her family upstairs. "Tandem houses," where parent and child live near each other, are also being tried. Special flats for the old often provide special services, such as alarm systems, maintenance, a caretaker, meals, and sometimes a resident nurse. All this costs money, but those currently retiring often have pensions above the minimum level.[24]

Every Dutch resident is entitled by law to long-term care in a nursing home.

Holland provides extensive social insurance for LTC services including nursing home, in-home personal care and prolonged institutional care.

Compulsory LTC was introduced in 1968. Prior to that date, nursing care costs had to be paid by the patient if not for a serious illness. The reform gave all elderly citizens who were chronically sick the right to a place in a state-registered nursing home. In the early 1970s, there were some 15,000 beds, mostly in small units of up to 150 beds. Even so there was already pressure to find places and an estimate was made that another 7,000 beds were needed. In order to hold the unexpected rise in costs, an income-related deductible was introduced. The state is now trying to make the old do more to provide for themselves. As more live to increasingly old age, there is sure to be a time when they cannot support themselves.[25]

The government supplies 90 percent of funding for home care through public subsidies. Clients must make a weekly income-based contribution for cost of service. Home help agencies are limited to specific conditions and must spend at least 75 percent of their budgets on services.[26]

A "Thuiszorg verzekering" product, which literally means, "home care insurance," was introduced in 1992. To date, only one insurance company has developed such a product. Benefit selections for home care range from a minimum of Dfl 10,000 to a maximum of Dfl 125,000 a year.[27]

The plan pays a monthly benefit, which depends on the amount insured, and the degree of loss of autonomy. The need for care, or the degree of loss of autonomy, is defined on the basis of the activities of daily living that a person can no longer perform alone.

As soon as the insured has been hospitalized or confined in a nursing home for more than ten days, benefit payments for this home care coverage stop.[28]

**Norway:** With a population totaling just 4.3 million in 1994, Norway's aging population is sizeable, with 688,000 citizens over age 65 (16 percent). Average life expectancy of men is 74 years; of women, 80 years.[29]

Nursing home residents in Norway must contribute their social security pensions plus between 60 and 80 percent of other private income, including that from interest, toward the cost of care. They are not, however, required to tap the principal of investment assets, liquidate investments, or sell their homes.[30]

Unlike the U.S., Norway offers publicly supported homemaker and personal care services to all citizens on a sliding scale, income-related fee basis.[31]

Nothing is currently known about the existence of long-term care insurance products in Norway.

**Sweden:** Sweden has the largest proportion of elderly persons to total population. In fact, Sweden has the world's highest ratio of older people relative to total population. The elderly (those aged 65 and over) today represent 18 percent of Sweden's total population (which numbers 9 million) and this percentage is anticipated to increase to 19.6 percent by 2010. Swedes aged 80 and over comprise 4.4 percent of the population and will likely increase to almost 6 percent by 2010. The number of persons age 80 and older increased by 44 percent from 1980 to 1990.[32, 33] The average life expectancy of men is 75 years; of women, 80 years.[34]

Since the early days of the social welfare state in Sweden, the state has assumed major responsibility for care of elderly persons, with little private or voluntary activity. Sweden has one of the world's most comprehensive programs of public care for older persons. Apart from care provided by family members, nearly all elder care comes from government providers.[35]

Sweden has historically financed long-term care as a socially insured benefit that is paid for through taxes, as acute health care is. Services are funded primarily by local governments; the national government's share of public spending for long-term care is less than 10 percent.[36]

In 1992, Sweden enacted the Adel Reform, which consolidated responsibility for long-term care at the municipal level. Municipalities assumed primary responsibility for all aspects of long-term care, including that provided in hospitals, nursing homes, people's homes, and the community. Municipalities also gained new taxing authority to fund services and additional staff resources to provide them.[37]

Despite a tradition of heavily subsidizing long-term care services, Sweden is shifting a greater share of the costs to consumers — from 4 percent in 1991 to about 10 percent in 1993. Officials expect consumer charges to increase further as a result of growing budgetary pressures and recent limits on the ability of municipalities to raise taxes. Income-related charges and copayments are increasingly being applied for home- and community-based care. These vary considerably among municipalities. Municipalities now are also charging individuals for the lodging component of residential or nursing-home care.[38]

Because municipalities finance most long-term care, they also control the supply of services. Recent reform efforts have concentrated on restricting the supply of institutional services, expanding home- and community-based services, and reducing the use of hospital beds for long-term care patients.[39]

Like Germany and some Canadian provinces, Sweden separates the costs of institutional care into a lodging component and a care component. Public funds generally pay for the care, while the individual generally pays for lodging.[40]

To stretch public resources and compensate families for the burden of providing long-term care at home, Sweden requires employers to grant up to thirty days of paid leave to provide home care. Sweden also pays salaries to family members who give full-time or part-time care. Under 1992 reform legislation, the national government expected to provide municipalities additional funds to support informal caregiving.[41]

In Sweden, little or no private long-term care insurance exists.[42]

**European Union Countries**

Because of the recent formation of the European Union, much that is currently being written addresses the E.U. as a whole, rather than on a country-by-country basis. Some interesting facts emerge, relative to the Union and long-term care:[43]

There are 68 million plus people aged 60 and over in the European Union. This represents about one in five of the total population. This figure is expected to rise rapidly in the coming decades so that by the year 2020 more than one-quarter of the Union's population will have reached their 60th birthday.

- Over 24 million people in the European Union suffer from some sort of disability. As the population ages, this figure will increase significantly.
- The family is overwhelmingly the main source of care for older people in the European Union. About two-thirds of the help provided to older people comes from within the family.
- Very little formal assistance is given to family caregivers in the European Union. In Southern Europe, there are almost no established programs or policies to help caregivers.
- Older people in countries with well-established welfare states are increasingly expressing a preference for professional care over family care, especially for conditions requiring a long-term commitment.
- There are also different financial and legal obligations on families to care for older people in the European Union. In Germany, the family is legally obliged to care financially for an older relative, whereas in Denmark the state takes

direct responsibility. In the U.K., the family is expected to provide care, but there is no legal requirement to do so.

According to Richard Thomas, Managing Director of RED ARC Assured Limited, whose long-term care program has been actively marketed in the U.K. for several years, "My impression overall is that the market in Europe is very much in its infancy. There are no big conclusions to draw at this stage, other than that the various governments have started to recognize the problem. Apart from Germany, there is little cohesion in terms of planning solutions. Countries that have tended towards government-funded social programs are beginning to see a rapid escalation in costs and are starting to pull them back."

**France:** In 1994, those ages 65 and over represented 15 percent of France's population numbering 8.7 million; by 2010, that figure is expected to rise to 16.3 percent. Life expectancy of French men is 73; of women, 81.[44]

In 1970, there were three employees working to every dependent relative, and the average contribution from the paycheck to support pensions was 17 percent. By 2010, there will be only 1.7 employees per relative, and the contribution will rise to 40 percent (*European*, February 18-21, 1993).

Like the rest of Western Europe, France is faced with an aging population. Estimates show that the current system of state pension insurance will not produce enough money to fund those eligible after the year 2005. In 1990 there were 2.3 people in the labor force for every person claiming a pension. Ten years from now, those who are working will not be enough to maintain the present level of pensions.[45]

In France, there is an extensive network of long-term care institutions run by the state, plus nursing homes and home help services. Private long-term care insurances still in its infancy, is principally targeted at the over age 60 group and, according to one source, is expensive.[46] In 1981, a law expanded health insurance coverage for home health care, including personal care.[47]

The LTC market in France came to life in the mid-1980s

when three companies launched products: two were true stand-alone LTC plans, the third was a life/annuity plan nearly identical to a scheme introduced in Germany at about the same time.

The life product met with little success, similar to the experience in Germany, with fewer than 100 policies sold by 1990. The reasons: lack of awareness and relative high price. One carrier offering the stand-alone LTC product withdrew from the market in 1988, having experienced rapidly deteriorating claims caused by underpricing.

By mid-1992, several private life and health insurers were offering contracts that paid an annuity in case of the need for medically recognized long-term care. Under these contracts, annuity payments may or may not be adjusted according to the seriousness of the insured's loss of independence. Benefits may be paid at the end of a one-year waiting period (extended to three years if long-term care is the result of mental causes; cancelled on the loss of independence following an accident) and/or a six-month period of consolidation after the need for long-term care arises (three months in the case of a need for long-term care resulting from an acute illness.) Basic monthly annuities can range from 2,000 to 8,000 FF per month.[48]

**Germany:** In 1994, those age 65 and over represented 15 percent of Germany's total population, which numbers 81.2 million. Life expectancy is currently 72 years for men; 79 years for women.[49] By 2010, those over age 65 are expected to represent 20.4 percent of the total population.

Germany's health system got its start in 1883, and survived the country's battering in two world wars. The big challenge now stems from West Germany's winning the cold war, and taking in East Germany. East Germany ran a centralized system, with government-owned hospitals and government-employed doctors. With difficulty, it is now being folded into the West German system, which features independent, nonprofit, government-regulated health insurers known as "sickness funds." Those funds collect premiums and pay medical bills.

As in the United States and the United Kingdom, a means-tested welfare program — basing eligibility on financial need — has been the source for most public funding for long-term care in Germany. Individuals have typically been required to have limited resources or to deplete assets before becoming eligible for public assistance to pay for long-term care. Public resources for long-term care support institutional services.[50]

Like the U.S., Germany has established initiatives to contain long-term care costs. Even while planning to add new funds ($7.3 billion annually), Germany has worked to develop a budget expressly for long-term care spending. Reforms scheduled for 1995/96 implementation were to convert Germany's financing of long-term care from welfare funds to a tax-based system of social insurance and to make long-term care services standard benefits provided through Germany's national health insurance plan.[51, 52]

The development of LTCI in Germany was much like the gestation of fraternal twins. As a life product, it sprang from the German Life Insurance Association, which, in 1985, commissioned a special committee to design a draft product. Insurers who entered this market followed the committee's recommendations so closely that a virtually uniform product is now offered. Using an ADL model, the plan provides both an annuity and a death benefit. Three points qualifies for 40 percent of the annuity benefit; 4 or 5 points, 70 percent; and 6 points, 100 percent. Following satisfaction of a six month elimination (deductible or "deferred") period, benefits are paid for care provided either by professionals or family. Premiums are not designed to remain level and have no guarantee, and there is no limit on future premium increases.

According to one source, these annuity products uniformly provide for the automatic payment of an old age pension instead of the LTC annuity from age 80 (or optionally from age 85) and a death benefit. These additional benefit elements make the product very expensive. No more than 5,000 policies had been sold by the end of 1992.[53]

As a health product, LTC took a form similar to stand-alone products in the U.S. Like the life product, an ADL model was used, with two main formats emerging: 1) a fixed daily benefit plan, with a point system and percentage payment method similar to the life products sold; and 2) a reimbursement plan, paying usually 80% of costs incurred for professionally provided care.

The health insurers were, according to one source, somewhat more successful than annuity sellers, with 300,000 policies in force by the end of 1993. The root cause of the failure of LTC products to make an impact, according to this source, lay in the reservations which life insurers themselves had about the subject. Long-term care insurance in many ways seemed an extremely risky new product. With traditional life insurance products booming, it was also considered unnecessary to market such a difficult product. In 1992, in the wake of the revived discussion on social LTC insurance, the association of life insurers developed new calculation bases. Since then, more and more life insurers have been offering second-generation products, which use these new calculation bases and are mainly additional benefit insurance. According to this source (1994), at present there are three types: a pure waiver of premium of the main policy, a deferred LTC annuity (i.e., payment of an LTC annuity from a specified age) linked to disability cover, and an LTC annuity, which begins immediately. These new products offered by life insurers give, according to this source, more comprehensive cover. Approximately 12,000 of these new products had been sold by fourth quarter 1994.[54]

Currently about twenty-six German insurers offer some form of nursing-care insurance, at premiums calculated according to the individual risks, with age and gender being the major factors. Insurance can be purchased either to cover the daily cost of long-term care or to cover a portion, up to 80%, of all costs for trained nurses.[55]

**Ireland:** In 1993, there were just over a half million people in Ireland aged 60 and over, representing about one in seven of the total population. There are some interesting differences between Ireland and most other countries, particularly those in the European Union.

Ireland has the lowest proportion of elderly in the E.U., with 11.3 percent over 65, and 4.5 percent over 75. The proportion of the very old, those aged 85 and over, is also lowest there. Increases in the relative number of those aged 75 and over in the last forty years were the smallest in Ireland, due partly to relatively high fertility rates and ongoing emigration. In addition, life expectancy of women in Ireland continues to be the lowest in the E.U.

The rate of older people living alone is not, however, as high as in other countries. Ireland is the only country in Europe with a fertility rate sufficient to reproduce its current population. Ireland also has a relatively low rate of one-parent families and of women in the conventional labor market, and a relative high mean household size (3.7).[56]

Between 1986 and 2011, one source estimates that the number of people aged 85 and older will increase by 55 percent, while the number aged 65 and over will rise by 14 percent. In the West and Northwest Regions, which in 1991 had the largest proportions of old people, the number of old people will decline. But in the Eastern region, they are expected to rise by 31 percent.[57]

In Ireland, geriatric long-stay hospitals and welfare homes are run by health boards. Patients are expected to make a means-related contribution towards their keep. If the patient has a social welfare pension, most of it will be paid over to the provider, with the patient retaining only a small portion. For care in private nursing homes — both those commercially profit-run and those run on a nonprofit basis, usually by religious bodies — government benefits are payable only where the patient is shown to be unable to meet the cost or has been assessed as needing nursing-home care by the health board and has passed a means test.[58]

There has, according to the National Council for the Elderly, been no support in Ireland for a major shift in financing care for the elderly. General taxation is, therefore, likely to continue as the main source of funding for public long-stay care and for sub-vented nursing home care.[59]

The third E.U. Directive on Non-Life Insurance — which provided for a completely open market within the E.U. for all forms of non-life insurance products including sickness or private medical insurance — became effective July 1994. At that time, the Irish authorities were required to remove the restrictions which gave VHI a virtual monopoly on private insurance.

Whether this type of control will extend to long-term care insurance is not known, although one source did speculate in 1994 that a number of insurers were soon expected to begin offering long-term care protection as an add-on to their mainstream policies and that VHI had expressed an interest in this area.[60]

**Italy:** Italy is rapidly graying. Today its population has the fourteenth highest proportion of elderly people in the world. Because of the current zero population growth, it will leap nearly to the top of the list by year 2000, with nearly 10 million people (17.5 percent of the population) over 65 years of age. More than half (58%) of Italy's elderly people stay at home or in a geriatric institution all the time. According to research by the Agnelli Foundation, nine out of ten elderly people feel abandoned by relatives, can't find anyone disposed to look after them, and complain about not being respected by young people. The changes to the extended family wrought by the urbanization and economic development of the post-Second World War period have deprived the elderly of the presence and care of children. The extended family survives mostly in the south, in communities emptied of most of their young people who emigrated to the north in the 1950s and 1960s.[61]

Italy has a comprehensive system of social benefits covering unemployment and disability as well as retirement pensions and family allowances. These benefits are all provided by the social security system (Istituto Nazionale della Previdenza Sociale.) Government expenditure on pensions in 1993 represented 15 percent of GDP. The pensionable age for men and women was to rise from 60 and 55 years respectively to 65 and 60 years by the year 2002. Major reductions in pension and welfare provision were expected in 1995. A comprehensive national health service, aiming to provide free medical care for all citizens, was introduced in 1980. However, minimum charges are still made for essential medicines, medical examinations, and hospital treatment. All workers are eligible for benefits under a unified national medical insurance scheme. In 1992, the state budget allocated 91,624,000 million lire to health.[62]

Development work on stand-alone LTC insurance plans had been going on in 1995 and 1996. Programs were to be launched initially in 1996 with a range of products available. More sophisticated reimbursement-type plans were to be sold by agents to individuals such as the self-employed and professionals. Simple programs with lesser benefits of an indemnity nature were to be marketed through third-party endorsements on a group basis.

**Spain:** In 1950, there were around 2 million people over 65 in Spain. Today, out of a total 39 million Spaniards, there are some 5.8 million, or 15 percent of the population. That figure is expected to increase to 16.4 by 2000.[63] Women predominate among the country's elderly; there are 2.7 million of them. Some 84 percent of old people live in cities and only 16 percent live in rural areas.

In Spain, private corporations of various types are being started. Publicly held businesses are being privatized. Insurance is one of the newer creations. Discussions within insurance organizations and between carriers and reinsurers now are in the early stages. Simple programs are expected to be part of first generation Spanish plans.

**Switzerland:** With a population totaling 7 million in 1994, Switzerland's aging population numbers just over 1 million (15 percent). The average life expectancy of men is 74 years; of women, 81 years.

Social insurance pays for health and medically related long-term care services provided to Swiss in institutions and at home. Co-payments for these services are income-related and average 5 percent for home care, 7 percent for long-term care hospitals, and 25 percent for old-age homes.

There are 900 private insurance companies in Switzerland. Ninety-six percent of all Swiss are privately insured for hospital costs, but requirements, restrictions, policy cancellations, and inadequate coverage constitute severe hardships for many older people. The cantons may pay all or part of insurance premiums for older people without adequate means. Most long-term care services are paid for with private resources.

Nothing is known currently about the existence of long-term care insurance products in Switzerland.

**United Kingdom:** In 1994, those age 65 and over represented 16 percent of the U.K.'s 58.4 million population; by 2010, that figure is expected to rise to 17.1 percent.[64]

Great Britain has the world's most centralized health care system. Most countries place some responsibility for care on states, provinces or the private sector, but Britain's is fully administered by the national government. The government owns most hospitals and employs most doctors. The system is almost fully financed by general taxes; very little money ever passes between providers and patients. The British plan also produces long waits for some elective services. The government embarked on a reform plan in 1990 designed to provide competition within the system and increase public satisfaction while keeping costs down.[65] In line with this goal in the new millennium, people age 65 and older who qualify will be able to receive direct care payments to purchase home care services of their choice if a recommendation of the Royal Commission on LTC is adopted by the Ministers.

The cost of long-term care in the U.K. could more than double in real terms over the next 40 years to £100 billion from the current £40 billion, according to one source. Over three-quarters of LTC in Britain is currently provided free of charge by family and friends. A study undertaken as part of the 1985 General Household Survey indicated that some 3 percent of the adult population — around 1.5 million people — spent more than twenty hours per week caring for someone.[66]

As in the United States and Germany, a means-tested welfare program — basing eligibility on financial need — has been the source for most public funding for long-term care in the U.K. Individuals are typically required to have limited resources or to deplete assets before becoming eligible for public assistance to pay for long-term care. (According to one source, "...everything over L8,000 will be swallowed in nursing home fees, before the local authority is obliged to step in and shoulder the cost."[67]) (The threshold for eligibility for public assistance was raised from L8,000 to L16,000 with the U.K. government's 1996 fiscal budget, announced in late November, 1995.[68])

During the 1980s, the U.K. reduced the supply of long-term care beds in National Health Service (NHS) hospitals and encouraged the growth of private sector, mostly for-profit nursing homes. This shift toward greater use of private nursing homes also brought about a shift in payment sources, since national health insurance only covered care in NHS facilities. A Social Security-based funding mechanism was established to subsidize care in private nursing homes, but only for those who could not afford to pay privately.[69]

Long-term care insurance was first sold in U.K. in 1991 by Commercial Union. The number of policyholders throughout the U.K. approached 10,000 at the end of 1994. Products are aimed at the age 65 to 75 market, with most carriers not offering below-age coverage.[70]

Two main funding methods have evolved: point-of-care (or "immediate funding") plans and pre-funding plans. Point-of-care plans are taken out either when the client is already in a home or on the point of entering one. In exchange for a single premium, the insurer, using an impaired life annuity, makes payments to the care provider for the rest of the client's lifetime.[71]

Pre-funding plans are monthly or annual premium payment plans, purchased prior to needing long-term care. The age at which clients utilize pre-funding plans seems to vary by carrier; one carrier reports average age of buyers at about 60, another age 67.[72]

Policies commonly aim to top-up existing resources to fund care fees. Typical LTC benefits, regardless of the funding method, might be up to 100 or 200 pounds per week, with most benefits paid directly to the care provider, either a residential home or home care provider.

According to one source, in many plans, the level of benefit payment depends on the number of ADLs failed. This also determines whether the benefit will be paid to provide care at home or in a nursing home.[73] Most insurers require three ADLs from a menu of six to qualify for full benefit, although some will provide partial benefits on failure of two ADLs.

LTC is treated in the U.K. as a medical insurance product. There is no tax relief on LTC insurance premiums as there is on pension and private medical insurance. However, if the benefits are paid to the nursing home, the client has no tax liability.[74]

Some "critical illness" products in the U.K. also cover long-term care under their loss of independence section. These plans, which pay out a cash lump sum to the policyholder, tend to be sold to a age range younger than that of those who purchase LTC.[75]

Where early LTC insurance plans offered only a comprehensive level of coverage, many now provide the opportunity for clients to select the type of coverage they require and the duration of benefit payment, thus providing considerable extra flexibility and very substantial cost savings.[76]

Great Britain saw the introduction of an annuity with a long-term care provision similar to the combo policies discussed in Chapter 5. To collect benefits for LTCI policyholders must be unable to do three out of six activities of daily living, contrary to stand-alone LTCI policies which require inability to do two out of six ADL's.

©Timothy Raab Northern Photo

Representatives of the British Consulate-General and U.K. Department of Social Security pose with the staff of the New York State Partnership for Long-Term Care at the Rockefeller Institute and guest author, S. Larry Feldman, front row, 2nd from the right.

## Eastern Bloc Countries

**Summary:** Insurance in general in Eastern block countries is quite embryonic, as are services for long-term care. Private acute and chronic care programs which, in every country, tend to receive the greatest attention and dollars, are only in the formative stages. Hungary and Poland are at the forefront in development of these types of programs. Government benefits, which focus on long-term care services and insurance to fill the gaps, will, no doubt, take a back seat to the more pressing issues of acute care.

## Africa

**South Africa:** With a population totaling 41.2 million in 1994, South Africa's aging population numbers just 4 percent (1.6 million). The average life expectancy of men is 62 years; of women, 67 years.[77]

South Africa's social security system provides old age, disability, and survivor benefits, funded completely by the government. Sickness, maternity, and unemployment benefits are provided to qualified insured workers. These are funded by unemployment contributions made by employees and employers.

Nothing is known currently about the existence of LTCI products in South Africa.

## Middle East

**Israel:** With a population totaling 5.5 million in 1994, Israel's aging population numbers 486,000 (9 percent). The average life expectancy of men is 74 years; of women, 78 years.[78]

LTCI is a fairly new program that, according to one source, has potential for reducing the number of older people in institutions and expanding home and community services available to severely disabled people. LTCI benefits are available to men age 65 or older and women age 60 or older "who are severely functionally disabled in activities of daily living or require constant attendance due to danger of harming themselves or their environment." The National Insurance Institute (NII), which oversees Israel's insurance programs, sets standards for eligibility. A nurse from the Ministry of Health assesses an older person's impairment level using an NII-approved dependency test.[79] Israel is distinguished from European countries by its much lower proportion of persons living alone and a higher proportion of couples. Couples without children and single females are the two main groups among elderly families.

Long-term care services under LTCI are available to severely disabled people who live at home or who live in an old-age home without public assistance. Location of services depends upon the older person's needs and the ability of the family to provide care. LTCI places substantial emphasis on home support services. There are two service benefit levels. People who are disabled in all activities of daily living receive services that can amount to 150 percent of the basic pension rate.

The Ministries of Social Affairs and Health and the *Kupat Holim Klalit* (a major sick fund) will continue to have responsibility for delivering home and community services outside of the LTCI system. The Ministry of Social Affairs provides personal care and domestic help to frail people in the community if their incomes are below a fixed amount and if social workers authorize the services. The Ministry of Health provides nursing care, if public health nurses authorize the services, to people who meet the program's income test. The Kupat Holim provides some long-term care services to people with insurance. The services available depend upon each region's policies.[80]

The primary objective of Israel's Long-Term Care Insurance (LTCI), a program based on principles of universality, personal entitlement, and equity, is to provide services to functionally dependent elderly (men aged 65 and up, women aged 60 and up) living at home. The program is funded by a contribution rate of 0.2 percent of employees' wages. LTCI is a needs-based program by design; costs are determined by the number of persons eligible, not by budgetary limitations. Eligibility for benefits is based on an aggregate score derived from assessment of dependency in basic activities of daily living and the need for constant attendance due to cognitive disability. The amount of services for which a person is eligible is set at one of two benefit levels according to his/her assessment score. The number of beneficiaries has risen significantly beyond projected budgets and has led to serious underfunding. This deficit has not been met either by a reduction in benefits or by an increase in tax rate. It has instead been funded by the transfer of funds from other programs.[81]

In the late 1980s, two Israeli carriers entered the long-term care market. Both plans were comprehensive in nature, covering both nursing home and home care (although one provided home care only following nursing home confinement), and providing a maximum benefit period of five years duration.

According to one source, most policies being marketed at the end of 1991 covered professional services both in institutions and at home and paraprofessional (personal care and home help) services. All policies provided coverage for at least up to five years, and two also offered benefits with an unlimited duration. Israeli policies also allow an individual who stops paying premiums to qualify for a lower level of benefit if nursing home or personal care is needed (equivalent in the U.S. to reduced, paid-up nonforfeiture benefits). This source noted two perceived faults with policies thus far: inadequate mechanisms for upgrading benefits (known as "inflation protection options" in the U.S.), and misunderstanding by policyholders of coordination of benefits provisions.[82]

The 1995 law requiring that sick funds offer a "basket of services," including LTCI, has shifted the direction toward simple group plans, with shortened benefit periods and amounts.

Initial Israeli products were of the individual form with an attempt at lifetime level pricing. Lifetime level pricing is, of course, higher, especially at younger issue ages. With the development of either an employer or a sick fund group approach, an annual type premium is being utilized on average premiums. These "pay-as-you-go" group premiums have made the individual premium approach look quite high, causing individual sales to suffer due to the success of the group approach.

## North America

**Canada:** Currently, 17 percent of Canada's population, which is in excess of 30 million, is over the age of 65. According to Statistics Canada, that number will increase to 25 percent by the year 2036. The segment of the population aged 80 and over will double in the next twenty years; triple in the next forty years.

On reaching age 65, Canadian men today can expect to live almost fifteen years more; women, more than 19. If they get to 75, men can expect to live another nine years; women, almost twelve.

For every severely disabled adult living in an institution there are three such adults living in the household population. In fact, in 1986/87, 12.2 percent of the entire Canadian population was disabled living in households. Thirty-nine percent of those 65 and older were similarly disabled (Statistics Canada).

Canada's health care system is an example of a single-payer system in which the government is the sole insurer. The system's broad outlines are dictated by the federal government, but the ten provinces and two territories handle details and administration. Physicians remain in private practice, and most hospitals are nonprofit rather than government-owned. The government raises revenues through personal, corporate, and sales taxes.[83]

Medicare, Canada's nationwide tax-funded social health insurance program — created to provide comprehensive, universal health care coverage to all Canadians — is popular among most Canadians, especially those who have not been seriously ill. To many, it appears to be totally free. In fact, it is very expensive. The average Canadian already pays 46 percent of his income in taxes. But Canada's health care spending is growing faster than inflation, faster than its population, and faster than the country's gross national product. The nation's commitment to health care consumes more than 10 percent of the GDP (about $72 billion) (Jane Fulton, Ph.D., The Health Group).

Many Canadians assume that like their medical expenses, their long-term care expenses will be covered quite extensively by their provincial health insurance plan. Currently, provincial health plans have rigorous eligibility criteria for long-term care, and some services require out-of-pocket payments. As demand increases, costs are expected to rise.

According to one source, many provinces are increasing support for long-term care by reallocating funds from acute care. However, to control costs of long-term care, provinces are also beginning to fix spending for certain services. Another source confirms that provincial governments are now focused on restraint, and restructuring of resources in health care, and that there is greater emphasis on rationing long-term care and home care services (Jane Fulton, Ph.D., The Health Group).

Long-term care is a priority for many Canadians. In the most recent annual study conducted by the Life Insurance Marketing &

Research Association (LIMRA), the government's continued ability to provide universal medical services ranked third in people's concerns about their financial futures. Right on the heels of that was an expressed concern by 59 percent of respondents about the costs of their long-term care needs and their ability to meet them.

Long-term care insurance products take one of two approaches in Canada: either they use nursing home care as the foundation of the plan (as U.S. plans do), or they use home care as the cornerstone benefit.

Development of products also takes one of two approaches: they are either manufactured by Canadian carriers themselves or with reinsurers, or are manufactured for Canadian carriers by U.S. carriers, reinsurers, and private labelers.

Carriers that build coverage around nursing home care appear to be cloning U.S. plans, with many of the same features, requirements, and limitations, including integration with other insurance and provincial health plans. Carriers using home care as a cornerstone are providing benefits on an indemnity basis rather than an expense incurred basis, with no regard for provincial health benefits.

The lack of regulation required in advance of the sale of an insurance product in Canada makes product development occur much more quickly than in the U.S. This lack of regulation also can allow for more creativity in plan design and funding methods and for more restrictive limitations than allowed in the U.S. (for example, AIDS exclusions.)

**Mexico:** With a population totaling 91.8 million in 1994, Mexico's aging population numbers just 4 percent (3.67 million). That figure is expected to increase to 4.8 percent by 2000. The average life expectancy of men is 67 years; of women, 73 years. More than half (53.3 percent) of Mexicans are under age 20; 38 percent are under age 15.[84, 85]

Nothing is known currently about the existence of long-term care insurance products in Mexico, although there are reports of nearly 20,000 beds in over 350 long-term care facilities.

## South & Central America

**Argentina:** With a population totaling 33.9 million in 1994, Argentina's aging population numbers just over 3 million (9 percent). The aging segment is expected to increase to 10 percent of the population by 2000. The average life expectancy of men is 68 years; of women, 74 years.[86, 87]

LTC insurance in Argentina is similar in design to products marketed in the U.S., using a reimbursement model and ADL basis, but with more limited benefit amounts and benefit periods. At least one domiciled insurer has actively marketed its stand-alone product for a couple of years. Recently, it has also begun adding a more limited long-term care benefit to its auto insurance coverages. National LTC Network member Gene Tapper is actively involved and has pioneered LTCI in Argentina.

**Brazil:** With a population totaling 155.3 million in 1994, Brazil's aging population numbers over 7.75 million (5 percent). The average life expectancy of men is 64 years; of women, 71 years.[88]

Nothing is known currently about the existence of long-term care insurance products in Brazil.

**Chile:** With a population totaling 14 million in 1994, Chile's aging population numbers 840,000 million (6 percent). The aging segment is expected to increase to 7.3 percent of the population by 2000. The average life expectancy of men is 69 years; of women, 76 years.[89, 90]

The LTC insurance market and products in Chile are expected to develop very much like those in Argentina

**Colombia:** With a population totaling 35.6 million in 1994, Colombia's aging population numbers 1.42 million (4 percent). The aging segment is expected to increase to 5 percent of the population by 2000. The average life expectancy of men is 68 years; of women, 73 years.[91]

Nothing is known currently about the existence of long-term care insurance products in Colombia.

**Peru:** With a population totaling 22.9 million in 1994, Peru's aging population numbers 916,000 million (4 percent.) The aging segment is expected to increase to 4.5 percent of the population by 2000. The average life expectancy of men is 63 years; of women, 67 years.[92, 93]

Nothing is known currently about the existence of long-term care insurance products in Peru.

**Uruguay:** With a population totaling just 3.2 million in 1994, Uruguay's aging population numbers a whopping 12 percent (384,000 million.) The average life expectancy of men is 70 years; of women, 76 years.[94] In 1999, more than seventeen percent of Uruguayans are over the age of 60, earning Uruguay the reputation as the "grayest" country in Latin America.

Uruguay has a long tradition as a welfare state, dating back to the beginning of the 20th century, when it had one of the highest per capita incomes in the world, based on livestock-related exports. Its economic prosperity allowed the development of a public infrastructure, financial institutions, and educational and social programs. Uruguay remains among those countries in South America that have the highest social security coverage, in terms both of benefits and population covered. Nevertheless, it has not been able to maintain an economic base to support its social protection policies. The social welfare system is financed by contributions from workers, employers, and the government. Grants for families are provided by the Family Subsidies Fund. Of total expenditure by the central government, in 1991, 275m. pesos uruguayos (4.8%) went for health services, and an additional 2,993m. pesos uruguayos (52.2%) for social security and welfare. In 1995, a major restructuring of the social security sector was identified as the main priority of the government in 1995.[95]

Nothing is currently known about the existence of long-term care insurance products in Uruguay, however with a state mandate that sons or daughters take care of their aging parents or provide for them financially, and half the taxes collected going to cover pensions and social services for the aged, the ingredients for an LTCI market are in place.

**Venezuela:** With a population totaling 21.3 million in 1994, Venezuela's aging population numbers 852,000 million (4 percent.) The aging segment is expected to increase to 4.7 percent of the total population by 2000. The average life expectancy of men is 67 years; of women, 73 years.[96, 97]

Nothing is currently known about the existence of long-term care insurance products in Venezuela.

## Succeeding in the International LTC Market
### by Gene Tapper

Growth and prosperity in the long-term care insurance market is something all who are in the business of selling long-term care insurance dream about. Not every day do administrators and agents receive an opportunity to offer programs in which they truly believe, without having to face difficult stumbling blocks. If you are in the business of telling people about the need, the cost, and the financing of long-term care and selling long-term care insurance, then the international marketplace may be the place to be. People are hungry to know about this subject and those who truly understand the need for long-term care insurance can be of service to mankind, help prevent financial ruin to many people and help people retain independence and peace of mind while realizing a profit from their efforts.

We in the United States have been fortunate to have had a long period of learning about long-term care, about the types and levels of care in our health care delivery system, and about these reimbursement insurance programs that have failed and succeeded in our country. It is time for those who have tenure in long-term care to share the wealth of information they have amassed with people on a global basis. There is much to communicate about the huge gaps that prevail in government insurance reimbursement systems and answers to these ever prevailing questions need to be provided: What is long-term care? How will it affect me? Why should I be concerned about long-term care? Also there is much to communicate about these misconceptions: "I will never need long-term care." "My government will pay for the cost." "My major medical plan will pay for the cost of care." "I will never go into a facility." "All I will need is home care." "My family will take care of me." Those who know better have heard these remarks, questions, and statements. These are comments heard across the United States. When I travel in Latin America, the British Isles, and the Far East, I hear the same statements. Long-term care is an issue for everyone — domestically *and globally*. Those of us who understand the need, the cost, and the financing of long-term care have an excellent opportunity for growth and prosperity in an ever-growing market for long-term care insurance.

In some countries where traditional caregivers have been family members, particularly the daughters-in-law, changes in sociological events are causing this phenomenon no longer to be true. As a result, formal caregivers are emerging to meet demands and needs. And, because of this change in cultural mores, the need for a means to pay for the cost of formal care is also emerging in many countries other than the United States.

We at GLOCAL Insurance Marketing have recognized that emerging need. As our name implies, we serve global communities through local people. We are helping global communities develop long-term care insurance policies commensurate with the need each country requires. We share our understanding with people; we help educate the people as to how we work so they can spread the word about long-term care to the local people in each country. It is amazing how it catches on. We have created an awareness of ways to help pay for the cost of prolonged care in communities far and near. We have reached millions of people with successful results — both for the consumer and the distributor of long-term care insurance.

As the environment of the international market for health care delivery changes, the senior population grows. The same trends that have been state-side with long-term care are happening in the international market. The long-term care insurance strategies already learned can be extrapolated and applied to this emerging market. Being in the right place at the right time was fortuitous for GLOCAL Insurance Marketing. We were introduced to foreign insurance outlets in need of long-term care insurance by people aware of our abilities. We were able to evaluate their stated needs. We were able to provide guidance based on knowledge of health care delivery systems, ability to structure insurance policy designs, contacts in the long-term care industry, our ability to provide products and procedures, ability to provide agent training programs, agent motivation, agent guidance, and ability to demonstrate how to educate the public about the need for long-term care insurance through seminars, newspapers, buffets, radio, TV, and more — all in the country's native language.

The steps we used to succeed in the international market included:

1. Finding an insurance outlet that was seeking help in implementing a long-term care insurance program and receiving authorization to proceed;

2. Listening to the outlet's goals and objectives with respect to long-term care insurance;

3. Developing a feasibility study pertaining to the country's need for long-term care and financial support systems already in place, or not in place, to pay for the cost of care;

4. Developing a marketing and business plan when the feasibility study demonstrates a favorable sales indication;

5. Designing a product for the needs of the country (including underwriting parameters, benefit language, and premium);

6. Integrating the new product into the existing structure of the outlet (organization, staffing, facilities, space requirements, equipment, etc.);

7. Developing and establishing the new product procedures for administration and claims adjudication of the product;

8. Developing and establishing product documentation and support items for distribution to sales force and consumer;

9. Making sure the product is admitted in the country of product sale;

10. Training staff and distribution system of the insurance outlet;

11. Advertising and selling the product through local people;

12. Processing new business;

13. Handling premium funds;

14. Performing policy holder services;

15. Adjudicating claims;

16. Making claim payments;

17. Providing continuous training;

18. Measuring the success of the program on a continuing basis with respect to the marketing plan, and redirecting functions to be performed by all parties to keep the program successful and prosperous.

As a result of extensive homework, marketing analysis, business planning, perseverance, lots of hard work, many miles of travel, hotels, and meetings, we have experienced growth and prosperity in a rewarding program. By helping people understand the need, the cost, and the financing of prolonged long-term care in the international community, success can be found in marketing international LTCI.

## A P P E N D I X   B

# SPECIMEN LONG-TERM CARE INSURANCE PLAN DOCUMENT
### (For Attorney's Use Only)

1. Purpose: This Plan is designed to provide long-term care insurance to certain key Employees. The presence of this Plan will relieve the minds of eligible Employees of the burdens and concerns involved in the costs and uncertainties resulting from from a chronic illness. This Plan is in exchange for the continued and loyal service by the Employee.

2. Effective Date: The Effective Date of this long-term care insurance plan is _____.

3. Definitions:

   a. Chronic Illness means Chronic Illness as defined in the Employee's Policy. The determination of whether an Employee has incurred a covered Chronic Illness shall be made by the Insurer. The Company shall determine whether the Employee has complied with all of the other conditions for receiving Premium Payments under this Plan.

   b. Company means _____, a corporation [or partnership] organized and existing under the laws of the State of _____.

   c. Employee means those employees of the Company as selected by the Company's Board of Directors [or Partners] to participate in this Plan. As of the Effective Date of this Plan, those Employees are attached hereto as Exhibit A. The Company shall have the sole and exclusive right to add additional Employees, to remove any Employees, and to terminate any Employee, with or without cause.

   d. Plan means this Long-Term Care Insurance Plan as in effect from time to time. This Plan may be terminated, modified, suspended, or amended in whole or in part at any time without the consent of the Employees.

e. Elimination Period means the number of days or months an Employee must be Chronically Ill before Benefits are payable under the Insurer's Policy.

f. Insurer means Continental Casualty Company (or Valley Forge Life Insurance Company in the State of Washington).

g. Policy means the individually-owned Long-Term Care Policy issued by the Insurer in the amount and duration(s) as the Employee, Company, and Insurer mutually agree. It shall be the sole responsibility of the Employee to secure the Policy, as defined in this paragraph. The Employee agrees to submit to any physical examination and to supply any additional information as may be requested by the Insurer. The failure of the Employee to meet these requirements or the failure to obtain a policy of long-term care insurance shall nullify all of the Company's obligations and liabilities under this Plan. Premium notices shall be forwarded to the Company and the Company agrees to pay such premiums as they become due.

4. Plan Administration: _____ is hereby designated as the "Plan Administrator" until designated otherwise by the Board of Directors [or Partners]. The Administrator shall be responsible for the management, control, and administration of this Plan and may allocate to others certain aspects of the management and operation responsibilities of the Plan.

5. Termination of Coverage: An Employee's coverage under this Plan shall terminate immediately upon the earliest of:

a. The date employment terminates, other than by reason of an Employee's Chronic Illness;

b. The date this Plan terminates or is modified to terminate coverage for any Employee; provided, however, that no termination or modification shall affect a previously Chronically Ill Employee's benefits;

    c. The date an Employee ceases to be eligible for coverage; or

    d. The date of an Employee's death.

6. Payment of Benefits:

    a. Premium Payments: The Company will pay to the Employee no benefits other than the premium for the policy described in this Plan.

    b. Policy Benefits: Following the Elimination Period, the Employee may receive "Policy Benefits" as defined and outlined in the Policy. The terms and conditions of the Policy are expressly incorporated herein. The Company's liability under this Plan shall be limited solely to paying, when due, the required premium under the Policy.

7. Company Benefit Provisions: The payment of Premium Payments is subject to all other applicable conditions and provisions of this Plan. Further, the Company may withhold from any Policy Premiums any federal, state or local taxes required to be withheld.

8. Termination of Benefits: The payment of Premium Payments shall cease upon the first to occur of any of the following events:

    a. The Employee dies;

    b. The Employee reaches age _____;

    c. The Employee fails to comply with the terms and conditions of this Plan; or

    d. The Employee leaves the Company's employ.

9. Claims: With respect to Policy Benefits, it shall be the sole duty and obligation of the Employee to notify the Insurer and to furnish any evidence or proof of disability that said Insurer may require. A detailed explanation of the Insurer's claim procedure will be found in the Policy. Payment or denial of Policy Benefits shall be made strictly in accordance with the terms of the Policy.

10. Communication: This Plan shall be communicated to each Employee by letter along with a copy of this

Plan. The letter and copy of this Plan shall constitute a Summary Plan Description.

11. Interpretation: This Plan shall be construed to comply with Sections 105, 106, and 162 of the Internal Revenue Code of 1986 and the Employee Retirement Income Security Act of 1974, as amended from time to time.

12. Nonguarantee of Employment: Nothing contained in this Plan shall be construed as a contract of employment between the Company and any Employee, or as a right of any Employee to be continued in the employment of the Company or as a limitation of the right of the Company to discharge any of its Employees with or without cause.

13. Right of Recovery: If Premium Payments have been paid in excess of the maximum amount payable under this Plan, the Company shall have the right to recover the amount of any such excess from the Employee, the Employee's estate, or the person to whom payments were made.

14. Funding: All Premium Payments paid under this Plan shall be paid from the general assets of the Company. Nothing contained in this Plan, and no actions taken under its provisions, shall create a trust of fiduciary relationship of any kind between the Company and an Employee.

15. Restriction of Alienability: Premium Payments payable to the Employee or beneficiary of the Employee shall not be subject to assignment, transfer, attachment, execution, or any other seizure under any legal or equitable process.

16. Communications: All communications regarding this Plan by and between the Company and the Employee shall be in writing. Communications shall be deemed given, made, delivered, or transmitted when mailed first class with postage paid. Communications addressed to the Employee shall be sent to the address

last appearing on the books of the Company; Communications addressed to the Administrator of this Plan should be addressed as follows:

_____

17. Governing Law: To the extent not pre-empted by federal law, the Plan shall be interpreted and enforced in accordance with the laws of the State of _____.

18. In Witness Whereof, the Company hereby executes this Plan as of this _____ day of _____.

## A P P E N D I X   C

# SPECIMEN LONG-TERM CARE INSURANCE PLAN
# BOARD OF DIRECTORS RESOLUTION

(For Attorney's Use Only)

WHEREAS,_____(Company) deems it to be in the best interests of the Company to provide certain long-term care insurance protection to certain key employees as may be designated by this Board from time to time; and

WHEREAS, Sections 105, 106, and 162 of the Internal Revenue Code of 1986 provide an incentive for Company-sponsored long-term care insurance protection for its employees.

NOW, THEREFORE, in consideration of the foregoing:

RESOLVED, that this Company shall hereby establish a Long-Term Care Insurance Plan effective _____, _____, (Plan) for certain key employees of the Company as may be designated by this Board from time to time. A copy of the Plan is attached to this resolution and the Board hereby ratifies and confirms said Plan.

FURTHER RESOLVED, that this Board hereby designates the following employees as participants (Employees) in said Plan effective as of the Effective Date of the Plan:

_____      _____

_____      _____

FURTHER RESOLVED, that the officers of this Company are hereby empowered to carry out the terms and provisions of the Plan including, but not limited to, the designation of a Plan Administrator.

FURTHER RESOLVED, that this Board reserves the right (i) to add or designate additional employees of the Company as Employees of the Plan, (ii) to remove any Employee from participation in the Plan, and (iii) to amend, modify, suspend, revoke, or terminate the Plan, in whole or in part, at any time or times.

IN WITNESS WHEREOF, the Directors of this Company hereby sign and seal the Resolution as of this _____ day of _____, _____.

## SPECIMEN LONG-TERM CARE INSURANCE PLAN
## LETTER TO COVERED EMPLOYEE
(For Attorney's Use Only)

Dear _____:

In view of your valuable services to the Company and as an additional incentive to your continued employment, the Board of Directors [Partners] has [have] approved the purchase of a Long-Term Care Insurance policy for you. The Plan Administrator of this Plan is _____. Any and all notices required or permitted to be given under the Plan should be directed to the Plan Administrator at the following address: _____ _____.

Any claim for Premium Payments (as defined in the Plan) should be directed to the Plan Administrator. Any claim for Policy Benefits (as defined in the Plan) should be directed to the Insurer of your individual long-term care policy.

If, for any reason, your claim for Premium Payments is denied, a procedure for claim review and appeal is established. This procedure is discussed in detail in the enclosed copy of the Plan. Your claim for Policy Benefits shall be governed exclusively under the terms and conditions of your Policy. We strongly advise that you review the claims procedure as contained in your policy. The Company shall in no way be liable for any benefits or payments under this Plan in excess of the Premium Payments as defined in the Plan.

In order to be covered under this Plan, you must make an application for long-term care insurance within the guidelines of the Plan or as otherwise mutually agreed upon by you, the Company, and the Insurer. You must co-operate with the Insurer and provide all information requested by the Insurer including submission to a physical examination, if necessary. Your failure to comply with these requirements and/or the failure to obtain a Policy (for any reason) shall void all of the Company's obligations and liabilities under the Plan. The Company will receive the premium notices and agrees to pay the premium due for so long as you comply with all of the terms and conditions of the Plan and you remain in the Company's employ.

We are pleased to provide this essential long-term care protection to you.

Sincerely,

(Title)

## EXHIBIT A

The following employees are hereby designated as participants ("Employees") in the Company's Long-Term Care Insurance Plan Dated _____, _____ ("Plan"). These Employees further agree to abide by and perform all of the terms and conditions as contained in said plan.


Employee                    Employee Signature

_____     _____

_____     _____

_____     _____

_____     _____


Permission to re-print granted from CNA Insurance Company.

# LONG-TERM CARE CITATIONS AT MDRT ANNUAL MEETINGS: 1989-2000

**THE AGE WAVE: GEARING UP FOR THE BUSINESS OF THE FUTURE**
Ken Dychtwald, Ph.D.
I/R Code: 5000.00
1989

**FOCUS ON SENIOR HEALTH CARE**
Gordon Kelley, CLU
I/R Code: 100.00
1989

**THE INTELLIGENT USE OF LONG-TERM CARE INSURANCE**
Richard F. Breen, Jr., LL.M., ChFC
I/R Code 100.03
1990

**GERI-HAT-TRICKS: FINANCING ELDER CARE**
Peter Strauss, Esq.
I/R Code: 100.071
1991

**THE FINANCIALLY MATURE: WHAT THEY WANT AND HOW TO HELP THEM GET IT**
Richard Breen, CLU, LL.M., CHFC
I/R Code: 2750.99
1991

**LONG-TERM CARE: MANAGING THE CHALLENGE OF THE 90S**
Phyllis Shelton
I/R Code: 100.041
1992

**HEALTH CARE IN THE '90s: ISSUES FOR AGENTS**
Arnold Katz, CLU
I/R Code: 100.07
1992

**LONG-TERM CARE PLANNING: WHY AND HOW TO USE IT**
S. Larry Feldman, CLU
I/R Code: 100.071
1994

**LONG-TERM CARE AND THE SENIOR MARKET**
Daryl S. Brockman
I/R Code: 100.071
C/R Code: 2500.20
1995

**MASTERING LONG-TERM CARE**
Susan E. Palla
I/R Code: 100.20
1997

**DO NOT GO GENTLE INTO THAT GOOD NIGHT**
Myra A. Bohme, CLU, RHU
I/R Code: 100.20
1998

**CRITICAL ILLNESS AND LONG-TERM CARE: TODAY'S INSURANCE PRODUCTS OF THE FUTURE**
Lisa McAree, CLU, Matthew S. Tassey, CLU, ChFC
1999

**INSURANCE SOLUTIONS FOR LONG-TERM CARE FUNDING**
Clifford P. Ryan, CLU, ChFC
1999

**THE CORPORATE LONG TERM CARE MARKET: IT'S NOT JUST FOR THE FORTUNE 500 COMPANIES**
Margie Barrie
2000

## A P P E N D I X    E

# NATIONAL LTC NETWORK

(*Contributing Authors)

**CFK LIFE Plans, Inc.**
784 Troy-Schenectady Road
Latham, NY 12110
*S. Larry Feldman, CLU**
*Ruth Hallenbeck**
(518) 786-6534
(800) 788-8852
Fax: (518) 785-6536
E-mail: lfeldman@cfklifeplans.com

**Individual Commercial Adm., Inc.**
9 Sylvan Way, Suite 170
Parsippany, NJ 07054
*Barry G. Eldridge*
*Susan Palla**
(973) 538-5511
(800) 422-0696
Fax: (973) 984-1091
E-mail: sue@ltcsource.com

**Gelbwaks Insurance Services, Inc.**
10051 N.W. 1st Court
Plantation, FL 33324
*Peter Gelbwaks**
(954) 236-9999
(800) 826-1686
(800) 546-2474
Fax: (954) 236-9993
E-mail: gelbwaks@gate.net

**Wisconsin Insurance World**
906 Ann Street
Madison, WI 53713
*Thomas L. Long**
(608) 283-6600
(800) 397-5186
Fax: (608) 283-6604
E-mail: wiwtll@wiwmktg.com

**Heartland Group**
1113 S. Milwaukee Avenue
Suite 300
Libertyville, IL 60048
*Thomas H. Riekse, Sr.**
(847) 680-8700
(800) 245-8108
Fax: (847) 680-9112
E-mail:
tomsr@theheartlandgroup.com

**Health Insurance Partners, Ltd.**
350 E. Michigan Avenue
Suite 400
Kalamazoo, MI 49005
*Richard B. Sanford**
(616) 385-4311
(800) 307-7798
Fax: (616) 385-6254
E-mail: amys@ligltd.com

**Health Insurance Partners, Ltd.**
5595 So. Harbor Ave.
Freeland, WA 98249
*Ronald F. Sanford*
(360) 331-4566
(800) 535-1310
Fax: (360) 331-4537
E-mail: seniors@whidbeyisland.com

**Schmidt Insurance, Inc.**
**S.I.A. Marketing Inc.**
Box 2384
Bismarck, ND 58502
931 S. 9th Street, Suite 201
Bismarck, ND 58504
*Gene G. Schmidt*
*Pamela Schmidt**
*Jonathan Spilde**
(701) 258-5894
(800) 544-5420
Fax: (701) 258-7989
E-mail: siamktg@btigate.com

When Caring Isn't Enough...

**GLOCAL Insurance Marketing, LLC**
10061 Riverside Drive #839
Toluca Lake, CA 91602
*J. Eugene Tapper* *
(818) 752-3635
Fax: (818) 980-6616
E-mail: gene.tapper@glocalim.com

**Master Care, Inc.**
6075 SW 124th Avenue
P.O. Box 1784
Beaverton, OR 97075
*Everett W. Thorne* *
(503) 626-2213
(800) 275-4582
Fax: (503) 627-9997
E-mail: ev@alveus.com

**The Heartland Group-Arizona**
6447 N. Palo Cristi Road
Paradise Valley, AZ 85253
*Robert Boyajian*
(602) 381-8500
(800) 381-8504
Fax: (602) 381-8503
E-mail: bob@heartlandltc.com

**LTCI Brokers, Inc.**
5015 Addison Circle, #515
Addison, TX 75001
*Thomas Collica* *
(972) 629-5824
(877) 696-5824
Fax: (972) 629-5555
E-mail: ltcibrokers@home.com

**Shields Brokerage**
21 Hampton Road
P.O. Box 1116
Exeter, NH 03833-1116
*Joe Anne Shields*
(603) 772-6700
(800) 972-0048
Fax: (603) 772-6714
E-mail:
jshields@shieldsbrokerage.com

**Stone Hill & Associates**
50 W. Broadway, #600
Salt Lake City, Utah 84101
*Harry "Hal" A. Stone, Jr.* *
*Gregory Hill* *
(801) 363-1215
(800) 748-4428
Fax: (801) 363-3932
E-mail: Hals@stonehill.net

**The Long Term Care Group, Inc.**
2270 Sharon Lane
Charlotte, NC 28211
*Melanie S. Steele* *
(704) 365-9330
(800) 582-4550
Fax: (704) 365-4551
Member 1995-1998, returned to Personal Production

**Allen B. Mansfield**
Executive Director National LTC Network
6190 Golfview Drive
Gurnee, IL 60031-4701
(847) 247-8514
(800) 996-6789
Fax: (847) 247-8212
E-mail: AMansfi919@aol.com

# CHAPTER NOTES

## Chapter 1

1. Rosalyn Carter, *Helping Yourself Help Others: A Book for Caregivers,* Time Books, Random House, 1994
2. *The Age Wave: The Challenges and Opportunities of an Aging America,* Dychtwald, Kenneth, New York: NY Bantam Doubleday Dell, 1990, Tarcher-St. Martins Press, NY, 1989
3. ASPE Research Notes, "Population Estimates of Disability and Long-Term Care," February 1995
4. *New England Journal of Medicine,* February 28, 1991
5. Ibid.
6. *65+ in the U.S.,* U.S. Department of Health and Human Services
7. Peter Kempner and Christopher M. Murtaugh, "Life-Time Use of Nursing Home Care," *The New England Journal of Medicine* 324, No. 9 (February 28, 1991; pp. 595-600)
8. "A Shopper's Guide to Long-Term Care Insurance," National Association of Insurance Commissions, Revised 1996 with 1997 insert
9. "Long-Term Care Insurance: An Employee's Guide," *Employee Benefit News,* April 1, 1997
10. Information received from the Department of Public Social Service, Los Angeles County, 1999
11. Based on $100 to $300 per day for nursing home care and $100 to $300 per day for an average of 3 days per week for home health care.
12. "Aging of America," 1991
13. "1998 Guide to Health Insurance for People with Medicare," National Association of Insurance Commissioners and the Health Care Financing Administration of the U.S. Department of Health and Human Services (page 5).
14. Premiums are based on an A+ Best's rated Long-Term Care insurance plan; Daily Maximum Benefit amount of $100; 1,095 days of benefit multiplier; Lifetime Maximum Benefit of $109,500; Elimination Period of 50 days; and no Benefit Increase Option. Note: There are many other choices of available benefits when you select your own long-term care insurance plan.

## Chapter 2

1. *Still Me,* Christopher Reeve, Random House, Inc., New York, 1998
2. Congressional Budget Office Calculations Based on Middle Series Projections. In Bureau of the Census, Current Population Reports, series P 25, No. 1018

## Chapter 3

1. "1998 Guide to Health Insurance for People with Medicare," Health Care Financing Administration
2. Department of Aging, State of California, 1997
3. "Long-Term Care Insurance: An Employee's Guide," *Employee Benefit News,* April 1, 1997
4. "1998 Guide to Health Insurance for People with Medicare," Health Care Financing Administration
5. *Financial Planning,* May 1995, The Care Givers 1995
6. Fortis Long-Term Care
7. Fortis Long-Term Care

8. Long-Term Care for the Elderly and State Term Policy, No. a-17
9. A Discussion on Home Health Care by Hamilton C. Scharff, MHA, RHU, LNHA, Fall 1997

## Chapter 4
1. *Guide to Health Insurance for People with Medicare*, Developed Jointly by the National Association of Insurance Commissioners and The Health Care Financing Administration of the U.S Department of Health and Human Services, 1995
2. 1987 Survey Funded by the Congressional Research Service
3. Elder Care Integral to Lifetime and Long Term Planning by Gary Mazart, Esq., Hannoch, Weisman, P.C. Roseland, NJ
4. Ibid.
5. The Corporation for Long-Term Care Certification, What Pays for Long-Term Care? Jan. 1999
6. "Will Nursing Home Bills Haunt Your Estate?" by Melynda Dovel Wilcox *Kipplingers Report*
7. Ibid.
8. State of Connecticut for Long-Term Care Quarterly Update, Dec. 1994
9. *Public and Private Responsibilities in Long-Term Care, Funding the Balance*, The John Hopkins University Press, Baltimore, 1998

## Chapter 8
1. LifePlans, Inc. LTC Claims Project sponsored by Departments of Health and Human Services and the Robert Wood Johnson Foundation
2. *The Wall Street Journal*, April 23, 1990
3. Ibid.
4. *New England Journal of Medicine*, February 28, 1991

## Appendix A: Long-Term Care Insurance Around the World
1. "Long-Term Care: Needs, Costs and Financing," Health Insurance Association of America
2. "Impact of Demographic and Socio-Economic Factors on the Changing Needs for Services for the Very Old," *International Social Security Review*, V.42, No.2, 1989
3. "Health Care for Elderly People in Developing Countries: A Case Study of Thailand," S. Jitapunkul, S. Bunnag, S. Ebrahim, *Age and Aging*, September 1993
4. "The Meaning of Activities of Daily Living in a Thai Elderly Population: Development of a New Index," S. Jitapunkul, P. Kamolratanakul and S. Ebrahim, *Age and Aging*, March 1994
5. "The Graying of Japan," *U.S. News & World Report*, September 30 1991
6. Ibid.
7. Ibid.
8. Ibid.
9. "Care of the Elderly in Japan: Changing Norms and Expectations," N. Ogawa and R.D. Retherford, *Journal of Marriage and the Family*, August 1993
10. 1994 World Population Data Sheet, Population Reference Bureau, Inc., Washington, D.C.
11. "Greying Australia: Future Impacts of Population Aging," Kendig and McCallum, 1986

12. "New Directions in Aging Policy in Australia," *Generations*, Winter '93
13. "International Perspectives on Long-Term Care Reform in the U.S.," Jane Tilly and Barbara Stucki, Public Policy Institute, *AARP*, 1991
14. See note 10 above
15. "A Crisis in Care? The Future of Family and State Care for Older People in the European Union," Family Policy Studies Centre, Centre for Policy on Aging, 1994
16. Ibid.
17. "European Models of Long-Term Care in the Home and Community," Barbara Coleman, Public Policy Institute, American Association of Retired Persons, September 1994
18. See note 16 above
19. "A Comparison of LTC Financing in the U.S. & Other Nations: Dispelling Some Myths," *Generations*, Spring 1990
20. Ibid.
21. See note 10 above
22. Statistical Abstract of the U.S., 1995
23. "Home Care: The Dutch Experience," Martin Kerkhof, Vice President, De Amersfoortse Verzekeringen, CCC/Elderly Matters Seminar, October 12, 1994
24. "Every Grey Hair Counts," *The Guardian*, February 13, 1993
25. International Healthcare Reform III, Interben, April 1995
26. See note 13 above
27. See note 23 above
28. Ibid.
29. See note 10 above
30. See note 19 above
31. Ibid.
32. GAO, Report to the Special Committee on Aging, U.S. Senate, "Long-Term Care: Other Countries Tighten Budgets While Seeking Better Access," August 1994
33. See note 17 above
34. See note 10 above
35. See note 17 above
36. See note 32 above
37. Ibid.
38. Ibid.
39. Ibid.
40. Ibid.
41. "Labor Market Programs and Part-Time Work: The Swedish Example," *Generations*, Winter '93
42. See note 32 above
43. See note 15 above
44. See note 10 above
45. See note 24 above
46. "European Market Development," Duncanson & Holt, October 1994
47. See note 13 above
48. "Summary Report, Long-Term Care Insurance," Life and Health Insurance Committees, Comite Europeen des Assurances, Paris, June 1993
49. See note 10 above
50. See note 32 above
51. Ibid.

52. GAO, Report to the Chairmen, Special Committee on Aging, U.S. Senate, "Long-Term Care: Current Issues and Future Directions," April 1995
53. "The German Government's Approach: Progress of Policy Initiative," Munchener Ruckversicherungs-Gesellschaft, CCC/Elderly Matters Seminar, October 12, 1994,
54. Ibid.
55. "Global Briefs," *Business Insurance*, July 26, 1994
56. Measures to Promote Health and Autonomy for Older People: A Position Paper, National Council for the Elderly, 1993
57. The Role and Future Development of Nursing Homes in Ireland, National Council for the Elderly, 1991
58. Ibid.
59. Ibid.
60. Ibid.
61. See note 24 above
62. Europa World Year Book, 1995
63. See note 22 above
64. See note 10 above
65. "Health Care Around the Globe," Thomas H. Moore, *Congressional Quarterly Weekly Report*, 9/25/93
66. "Financing Long-Term Care in Great Britain," Nuttall et al., Institute of Actuaries, October 25, 1993
67. "What Shall We Do With Granny?" *Post Magazine*, October 12, 1995
68. *The National Underwriter*, December 11, 1995
69. "International Long-Term Care Reform: A Demographic, Economic and Policy Overview," Pamela Doty, U.S. Department of Health and Human Services, May 1993
70. "Latin American Pensions: Paying for Greying," *The Economist*, November 26, 1994
71. See note 67 above
72. Ibid.
73. "Taking Care of Long-Term Care," *Pensions Management*, June 1995
74. Ibid.
75. Ibid.
76. "Long-Term Care Insurance, Market Analysis: A Review of Current U.K. Policies," Brunswick Marketing Consultants, January 1996
77. See note 10 above
78. Ibid.
79. See note 13 above
80. Ibid.
81. "Long-Term Care Insurance in Israel: Three Years Later," *Aging International*, Vol. 20, No. 2, 6/93
82. "Private Outlets for Public Limitations: The Rise of Commercial Health Insurance in Israel," *Journal of Health, Politics, Policy and Law*, 1992
83. See note 65 above
84. See note 10 above
85. See note 22 above
86. See note 10 above
87. See note 22 above
88. See note 10 above
89. Ibid.
90. See note 22 above

91. See note 10 above
92. Ibid.
93. See note 22 above
94. See note 10 above
95. See note 62 above
96. See note 10 above
97. See note 22 above

# G L O S S A R Y

**Activities of Daily Living (ADL's):** The activities or tasks that an individual must be able to perform to live independently. Long-term care needs are often evaluated on an individual's ability to carry out basic activities of daily living such as bathing, elimination (control of bowel and bladder), dressing, eating, getting in and out of a chair or bed, and personal hygiene activities.

The following are examples of what constitutes ADL dependency:

| ADL | Independence | Dependence |
|---|---|---|
| Bathing | Needs assistance or assistance only in bathing a single part (such as back). | Needs assistance in bathing more than one part; does not bathe self, needs assistance into and out of tub. |
| Dressing | Gets clothes from closet or drawers, puts on clothes, manages buttons or fasteners. | Does not dress self or can only partly dress. |
| Eating | Conveys food from plate, or its equivalent, into mouth. Does not include preparation. | Needs assistance in the act of eating, or being fed by mouth. |

ADLs define the disability in long-term care insurance and are the essence of all long-term care insurance policies. For example, the inability to perform two of the five ADLs will qualify an insured to go on claim for benefits.

**Acute Care:** Care for an illness or injury that develops rapidly, has pronounced symptoms, and is finite in length. Traditional medical insurance, Medicare, and Medicare Supplements are designed to provide coverage for acute illnesses. Acute care can be provided in a physician's office, clinic, or hospital setting.

**A.A.R.P:** American Association of Retired Persons, both an entrepreneurial and advocacy organization; competes with the sale of LTCI and Medigap insurance directly through the mail.

**Adult Day Care:** Programs provide recreation and some medical services in specified centers. The cost is much lower than home health care.

**Adult Day Health Care:** Care and services provided in a residential health care facility or approved extension site, on an outpatient basis, under the medical direction of a physician (in the medical model). Personnel of the adult day health care program in accord provide these with a comprehensive assessment of care needs and an individualized health care plan. Ongoing implementation and coordination of the health care plan and transportation are also included.

**Adult Home:** A licensed adult-care facility that provides long-term residential care, room, board, housekeeping, personal attention, and supervision for five or more eligible adults, who are not related to the operator. These do not require continual medical or nursing care. Such facilities are eligible to receive SSI payments for room and board, but are not eligible to receive payment for any service under the Medicaid program.

**Alternate Plan of Care:** If a claimant would otherwise require confinement in a longterm care facility, the insurance company may pay for medically appropriate services and supplies in another setting.

**Assisted Living Facility:** A nonmedical institution providing room, board, laundry, some forms of personal care, and possibly recreational and social services. Licensed by the department of social services in most states, these facilities exist under several names including domiciliary care facility, sheltered house, board and care, community-based residential facility, and so on.

**Assisted Living Facility (Unlicensed):** A residential facility which provides room, board, housekeeping, personal services, and supervision to private pay residents but is not licensed by the state. Health services may be provided to residents, at their request, through a licensed or certified home health care agency which may or may not be owned by the operator. These facilities are not eligible to receive Medicare or Medicaid payments for any service. They are often referred to as assisted living "look-alikes."

**Assisted Living Program (DOH/DSS Licensed):** An entity that is licensed to operate either as an adult home or enriched housing. It may also be licensed as or have a contractual arrangement with a licensed home health care agency or a certified home health care agency, and provide long-term residential care, room, board, housekeeping, personal care, and supervision to five or more eligible adults not related to the operator. These facilities are eligible to receive Medicaid and SSI payment for services.

**Artificial Impoverishment:** See Medicaid Trust

**Bed Reservation Benefit:** Pays cost of reserving policyholder/resident's place in a care facility should the need for hospitalization arise.

**Benefit Period:** The length that benefits will continue to be paid, once the elimination period has been met.

**Care Coordinator:** A person designated by an insurer to organize a plan of care either prior to or at the time of claim between the insured, medical providers, and family members. The care coordinator does not restrict a policyholder's access to care, nor does she mandate the use of specific providers or facilities.

**Caregiver:** Usually a relative of a chronically ill person who provides constant help and care. Caregivers can undergo extreme stress, sacrificing sleep, vacations, relationships, jobs, and even their own health.

**Case Management:** An approach that makes use of a team of specially trained social workers, nurses, and medical personnel. Following a comprehensive assessment, the case manager makes recommendations on the facilities or package of services that best suits the individual and minimizes out-of-pocket expenses. The program is monitored with periodic follow-ups. The individual, a family member, and the personal physician are included in all decisions.

**Certified Home Health Care:** A form of care which provides, as a minimum, certain services of a preventative, therapeutic, health guidance, and/or supportive nature to persons at home. These include nursing services, home health aide services, medical supplies, equipment and appliances suitable for home use, and at least one additional service which may include, but not be limited to, physical therapy, speech/language pathology, nutritional services, and social work services. The home health care provider has received appropriate approval to bill Medicare and/or Medicaid for said services.

**Chronically Ill:** The definition under which an individual qualifies for favorable tax treatment for long-term care expenses, whether self-insured or reimbursed by an insurance company. To be chronically ill, the person must be unable to perform two of six activities of daily living for at least 90 days, or suffer a severe cognitive impairment.

**Cognitive Impairment:** Deterioration or loss of intellectual capacity as reliably measured by clinical evidence and standardized tests to judge the areas of memory; also orientation supervision. Such memory loss can result from Alzheimer's disease or similar forms of senility or irreversible dementia.

**Community Spouse:** The spouse who continues to live at home, as opposed to the spouse who is confined in a nursing facility.

**Continuing Care Retirement Community:** A facility or facilities approved by the Life Care Community Council. Pursuant to a contract, these provide a comprehensive cohesive living arrangement for the elderly in independent living units (townhouse and/or apartment-style living). These provide board, a range of health care and social services, including home care, nursing care, and at least sixty days of on-site or affiliated nursing facility care. Access to health services, prescription drugs, and rehabilitation services is also provided.

**C.P.I. (Consumer Price Index):** The price index for all urban consumers, published by the U.S. Department of Labor.

**Custodial Nursing Care:** Care that primarily provides

assistance in the activities of daily living, such as bathing, dressing, or eating. This care can be provided by someone without professional medical skills or training, but must be based on a doctor's orders.

**Daily Benefit Amounts:** An insurance policy term that refers to daily benefits for various types of long-term care. Benefits are usually purchased in dollar increments up to the maximum allowed by the policy.

**Dementia:** Not a disease, but a group of symptoms resulting from disease and/or deterioration, characterized by intellectual decline that impairs even routine functions.

**Diagnostic Related Group:** A method used to calculate Medicare Part A payments to hospitals, based on patient diagnosis rather than the length of the hospitalization. There are 490 classifications of DRG's. (June 1991: Medicare proposed 297 categories of ambulatory DRG's).

**Durable Medical Equipment:** Includes physician/approved items such as wheelchairs, walkers, ramps, and respirators, that may be purchased or rented.

**Eden Alternative:** A program in which nursing home residents live in close contact with companion animals, plants, and children, in order to improve their quality of life.

**Elimination Period:** The length of time that one would have to wait and be responsible for payment for services, until benefits are payable under a policy. This is usually measured from date of confinement (the day one begins to receive coverable care). Also referred to as the "waiting period."

**Emergency Alert System:** A radio transmitter worn on the person which provides reassurance to a patient who can then signal a monitoring center, in case of emergency.

**Enriched Housing:** A licensed adult care facility established and operated for the purpose of providing long-term care to five or more adults, primarily persons 65 years of age or older, in community-integrated settings. These resemble independent housing units. Such programs must provide or arrange for the provision of room and board, housekeeping, personal care, and supervision.

**Expense-Incurred:** A definition of daily benefit payments based on the actual expenses incurred for the necessary long-term care service.

**Functional Assessment:** A medical and psychological evaluation of an individual showing how well they can cope with everyday chores, routines, and responsibilities; also identifies the causes of any problems and suggests remedies.

**Geriatric Care Manager:** A person who coordinates the care of an elderly or disabled person.

**"Granny Dumping":** The abandonment of elderly people in emergency rooms, under the pretext of illness, usually by relatives who are too poor, too tired, or too stressed to continue providing care.

**Guaranteed Renewability:** Assurance that once a person is issued a policy, the insurer cannot cancel coverage for any reason except failure to pay premiums when due. Premiums may only be increased by the insurer on a class basis.

**Health Care Finance Administration:** The federal agency (part of the Department of Health and Human Services) responsible for Medicare and Medicaid rulemaking and administration.

**Health Insurance Portability and Accountability Act (HIPAA):** Portions of this Federal legislation passed in 1996 clarified the tax treatment of long-term care insurance premium payments and defined the parameters under which benefits and expenses are received tax-free.

**Home Care:** Services provided in the home of a chronically ill person. Benefits may include service and supplies provided by a home health care practitioner. These include part-time skilled nursing care, home health care aide services, therapy by a licensed therapist, hospice and personal care services. The unaffordability of home care causes many unnecessary admissions to nursing homes.

**Homemaker Services:** Services such as meal preparation, shopping, laundry, dusting, vacuuming, and so forth, provided by an informal caregiver.

**Hospice Care:** A unique form of medical and social service care for terminally ill patients that emphasizes pain control, symptom management, and emotional support, rather than life sustaining technology.

**Hospice Care (Through a Certified Hospice):** The provision of short-term inpatient services for pain control and management of symptoms related to terminal illness. Such services shall be provided by a hospice as defined in Part 40 of the Public Health Law possessing a valid certificate of approval issued by the State Commissioner of Health.

**Indemnity Benefits:** Pays scheduled daily benefits as long as some charge is incurred.

**Instrumental Activities of Daily Living (IADL's):** Cooking, shopping, housekeeping, laundry, bill paying, telephoning, medication management.

**ICF/MR:** A licensed facility the primary purpose of which is to provide health or rehabilitative services for mentally retarded individuals or persons with related conditions.

**Incontinence:** Inability to control bladder or bowel functions, which can result from any of a large number of underlying causes often associated with old age.

**Inflation Protection:** Rider added to a policy to help keep up with the rising cost of care over the years by increasing the original dollar amount of coverage. Depending on the insurance company option, increases may occur at a stated annual percentage, simple or compounded (number of years may be limited or based on the Consumer Price Index (CPI)). You must be aware of the different premium options for this rider.

**Intermediate Nursing Care:** The mid-range of care, usually delivered in a nursing home, involving a lesser degree of medical services and a greater degree of custodial care (assistance with normal daily living activities).

**Licensed Home Care:** A form of service that provides, as a minimum, the following preventative, therapeutic, health guidance, and/or support to persons at home: nursing services; home health aide services; medical supplies, equipment, and appliances suitable for use in the home. Though licensed by the state, an agency cannot bill Medicare for services rendered, and can only bill Medicaid under a contract with a state agency or its locally designated office.

**Long-Term Home Health Care Program:** A coordinated plan of care and services provided at home for an extended period of time to invalid, infirm, or disabled persons, who are medically eligible for placement in a hospital or residential health care facility, if such program were unavailable. This program shall be provided in the person's home or in the home of a responsible relative or other responsible adult, but not in a private proprietary home for adults, private proprietary convalescent home, residence for adults, or public home.

**Long-Term Care:** Refers to health care, rehabilitative services, and personal care for people who need help and supervision with ordinary tasks of daily living for an extended period of time. These needs may be due to a heart attack, stroke, or a disabling health condition such as Alzheimers' disease. Long-term care can be provided in the home or in a nursing facility.

**Long-Term Care Insurance:** Private insurance designed to provide reimbursement or indemnity for costs associated with long-term care. Options include amount of daily benefit (after an elimination period), up to a maximum benefit period. Home health care and inflation riders are available. Insurance benefits to cover these expenses also help provide asset protection, freedom of choice, and dignity, during difficult health situations, and family caregiver relief.

**Long-Term Care Rider:** An optional benefit that can be added to a life insurance policy, disability income policy, or annuity, to provide benefits for long-term care.

**Managed Care:** A type of claims management system for long-term care insurance policyholders which uses preselected providers who have agreed to treat policyholders at time of claim on a reduced cost basis. The cost savings may be used to extend the benefit period of the insured/claimant.

**Medicaid:** A federal program that states have adopted to provide payment for health care services to lower income people.

Often referred to as a poverty program to provide very basic insurance for the neediest Americans. In order to qualify for nursing home care, some persons must spend themselves into poverty to prove eligibility. (Title XIX of the Social Security Act.)

**Medicare:** The federal health insurance program financed by Social Security tax and personal contributions. It is designed to provide financial assistance for hospital and medical expenses to those over age 65, as well as some disabled persons. Medicare pays for almost none of the long-term care costs, which, if covered following a hospital stay, must be in a skilled nursing facility certified by Medicare. Less than half of the nursing homes in the U.S. are certified, and less than one-fourth of them are participating in Medicare.

**Medicare Supplement Insurance (Medigap):** Individual insurance policies designed to cover some or all of the co-payments and deductibles associated with Medicare. At time of purchase, insureds may have a choice of policy options, which are not intended to cover long-term costs.

**NAIC Model Regulations:** The National Association of Insurance Commissioners promulgates and continually amends a body of model law and regulations governing long-term care insurance and Medigap insurance, as a guide to state legislation and regulation of this market.

**National Academy of Elder Law Attorneys:** A specialty organization created to promote the development of Elder Law as a specialty and to disseminate Elder Law information. Elder Law deals with the specific body of laws pertaining to the rights of the elderly.

**Nonconfined Care:** Care received at an Adult Day Care Center, Home Health Care, and Home Hospice Care.

**Nonforfeiture Values (LTC Policies):** May take the form of cash value, via return of premium rider or paid-up insurance or extended benefit insurance or a combination thereof. (NYS Department Insurance prohibits the return of a cash value.)

**Non-Tax-Qualified Plans:** Refers to the sale of long-term care insurance policies that do not meet the required definitions under HIPAA federal legislation. There could be adverse tax consequences for these plans sold from January 1, 1997 forward. (Pre 1/1/97 policies received "Grandfather" status.)

**Nursing Home:** A skilled nursing facility that provides a full range of board, care, and medical services to those recovering from hospitalization and those unable to live at home.

**Paid Up or Limited Premium Payment LTC Policies:** All LTC insurance companies offer lifetime premium payment schedules, yet some offer limited premium payment schedules, such as ten or twenty year, or paid up at age 65 options.

**Part A:** The part of the Medicare program that pays hospital bills as well as certain skilled nursing facility and home care costs.

**Part B:** The part of the Medicare program that pays physicians' bills.

**Partnerships:** A joint public and private sector program that allows residents of a state to buy approved long-term care insurance policies that would pay benefits during a long-term care claim and enable these residents to conserve some assets that otherwise would have to be spent down to obtain Medicaid. States introducing partnerships thus far are Connecticut, New York, Indiana, and California, but several other states are expected to introduce versions in the near future. New York's Partnership is known as a Time Element plan. Connecticut and California plans are referred to as Dollar For Dollar plans. Indiana's Partnership has incorporated both concepts.

**Personal Care Services:** Services such as grooming and dressing, provided by an informal caregiver.

**Per Diem:** A method for paying the daily benefit amount based on an elected amount and not on the actual expenses incurred. Long-term care insurance policies that are tax-qualified have a $190 tax-free per diem cap in 1999.

**Pre-Existing Conditions:** Any sickness or injury for which one consults a physician and is diagnosed, treated, or recommended for treatment prior to an effective date of application for coverage. (Check Company policy for pre- and post-time elements regarding pre-existing conditions.)

**Pool of Money:** Long-term care insurance policies that

rather than designate a period of time to receive benefits, create a lump sum of money to be used as needed during a long-term care claim. The claim ceases when services are no longer needed or the lump sum of money runs out.

**Reasonable, Customary, and Usual Charges (RCU's):** Refer to a geographical table of normal expenses for the particular service delivered.

**Reimbursement Benefits:** Pays benefits based on the actual amount of expenses incurred up to the chosen daily or monthly limit (in contrast to Indemnity Benefits).

**Respite Care:** Respite care is scheduled short-term care provided on a temporary basis to an individual who needs this level of care, but who is normally cared for in the community. The goal of scheduled short-term care is to provide relief for the caregivers while providing care for the individual. Care can be provided in the community or in a nursing facility.

**Restoration of Benefits:** Usually a limited benefit to restore the original policy maximum, if an insured is treatment free for a stated period of time.

**Sandwich Generation:** A popular phrase for those who were born in the 1940s and 1950s and who are sandwiched between caregiving responsibilities for their children and for their aging parents.

**Senility:** Also called "dementia." Once considered a normal part of aging, now doctors view this as the result of disease and deterioration.

**Senior Housing:** Independent living units, generally apartments. Any supportive services, if needed, are through contract arrangement between tenant and service provider.

**Skilled Nursing Care:** The highest level of care, usually provided in a skilled nursing facility or special department of a hospital. This involves the continual medical services of a skilled care nurse or technician.

**Skilled Nursing Facility:** A nursing facility serving residents whose medical conditions require round-the-clock skilled professional care from doctors and nurses.

**Spend-Down:** Term used for depletion of one's assets to the point of qualifying for public assistance.

**Spent Down:** Refers to the depleted physical and emotional state of care givers, such as family and friends, who provide care up to and beyond their own ability to continue providing care.

**Spousal Benefit Transfer:** When both spouses buy a policy, the surviving spouse inherits any benefits left by the deceased spouse, or if one spouse exhausts benefits, they can be transferred over from the second spouse's policy.

**Sub-Acute Care:** Relates to short-term care provided in nursing facilities to individuals who nowadays seem to be released from hospitals "quicker and sicker." (See DRG's.)

**Supplemental Security Income:** A Federal program of cash assistance to the aged, blind, and disabled (Title SVI of the Social Security Act). SSI terminology and methods are very influential in Medicaid procedures.

**Survivorship:** If both spouses apply for coverage at the same time and one spouse dies, the policy for the survivor becomes paid up after a time period determined by the insurance company.

**Tax-Qualified LTC Plans:** Long-term care insurance policies that meet the definitions required by HIPAA to be eligible for favorable tax treatment.

**Third Party Notification:** Gives policyholder the option to have the "premium due notice" sent to a third party of his or her choice as a precaution to make sure the premium is paid.

**Viatical Settlement:** Purchase of a life insurance policy owned by a terminally ill person (or high net worth healthy policyholder over the age of 70) by a Viatical Settlement Company, for an amount less than the original death benefit.

**Waiver of Premium:** A policy provision that will keep the policy in force during a period in which benefits are claimed or paid under the policy, without the requirement that one continue to pay premiums for long-term care insurance. Waiver of Premium could begin as early as the first day of benefit, up to the 90th day of benefit depending on the insurance company.

**Worksite:** Because of an individual's direct or indirect relationship to a sponsoring worksite (employer) or association, (s)he is eligible to apply for long-term care insurance offered only to employees and their families or association members and their families.

# E D I T O R ' S   B I O G R A P H Y

## Paul Elisha

Paul Elisha holds a Bachelor's degree in Journalism and Music from Indiana University and a Master's degree in Psychology from Adelphi University. He has participated in master classes with major poets at Bennington and Skidmore Colleges, SUNY Albany and Frost Place in New Hampshire. Currently, Mr. Elisha is best known as a commentator for WAMC-Northeast Public Radio (Albany, NY) and host of Northeast Public Radio Network's morning music program "Performance Place."

Over a forty-year writing career, Mr. Elisha was a program annotator for the NBC Symphony broadcasts under maestro Arturo Toscanini and music reviewer for the *Albany Knickerbocker News* and the *Schenectady Gazette*. He's also been an editor and copywriter and served as a public relations officer in the administrations of five New York governors. He also served as executive director of New York State Common Cause. But before, during, and since all of these activities, he was and continues to be a practicing poet.

A collection of Mr. Elisha's poems (many based on World War II combat experiences) has been completed. Some of these have been published in the *International Journal of War, Literature and the Arts*. A performance piece titled "Drums and Echoes," for solo readers and spoken chorus (with percussion accompaniment), received its premiere performance by the SUNY Albany Collegiate Chorale and Percussion Ensemble, in November 1994. Most recently, Mr. Elisha was the recipient of a State Arts Council grant to create a series of poems from interviews with WWII Pacific combat veterans from New York's Capital District.

## CO-AUTHOR BIOGRAPHY

### National LTC Network

At a Long-Term Care Insurance conference in San Francisco in 1992, two participants who specialized in the marketing of long-term care insurance talked about the need for a forum at which marketers could exchange ideas. This conversation led them and others they enlisted to contact their peers and determine interest in forming a study group or "network" of firms that specialized in the marketing of long-term care insurance.

In November 1994, representatives of seven firms met in St. Louis, Missouri, and discussed ideas for an organization of brokerage agencies specializing in long-term care insurance. At the conclusion of the meeting, all agreed to proceed with the formation of a network. In January 1995, after a review of the proposed by-laws, the firms agreed to form the National Long-Term Care Network. It was also agreed that membership in the Network would be limited and based on review of an applicant firm's productivity, experience, and integrity.

The founding firms in the National Long-Term Care Network listed these as their purposes:

1.  To place a national focus on long-term care education and ethics for professional LTC agents and the clients they serve.
2.  To create new long-term care products with new benefits in response to consumer demand.
3.  To exchange distribution and administrative ideas among top long-term care producers to analyze and accommodate product and market changes and their ultimate effect on the industry.
4.  To provide industry leadership in the formation of comprehensive long-term care laws.
5.  To reach out to the Network's 50 state broker membership, in order to facilitate the enrollment of national groups.
    Based on these purposeful particulars, mission and vision statements for the National Long-Term Care Network were developed and approved.

## Mission Statement

The National Long-Term Care Network is dedicated to improving the design, distribution, and marketing of private long-term care insurance and the quality of long-term care education, for the benefit of the consumer and the agent.

## Vision Statement

We envision a country in which every individual is assured of maintaining his or her personal dignity, freedom of choice, and financial independence, when faced with the increasing costs of long-term health care.

We envision a more responsive marketplace where agents, companies and consumers work together to create solutions that address the rapidly evolving needs of an aging population.

We pledge resources, knowledge, and the strength of members, in promoting private long-term care insurance as a means to achieve these ideals.

In fulfilling its mission and vision statements, since its formation, the National Long-Term Care Network has accomplished the following:

1. Developed and published quarterly newsletters for producers of long-term care insurance.
2. Members have become state certified continuing education instructors.
3. Planned and co-sponsored the first Producers' Long-Term Care Insurance Conference with the National Association of Health Underwriters (October 1996).
4. Members are frequent contributors of articles on long-term care insurance issues to local, state, and national publications.
5. Members have made presentations to local, state, and national producer groups and at many Long-Term Care Forum meetings.
6. Designed a worksite long-term care insurance policy for employees and extended family, for distribution through members by independent agents and financial planners.
7. Members have contributed to many chapters in this book.

These accomplishments best describe the National Long-Term Care Network as a cohesive group of fifteen reliable brokerage/distribution agencies, with experienced and dedicated individuals, who believe comprehensive long-term care coverage can help to shape the economic future of this country.

Thomas L. Long, President
National LTC Network

# AUTHOR'S BIOGRAPHY

## Samuel Larry Feldman, CLU

S. Larry Feldman holds a Bachelor of Science degree from Rider University in Lawrenceville, NJ, where he majored in business administration and minored in insurance. He received his Charter Life Underwriter degree from the American College of Life Underwriters in Bryn Mawr, PA. Mr. Feldman is President of CFK LIFE Plans, Inc., a Managing General Agency representing several of the nation's leading long-term care insurance companies.

A nationally known speaker, lecturer, and panelist on the topic of long-term care and long-term care insurance, his focus is on educating and training agents and financial planners, believing the extra time spent now will benefit clients for many years to come. He is a life member of the Million Dollar Round Table, having made presentations at two annual meetings. Larry was a main platform speaker at the first annual Long-Term Care Producers' Conference, sponsored by the National Association of Health Underwriters Education Foundation. He was twice invited to be a panelist at the Annual Private Long-Term Care Insurance Conference, most recently the 2000 Meeting, to discuss "New Directions in Long-Term Care Insurance Distribution Systems." This conference is made up of representatives from the public and private sectors, the for-profit and not-for-profit provider worlds, and from consumer and provider organizations.

Mr. Feldman was the producer and a panelist for the public announcement of the New York State Partnership for Long-Term Care Insurance, broadcast over New York State Public Broadcasting Stations. He was appointed to the New York State Task Force on Long-Term Care Financing in 1996. The eleven member bipartisan panel supported by the Governor and the Legislature was given the opportunity to guide the State (which leads the nation in its reliance on Medicaid to finance long-term care services) in meeting the challenge to reform the financing and delivery of long-term care.